METRIC PATTERN CUTTING

Also from Blackwell Publishing

Metric Pattern Cutting for Menswear
THIRD EDITION
Winifred Aldrich
ISBN-10: 0 632 04113 7
ISBN-13: 978 0 632 04113 8

*Metric Pattern Cutting for Children's Wear
and Babywear*
THIRD EDITION
Winifred Aldrich
ISBN-10: 0 632 05265 1
ISBN-13: 978 0 632 05265 3

Fabric, Form and Flat Pattern Cutting
Winifred Aldrich
ISBN-10: 0 632 03917 5
ISBN-13: 978 0 632 03917 3

Pattern Cutting for Women's Tailored Jackets
Winifred Aldrich
ISBN-10: 0 632 05467 0
ISBN-13: 978 0 632 05467 1

Fashion Source Book
Kathryn McKelvey
ISBN-10: 0 632 03993 0
ISBN-13: 978 0 632 03993 7

Fashion Design
Kathryn McKelvey and Janine Munslow
ISBN-10: 0 632 05599 5
ISBN-13: 978 0 632 05599 9

Illustrating Fashion
Kathryn McKelvey and Janine Munslow
ISBN-10: 0 632 04024 6
ISBN-13: 978 0 632 04024 7

Introduction to Clothing Product Management
SECOND EDITION
A. J. Chuter
ISBN-10: 0 632 03939 6
ISBN-13: 978 0 632 03939 5

Colour Forecasting
Tracy Diane and Tom Cassidy
ISBN-10: 1 4051 2120 3
ISBN-13: 978 1 4051 2120 0

*Carr and Latham's Technology of
Clothing Manufacture*
THIRD EDITION
David Tyler
ISBN-10: 0 632 05248 1
ISBN-13: 978 0 632 05248 6

Introduction to Clothing Manufacture
Gerry Cooklin
ISBN-10: 0 632 02661 8
ISBN-13: 978 0 632 02661 6

Fashion Marketing
SECOND EDITION
Edited by Mike Easey
ISBN-10: 0 632 05199 X
ISBN-13: 978 0 632 05199 1

Understanding Fashion
Elizabeth Rouse
ISBN-10: 0 632 01891 7
ISBN-13: 978 0 632 01891 8

Fashion Design and Product Development
Harold Carr and John Pomeroy
ISBN-10: 0 632 02893 9
ISBN-13: 978 0 632 02893 1

Fashion Buying
Helen Goworek
ISBN-10: 0 632 05584 7
ISBN-13: 978 0 632 05584 5

METRIC PATTERN CUTTING

Fourth Edition

WINIFRED ALDRICH

Blackwell
Publishing

Editorial Offices:
Blackwell Publishing Ltd, 9600 Garsington Road, Oxford OX4 2DQ, UK
 Tel: +44 (0)1865 776868
Blackwell Publishing Professional, 2121 State Avenue, Ames, Iowa 50014-8300, USA
 Tel: +1 515 292 0140
Blackwell Publishing Asia, 550 Swanston Street, Carlton, Victoria 3053, Australia
 Tel: +61 (0)3 8359 1011

First published in Great Britain in 1976 by Mills & Boon Ltd, in 1981 by Bell & Hyman Ltd, and in 1987 by Unwin Hyman Ltd
Revised edition 1979, reprinted 1980
Revised edition 1982, reprinted 1983, 1984
Revised edition 1985, reprinted 1986, 1987, 1988 (twice), 1989, 1990
Reprinted by HarperCollins Publishers 1991
Reprinted by Blackwell Scientific Publications 1992, 1993
Third edition 1994
Reprinted by Blackwell Science Ltd 1994, 1995
Revised edition 1997, reprinted 1998, 1999
Fourth edition 2004
Reprinted 2006

ISBN-10: 1-4051-0278-0
ISBN-13: 978-1-4051-0278-0

Library of Congress Cataloging-in-Publication Data
Aldrich, Winifred
 Metric pattern cutting / Winifred Aldrich.-- 4th ed.
  p. cm.
 Includes index.
 ISBN 1-4051-0278-0 (alk. paper)
 1. Dressmaking--Pattern design. I. Title
 TT520.A43 2004
 646.4′072--dc22

                                      2004049690

A catalogue record for this title is available from the British Library

Set in 9.25 on 11pt Times NRMT
by SNP Best-set Typesetter Ltd., Hong Kong
Printed and bound in Great Britain
by TJ International Ltd, Padstow, Cornwall

The publisher's policy is to use permanent paper from mills that operate a sustainable forestry policy, and which has been manufactured from pulp processed using acid-free and elementary chlorine-free practices. Furthermore, the publisher ensures that the text paper and cover board used have met acceptable environmental accreditation standards.

For further information on Blackwell Publishing, visit our website:
www.blackwellpublishing.com

ACKNOWLEDGEMENTS

I would like to thank:
Hilary Candler and Alec Aldrich for their help with the original edition.
Stephen Chalkley for his provision of my CAD system.
The British Standards Institution for their information on the future size designation of women's wear.
The SATRA footwear Technology Centre for their information.
The following people and companies who supplied information and photographs for the chapter on Computer-Aided Design:
assyst bullmer, Germany
Browzwear International Ltd, Israel
CAD for CAD, Oxford
Gerber Technology, Manchester
Investronica, Spain
Katherine Townsend, Nottingham Trent University
Lectra, France
NedGraphics B.V., The Netherlands

CONTENTS

Part One: Classic Form Cutting
(Cutting to create shape for the female figure)

Part Two: Flat Cutting
(Cutting flat shapes for casual and jersey garments)

Part Three: Size and Fit

Part Four: Computer-Aided Design

INTRODUCTION

Revised Edition 2004   This third major revision of the original book, written in 1975, remains true to its original concept. It offered a range of good basic blocks, an introduction to the basic principles of pattern cutting and gave a few examples of their application into garments. The principal aim was to give students confidence in their ability to develop a unique style of pattern cutting and to offer tutors a starting point from which they could extend their students' knowledge.

The new edition responds to the way fabrics and fashion have changed the cut and sizing of garments in different manufacturing processes. The great expansion of casual wear, in jersey or stretch fabrics, has led to the expansion of *flat cutting* with no darting to create the shape. This edition devotes a whole section to this type of cutting. However, students have to understand how to create shape through cutting alone, in fact, *form cutting*, and therefore the first section of the book still covers this technique. The sections on computer-aided design and grading have been updated. The size charts of body measurements have been revised; they acknowledge the changing shape of women's bodies.

The book remains written for beginners, students who are starting practical pattern cutting as a part of Fashion Degree or Diploma courses or for City and Guilds Examinations; it is also for students in upper schools who are studying advanced dress subjects. One chapter deals specifically with drafting the block for individual figures. This will be useful for women who make clothes for themselves in order to create and develop their own individual style, or women who find mass-produced clothes an uneasy fit.

Some garment patterns, particularly in couture design, are constructed by draping on the dress stand. However, pattern cutting from blocks or adaptation of existing patterns is now widely used by the dress trade because of its accuracy of sizing and the speed with which ranges can be developed. Pattern cutting by this method is a means of achieving a shape around the body so that although the body and therefore the body blocks remain constant, there is no limit to the ideas that can be followed through into workable designs. However, the designer must always be conscious that the body is a form. This can be difficult when one has to relate flat pieces of paper to a design that is basically sculptural when it is completed. In addition, the form will move; this must be exploited in the cut of the garment. A moving shape is more visually exciting than a still form. But there are practical problems to be considered in allowing for this movement. The system of pattern cutting offered in this book attempts to make the student more fully aware of designing round the figure rather than seeing it as a body that possesses only a front view.

Pattern cutting should be used in conjunction with a dress stand. This means that as the design evolves, proportion and line can be checked and corrected. Pattern cutting can achieve a shape quickly, but more complicated styles should be made up into a muslin or calico toile so that the result can be assessed on a form or a moving figure.

PATTERN CUTTING AND DESIGN

Pattern cutting by adapting shapes from block patterns can be traced back to the middle of the nineteenth century. As the craft developed the basic rules evolved, but rules can be broken or changed if this comes from new creative directions. This concept of design has been responsible for the most exciting changes in shape and cut during the 20th century. Poiret, Vionnet and Chanel, sensitive to social and aesthetic influences, 'discovered the body' after it had been enclosed in structures for a century. Although their interpretations differed, they were the innovators of soft easy fitting clothes. Today the changing social attitudes of many women have changed their attitudes to fashion, they buy clothes to satisfy themselves, they are not prepared to be restricted to a dictated line for a season or by an outdated image of femininity.

Marrying design with fashion has always been a difficult process; it can be overwhelmed by gimmicks and the bizarre effects that are a part of fashion. Whilst these are necessary because they inject wit, pleasure and excitement, translating them into wearable fashion is a creative art. Designing at the level of couture or small designer collections is very different from that of designing for a mass market. Garments created for an individual client give a designer more freedom. The cost factor becomes less important, and this allows the original idea to be carried through. Interesting fabrics that are difficult to handle can be used, their surface qualities emphasized by decorative techniques. The 'cut' of the garment is usually determined by draping on the stand where the intricacies of the cut can be developed. Designing for individual clients allows the personality of the wearer to be fused with the original idea. The rise of the celebrity in the music industry and the media has developed a new exciting market for some top designers; it is a means by which they can promote their designs and their name. Most major designers also create 'designer collections' which are produced by manufacturing processes, but the high price of the garments allows the 'signature' of their cut to remain and limited runs of specially printed or woven fabrics to be used.

The most limiting factors in designing for mass production are price and the production processes. Clothes also have to have 'hanger appeal'; that is, people will be tempted to try them on or buy them for their look alone. Often dresses that look sensational on a moving body can look limp and featureless on a clothes rail. There are two types of successful designers in the mass production fashion trade. The first group are employed by 'production-led' manufacturers: these designers can develop current fashion shapes, but recognize that fabric economy and repeat making-up methods are the priority. The second group are employed by 'design-led' manufacturers: they are able to produce original ideas and are able to experiment with new fabrics and production processes.

There are some basic elements of design that affect or may limit a designer in any field.

Colour and pattern These are the most dominant features in a fashion trend. Each season a colour theme emerges, occasionally spontaneously, sometimes influenced by top designers. However, most mass retailers rely on the style and colour predictions of the major forecasting agencies. New technologies now offer a revolution in printed textiles. Instead of all-over repeat designs, unrepeating patterns and new scales of pattern can be achieved, thus offering new concepts in which decoration is integral to the whole design.

Fabric quality New technologies have also expanded the range of fabrics available to a designer. The aesthetic qualities of a fabric are often the inspiration that initiates a design. However, in creating a new shape a designer has to consider five crucial fabric qualities which could realize it or destroy it. These are: *weight, thickness, shear, drape* and *stretch*. Whilst large companies have testing procedures that can determine technical measures, the designer often has to make instant judgements and therefore has to be able to estimate the qualities of a fabric and idealize the final effect.

Shape Whilst recognizing the crucial role that fabric choice plays in the realization of design, its success rests with the quality of the pattern cutting. The domination of stretch fabrics in the mass market has meant an expansion of simple *flat pattern cutting* techniques which rely on the stretch to create the body shape. But stretch fabrics can be married with 'form' cutting to give quite different effects. Bias cutting adds to the drape quality of fabrics, and the use of layers can affect the weight and thickness of the design. *Form cutting* of close fitting garments in fabrics without shear or drape, such as stiff silks, requires great skill.

Line The interpretation of line and cut is the most complex part of a designer's work. Once a fashion shape becomes established, the variations in cut to achieve it are infinite. The designer must use his or her skill to produce a range that will translate the latest fashion across a range of sizes.

FABRICS

Designers have to acquire a deep understanding of the qualities of fabrics. Many designers specialize in designing a particular product, for example lingerie or sportswear. This means that they have to understand the basic properties of fabrics and testing procedures and be assured that the fabric will perform well for their particular product.

The designer has to become familiar with the types of woven and knitted structure of fabric. Knowledge of the basic source of fabrics has to be acquired and how this affects the enormous number of finishes that can be applied to fabrics.

However, the most important qualities that a designer must consider when creating a design are: *weight, thickness, drape, stretch* and *shear* (the amount the fibres distort in the warp and weft). These qualities will affect quite dramatically how a pattern will be cut and how the final shape will be realized. A list of fabrics is shown below, which is categorized into the different fabric weights. Weight and thickness are generally closely linked, but some thick pile fabrics constructed with man-made fibres can be deceptively light. Shear and drape are also often closely linked; these qualities allow the cutting of soft body skimming shapes. Today the popularity of stretch fabrics, both woven and knitted, has been the most influential factor in cutting for mass-produced garments. In the edited list of fabrics below, knitted fabrics are listed in all columns because of the huge variety in different weights.

LIGHT–MED	MEDIUM	MED–HEAVY	HEAVY
Afgalaine	Alpaca	Bedford cord	Astrakhan
Angora	Bagheera	Bouclé	Beaver
Bengaline	Barathea	Broadcloth	Double
Cashmere	Bark crepe	Burlap	Duffle
Chino	Brocade	Camel hair	Felt
Chintz	Butcher	Canvas	Fur fabric
Cire	Calico	Chenille	Knitted fabrics
Crepon	Cavalry twill	Cheviot	Loden cloth
Dupion	Cloque	Corduroy	Melton
Faille	Coutil	Donegal tweed	Plush
Foulard	Covert	Drill	Quilted
Gingham	Crepe	Duck	
Homespun	Damask	Dungaree	
Honan	Denim	Duvetyn	
Knitted fabrics	Doeskin	Flannel	
Lame	Faconne velvet	Fleece	
Matelasse	Gabardine	Flock	
Mohair	Grenadine	Fustian	
Moire	Grosgrain	Harris tweed	
Ottoman	Haircord	Honeycomb	
Panama	Hopsack	Intarsia	
Percale	Jacquard	Knitted fabrics	
Pique	Jean	Llama fabrics	
Sateen	Knitted fabrics	Moleskin	
Satin	Panne velvet	Tapestry	
Shantung	Repp	Ticking	
Sharkskin	Sailcloth	Tweed	
Slipper satin	Saxony	Velour	
Surah	Serge	Venetian	
Taffeta	Suitings	Vicuna fabrics	
Tricot	Tartan	Whipcord	
Tussore	Velvet		
	Velveteen		
	Worsted		

Part One: Classic Form Cutting
1 THE BASIC DARTED BODICE BLOCKS

Tools and Equipment for Making Patterns

A student should aim to acquire a good set of equipment. However, some items are very expensive. The items marked with an asterisk (*) denote those that are not essential immediately.

Working Surface   A flat working surface is required. Ideally, it should be 90–92 cm high.

Paper   Strong brown paper is used for patterns. Parchment or thin card should be used for blocks that are used frequently.

Pencils   Use hard pencils for drafting patterns (2H), coloured pencils for outlining complicated areas.

Fibre Pens   For writing clear instructions on patterns.

Rubber

Metric Ruler

Curved Rules   For drawing long curves.

Metre Stick

Set Square   A large set square with a 45° angle is very useful; metric grading squares can be obtained.

Metric Tape Measure

Tracing Wheel

Shears   Use separate shears for cutting cloth and paper as cutting paper will blunt the blades.

Sellotape

Pins

One-quarter and One-fifth Scale Squares   These are essential for students to record pattern blocks and adaptations in their notebooks.

Stanley Knife

Tailor's Chalk   For marking out the final pattern onto the cloth and for marking fitting alterations.

Toile Fabrics   Calico is used for making toiles for designs in woven fabrics. Make sure the weight of the calico is as close to the weight of the cloth as possible. Knitted fabric of the same stretch quality must be used for making toiles for designs in jersey fabrics.

Metric Square

Calculator   The calculator is now a common tool in all areas of skill. If a calculator is not available use the table of aliquot parts (see Appendix, page 197).

French Curves   Plastic shapes and curves are available in a range of sizes; they are useful for drawing good curves. A flexicurve which allows a shape to be manipulated is also available.

Pattern Notcher   This is a tool that marks balance points by snipping out a section of pattern paper.

Pattern Punch

Pattern Hooks

Pattern Weights   These keep pieces of pattern in position on paper or cloth.

Model Stands   Although not essential for a beginner, they are invaluable to the serious student for developing designs.

Computer Equipment   A description of computer equipment can be found on pages 183–196.

The equipment can be obtained at:
Franks Ltd., Kent House, Market Place, London W1W 8HY
Morplan, 56 Great Tichfield Street, London W1W 7DF
Staples Group, Lockwood Road, Huddersfield HD1 3QW

Industrial Sizing Systems

Measurement surveys collect measurement data to produce sizing systems. They are very costly. To obtain reliable data, thousands of subjects have to be measured and it is very difficult to obtain public money for the task. The last survey, which was totally funded by the government and made publicly available, was in 1957. Recent surveys have been private ones done by individual companies or have been joint enterprises between the government and large retailers. As the companies have borne all, or a proportion, of the costs, they see the information as commercially valuable and therefore it is withheld from public use. This has happened to the data from the latest British survey which took place under the direction of the Department of Computer Science, University College, London. The survey was carried out using computer scanning equipment. A number of systems are now available to companies. Although some problems remain, the scanners can now make reliable recordings of most of the principal body measurements required for clothing. They can also create 3D images of the body which give useful information about the changing shape of the population. The biggest problem remains the cost; in the present financial climate few companies are willing to invest in such innovative technology and they are nearly all in operation in government-sponsored projects. A large number of surveys, particularly those in developing countries, are undertaken using manual techniques. A researcher from Manchester Metro University has developed a system of manual measurement using an anthropometric stand and a special harness.

BRITISH AND EUROPEAN STANDARDS
The British Standards Institution has usually been a main guide to sizing, measurements and labeling. Their new Standards have been adopted from CEN, the European Committee for Standardization. Most European countries including the UK have signed to adopt the standards agreed. The standards offered by BSI at present are BS EN13402-1:2001 and BS EN13402-2:2002. These define terms, definitions and body measurement procedures and the primary and secondary dimensions used for garment labeling. BSI has also published a CEN discussion paper BS EN13402-3 which actually lists proposed body measurement size charts, and shows a pictogram of

a figure with basic body measurements to use on labels. A final revision and publication of this discussion paper as a European or British Standard is not expected until the end of 2004. A further Standard is proposed, EN13402-4; this will designate a coding system which will be circulated for discussion in 2004. As European coding is quite different from UK coding this could be contentious.

The use of standards by manufacturers is voluntary and explains the anarchic systems of sizing that are found in High Street fashion. Despite the work taking place to obtain more consistent sizing both in the UK and Europe, the garments on sale in both large and small retail outlets appear to be giving less and less information. Pictograms and body measurements have virtually disappeared, the labels only display a size code. Many retail outlets do not have in-store size charts to relate the codes to body measurements. Translations to European code sizes vary between manufacturers. Although the mail order catalogues offer customers body size charts with the codes, it is apparent that these vary with reference to their niche markets.

OTHER DATA SOURCES
The Handbook of Adult Anthropometric and Strength Measurements is another source from which measurement data are available for designers and manufacturers. It was produced by the Consumer Safety Unit (CSU) of the UK Department of Trade and Industry. The handbook is a design resource produced by the Institute of Occupational Ergonomics at the University of Nottingham. The handbook brings together all available anthropometric and strength data on 266 anthropometric dimensions and 28 strength measurements. Data are presented from a range of countries from Europe, Asia and the USA.

SIZE CHARTS OF BODY MEASUREMENTS IN THIS BOOK
Three charts are offered:
1. Body measurements – 4 cm and 6 cm increments (most European sizing)
2. Body measurements – 5 cm increments (most current UK sizing)
3. Body measurements – S M L XL (young fashion)

Standard body measurements

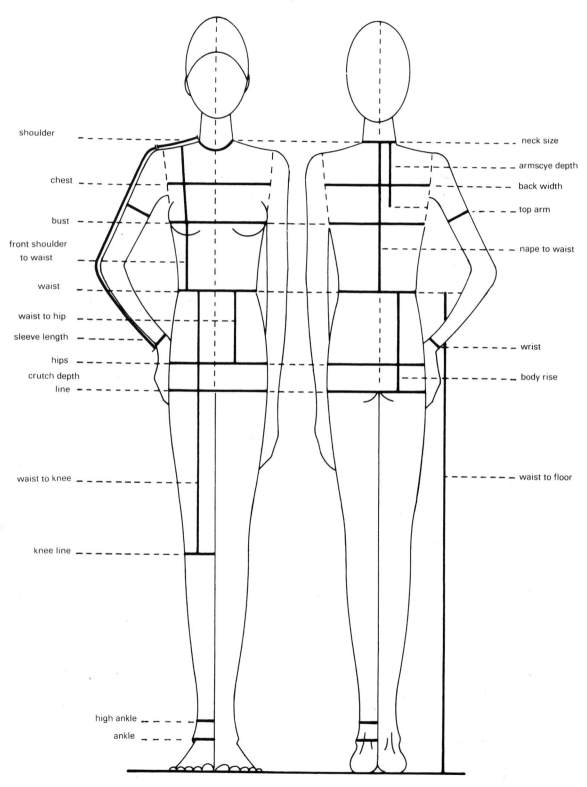

shoulder

chest

bust

front shoulder
to waist

waist

waist to hip

sleeve length

hips

crutch depth
line

waist to knee

knee line

high ankle

ankle

neck size

armscye depth

back width

top arm

nape to waist

wrist

body rise

waist to floor

Standard Body Measurements – 4cm and 6cm Increments (European Sizing)

(See page 12 for 5cm increments – current British sizing)

This chart is based on European body measurement size charts which follow the system of bigger intervals between the larger sizes. **Note** The greatest percentage of the population falls into medium height range. Although the girth of women varies, the general trend is for weight to increase with height within this group. See the table below for shorter or taller women.

Size code	Women of medium height 160cm–172cm (5ft 3in–5ft 7½in)									
	8	10	12	14	16	18	20	22	24	26
BUST	80	84	88	92	96	100	104	110	116	122
WAIST	62	66	70	74	78	82	86	92	98	104
HIPS	86	90	94	98	102	106	110	116	122	128
BACK WIDTH	32.4	33.4	34.4	35.4	36.4	37.4	38.4	39.8	41.2	42.6
CHEST	30	31.2	32.4	33.6	34.8	36	37.2	39	40.8	42.6
SHOULDER	11.75	12	12.25	12.5	12.75	13	13.25	13.6	13.9	14.2
NECK SIZE	35	36	37	38	39	40	41	42.4	43.8	45.2
DART	5.8	6.4	7	7.6	8.2	8.8	9.4	10	10.6	11.2
TOP ARM	25.6	27	28.4	29.8	31.2	32.4	33.8	35.8	37.8	39.8
WRIST	15	15.5	16	16.5	17	17.5	18	18.5	19	19.5
ANKLE	23	23.5	24	24.5	25	25.5	26	26.7	27.4	28.1
HIGH ANKLE	20	20.5	21	21.5	22	22.5	23	23.7	24.4	25.1
NAPE TO WAIST	40	40.5	41	41.5	42	42.5	43	43	43	43
FRONT SHOULDER TO WAIST	40	40.5	41	41.5	42.3	43.1	43.9	44.7	45.5	46.3
ARMSCYE DEPTH	20	20.5	21	21.5	22	22.5	23	23.7	24.4	25.1
WAIST TO KNEE	57.5	58	58.5	59	59.5	60	60.5	61	61.5	62
WAIST TO HIP	20	20.3	20.6	20.9	21.2	21.5	21.8	22.1	22.4	22.7
WAIST TO FLOOR	102	103	104	105	106	107	108	109	110	111
BODY RISE	26.6	27.3	28	28.7	29.4	30.1	30.8	31.8	32.8	33.8
SLEEVE LENGTH	57.5	58	58.5	59	59.5	60	60.5	60.8	61.1	61.4
SLEEVE LENGTH (JERSEY)	51.5	52	52.5	53	53.5	54	54.5	54.8	55.1	55.4
Extra measurements (garments)										
CUFF SIZE SHIRTS	21	21	21.5	21.5	22	22.5	23	23.5	24	24.5
CUFF SIZE, TWO-PIECE SLEEVE	13.25	13.5	13.75	14	14.25	14.5	14.75	15	15.25	15.5
TROUSER BOTTOM WIDTH	21	21.5	22	22.5	23	23.5	24	24.8	25.6	26.4
JEANS BOTTOM WIDTH	18.5	18.5	19	19	19.5	20	20.5			

Size charts for short and tall women have each vertical measurement adjusted as follows:

	Short women 152cm–160cm (5ft–5ft 3in)	Tall women 172cm–180cm (5ft 7½in–5ft 10½in)
NAPE TO WAIST	–2cm	+2cm
SCYE DEPTH	–0.8cm	+0.8cm
SLEEVE LENGTH	–2.5cm	+2.5cm
WAIST TO KNEE	–3cm	+3cm
WAIST TO FLOOR	–5cm	+5cm
BODY RISE	–1cm	+1cm

Standard Body Measurements – 5 cm Increments

Many British companies are, for commercial reasons, using 5 cm intervals between all sizes. This simplified size chart from size 10 to size 24 eliminates the size 8 and allows increments to remain the same across the size range and therefore creates easier size grades. (A 'half size' −2.5 cm increment can be created for size 8.)

	Women of medium heigh 160 cm–172 cm (5 ft 3 in–5 ft 7½ in)							
Size code	10	12	14	16	18	20	22	24
BUST	82	87	92	97	102	107	112	117
WAIST	64	69	74	79	84	89	94	99
HIPS	88	93	98	103	108	113	118	123
BACK WIDTH	33	34.2	35.4	36.6	37.8	39	40.2	41.4
CHEST	30.5	32	33.5	35	36.5	38	39.5	41
SHOULDER	11.9	12.2	12.5	12.8	13.1	13.4	13.7	14
NECK SIZE	35.6	36.8	38	39.2	40.4	41.6	42.8	44
DART	6.4	7	7.6	8.2	8.8	9.4	10	10.6
TOP ARM	26.4	28	29.6	31.2	32.8	34.4	36	37.6
WRIST	15.5	16	16.5	17	17.5	18	18.5	19
ANKLE	23.4	24	24.6	25.2	25.8	26.4	27	27.6
HIGH ANKLE	20.4	21	21.6	22.2	22.8	23.4	24	24.6
NAPE TO WAIST	40.5	41	41.5	42	42.5	43	43.5	44
FRONT SHOULDER TO WAIST	40.5	41	41.8	42.6	43.4	44.2	45	45.8
ARMSCYE DEPTH	20.5	21	21.5	22	22.5	23	23.5	24
WAIST TO KNEE	58	58.5	59	59.5	60	60.5	61	61.5
WAIST TO HIP	20.3	20.6	20.9	21.2	21.5	21.8	22.1	22.4
WAIST TO FLOOR	103	104	105	106	107	108	109	110
BODY RISE	27.3	28	28.7	29.4	30.1	30.8	31.5	32.2
SLEEVE LENGTH	57.5	58	58.5	59	59.5	60	60.5	61
SLEEVE LENGTH (JERSEY)	51.5	52	52.5	53	53.5	54	54.5	55

Note Mainstream garments, such as those in mail order catalogues, will be offered in the following size codes:
Small = 8–10   Medium = 12–14   Large = 16–18   XLarge = 20–22.
Use the measurements from the columns 10, 14, 18, 22 for each of the size codes.

Standard Body Measurement Chart for High Street *Fashion* Garments

Small = approx. size 8–10
Medium = approx. size 12
Large = approx. size 14–16
XLarge = approx. size 18

	SML MED LGE XLGE			
Size symbol	S	M	L	XL
BUST	82	88	94	100
WAIST	64	70	76	82
HIPS	88	94	100	106
BACK WIDTH	32.8	34.4	36	37.6
CHEST	30.6	32.4	34.2	36
SHOULDER	11.8	12.2	12.6	13
NECK SIZE	35.5	37	38.5	40
DART	6.1	7	7.9	8.8
TOP ARM	26.4	28.4	30.4	32.4
WRIST	15.3	16	16.7	17.4
ANKLE	23.1	24	24.9	25.8
HIGH ANKLE	20.1	21	21.9	22.8
NAPE TO WAIST	40.4	41	41.6	42.2
FRONT SHOULDER TO WAIST	40.4	41	41.6	42.2
ARMSCYE DEPTH	20.4	21	21.6	22.2
WAIST TO KNEE	57.7	58.5	59.3	60.1
WAIST TO HIP	20.2	20.6	21	21.4
WAIST TO FLOOR	102.5	104	105.5	107
BODY RISE	27	28	29	30
SLEEVE LENGTH	57	58	59	60
SLEEVE LENGTH (JERSEY)	51	52	53	54

Constructing Blocks

BLOCK PATTERNS

A block pattern is a foundation pattern constructed to fit an average figure. The average measurements of women are obtained by clothing manufacturers from sizing surveys.

Designers use a foundation pattern (block) as a basis for making the pattern for a design. They may introduce style lines, tucks, gathers, pleats or drapes, but still the basic fit of the pattern will conform to the block used. The finished pattern is made up into a calico toile to check the proportions and shape. The design is then cut out in fabric and made up. This is termed a sample. If it is accepted by buyers and orders are received, the pattern is then graded into the sizes required.

BLOCK PATTERNS – GENERAL INFORMATION

Instructions are given for a wide range of basic garments. The blocks include the basic amount of ease required for the function of the block; for example, a dress block requires less ease than a jacket block. Some blocks offer a further choice of ease; for example, the overgarment block can be drafted to be close fitting for a formal coat or to be an easier fitting coat. It is important that the correct block is chosen for the design; this not only saves time during adaptation but also can affect the final shape. For example, the close fitting bodice block has a wide dart to produce shaping for the bust; this shaping is too acute for many easy fitting designs; the easy fitting block would provide a better base.

Special Note   The basic blocks should be drafted in full scale; students then find it easier to understand block construction and become aware of body proportions.

INTERMEDIATE BLOCKS

Some manufacturers construct intermediate blocks; these are basic shapes that are in use continually, for example the kimono block, the 'A' line skirt block, or a particular shape on which a range of designs has been based. The latter is often developed for a particular fashion shape; this type of 'fashion block' may only be used for one season. As manufacturers change to computer grading systems and to computer-aided design, intermediate blocks will be used increasingly. Their data can be stored and recalled for rapid adaptation and grading, thus improving efficiency.

BLOCK PATTERNS – INDIVIDUAL FIGURES

The basic blocks can be drafted to fit individual figures by using personal measurements instead of the standard ones listed in the size chart. Methods of taking personal measurements and alterations for difficult figures are included in Chapter 13.

SEAM ALLOWANCES

There is no seam allowance included in the blocks. These are added after the pattern is constructed. See the section on seam allowances on page 32.

TYPES OF BASIC BLOCKS AVAILABLE IN THE BOOK

Blocks for Form Cutting

1. The Close Fitting Bodice Block (page 14).
2. The Easy Fitting Bodice Block (page 16).
3. The Tailored Jacket Block – close or easy fitting (page 18).
4. The Classic Coat Block – close or easy fitting (page 20).
5. The One-Piece Sleeve Block   The block can be constructed for all the above blocks (page 22).
6. The Two-Piece Sleeve Block   The block can be constructed for all the above blocks (page 24).
7. Block modification for sleeveless and waist shaping (pages 26 and 27).
8. The Dress Blocks: one-piece and two-piece (page 28).
9. The Shaped Kimono Blocks (page 60).
10. The Tailored Skirt Block (page 78).
11. The Classic Tailored Trouser Block (page 98).
12. The Very Close Fitting Trouser/Jeans Block (page 104).

Blocks for Flat Cutting

1. The Easy Fitting Trouser Block (page 128).
2. The Simple Trouser Block (page 130).
3. The Simple Skirt Block (page 130).
4. The Basic Shirt Block (page 134).
5. The Basic 'Flat' Overgarment Blocks (page 136).
6. The 'Flat' Kimono Block (page 136).
7. Tee Shirt and Track Suit Blocks (page 144).
8. A Range of Knitwear Blocks (pages 150–153).
9. A Range of Body Shape Blocks – for stretch fabrics (pages 156–162).

The Close Fitting Bodice Block

This is a close fitting block. If easy fitting styles with less dart shaping are required use the easy fitting block on page 16.

MEASUREMENTS REQUIRED TO DRAFT THE BODICE BLOCK (example size 12)
Refer to the size chart (page 11) for standard body measurements.

bust	88 cm	shoulder	12.25 cm
nape to waist	41 cm	back width	34.4 cm
waist to hip	20.6 cm	dart	7 cm
armscye depth	21 cm	chest	32.4 cm
neck size	37 cm	front shoulder	
		to waist	41 cm

Square down from 0; square halfway across the block.
0–1 1.5 cm.
1–2 armscye depth measurement plus 0.5 cm; square across.
2–3 half bust plus 5 cm [i.e. for 88 cm bust: (88 ÷ 2) + 5 = 49]. Square up and down; mark this line the centre front line.
3–4 = 0–2 (add 0.3 cm for each size 16, 18 and 20: add a further 0.8 cm for each of the remaining larger sizes.) Example for size 20, 3–4 = 0–2 plus 0.9 cm.
1–5 nape to waist measurement; square across to 6.
5–7 waist to hip measurement; square across to centre front line. Mark point 8 (this gives half hip measurement plus 2.5 cm ease).

Back

0–9 one fifth neck size minus 0.2 cm; draw in back neck curve 1–9.
1–10 one fifth armscye depth measurement minus 0.7 cm; square halfway across the block.
9–11 shoulder length measurement plus 1 cm; draw back shoulder line to touch the line from 10.
12 centre of shoulder line.
12–13 draw a dotted line 5 cm long and sloping inwards 1 cm. Construct dart 1 cm wide with this line as centre (make both sides of dart the same length).
2–14 half back width measurement plus 0.5 cm ease; square up to 15.

14–16 half the measurement 14–15.
17 midway between 2 and 14; square down with a dotted line to point 18 on waistline, and point 19 on the hipline.

Front

4–20 one fifth neck size minus 0.7 cm.
4–21 one fifth neck size minus 0.2 cm; draw in front neck curve 20–21.
3–22 half chest measurement plus half width of dart; square up.
3–23 half the measurement 3–22; square down with a dotted line to point 24 on waistline and 25 on hipline.
26 is the bust point 2.5 cm down from 23; draw a line joining 20–26.
20–27 dart width measurement; draw a line joining 26–27.
11–28 1.5 cm; square out approx. 10 cm to 29.
27–30 draw a line from 27, shoulder length measurement, to touch the line from 28–29.
22–31 one third the measurement 3–21.
32 is midway between 14 and 22; square down with a dotted line to point 33 on the waistline and point 34 on the hipline.
Draw armscye as shown on diagram touching points 11, 16, 32, 31, 30; measurement of the curves:

sizes	8–14	from 14	2.5 cm	from 22	2 cm
sizes	16–20	from 14	3 cm	from 22	2.5 cm
sizes	22–26	from 14	3.5 cm	from 22	3 cm

Draw round the outer edge of the shape from 1–21 to complete the block. When shoulder seams are joined it is essential that the neck and armscyes are smooth curves.

Sleeve Draft a one-piece sleeve (page 22) or a two-piece sleeve (page 24) to fit the armscye measurement.

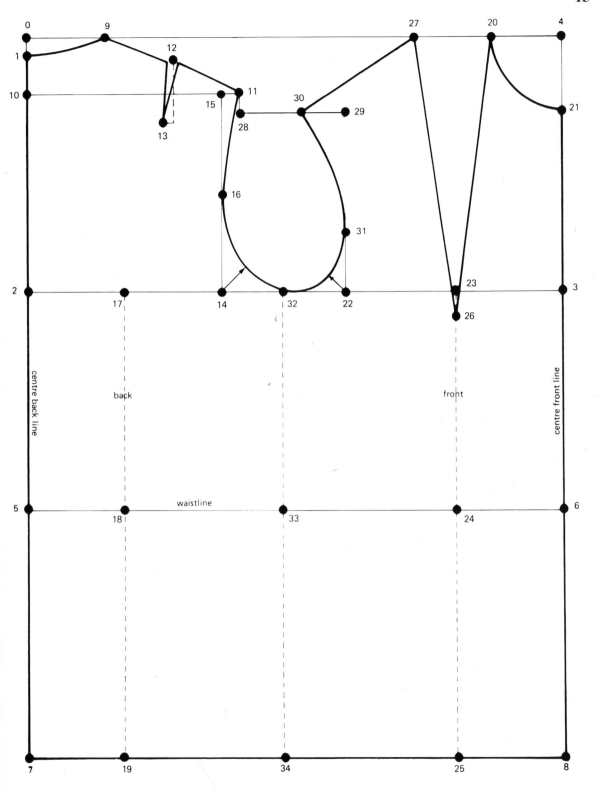

The Easy Fitting Bodice Block

For easy fitting dress styles and easy fitting raglan and kimono shapes.

MEASUREMENTS REQUIRED TO DRAFT THE BLOCK (example size 12)
Refer to the size chart (page 11) for standard measurements.

bust	88 cm	shoulder	12.25 cm
nape to waist	41 cm	back width	34.4 cm
waist to hip	20.6 cm	dart	7 cm
armscye depth	21 cm	chest	32.4 cm
neck size	37 cm	front shoulder to waist	41 cm

Square down from 0; square halfway across the block.

0–1 1.5 cm.

1–2 armscye depth measurement plus 2.5 cm; square across.

2–3 half bust plus 7 cm [i.e. for 88 cm bust: (88 ÷ 2) + 7 = 51]. Square up and down; mark this line the centre front line.

3–4 = 0–2 (add 0.3 cm for each size 16, 18 and 20: add a further 0.8 cm for each of the remaining larger sizes.) Example for size 20, 3–4 = 0–2 plus 0.9 cm.

1–5 nape to waist measurement; square across to 6.

5–7 waist to hip measurement; square across to 8.

Back

0–9 one fifth neck size minus 0.2 cm; draw in back neck curve 1–9.

1–10 one fifth armscye depth measurement minus 1 cm; square halfway across the block.

9–11 shoulder length measurement plus 1 cm (0.5 cm ease and 0.5 cm extra length). Draw back shoulder line to touch the line from 10.

2–12 half back width measurement plus 1 cm ease; square up to 13.

12–14 half the measurement 12–13.

Front

4–15 one fifth neck size minus 0.7 cm.

4–16 one fifth neck size minus 0.2 cm; draw in front neck curve 15–16.

15–17 half the standard dart measurement.

3–18 half chest measurement plus 1 cm, plus half the measurement 15–17; square up.

18–19 half the measurement 3–16 minus 2 cm.

3–20 half the measurement 3–18; join 15–20 and 17–20 to form a dart.

11–21 1.5 cm; square out 15 cm to 22.

17–23 draw a line from 17, shoulder length measurement plus 0.5 cm, to touch the line from 21–22.

18–24 half the measurement 12–18; square down to point 25 on the waistline and 26 on the hipline. Draw armscye as shown on diagram touching points 11, 14, 24, 19, 23; measurement of the curves:

sizes		from 12		from 18	
sizes	8–14	from 12	2.5 cm	from 18	2.25 cm
sizes	16–20	from 12	3 cm	from 18	2.75 cm
sizes	22–26	from 12	3.5 cm	from 18	3.25 cm

Sleeve Draft a one-piece sleeve (page 22) or a two-piece sleeve (page 24) to fit the armscye measurement.

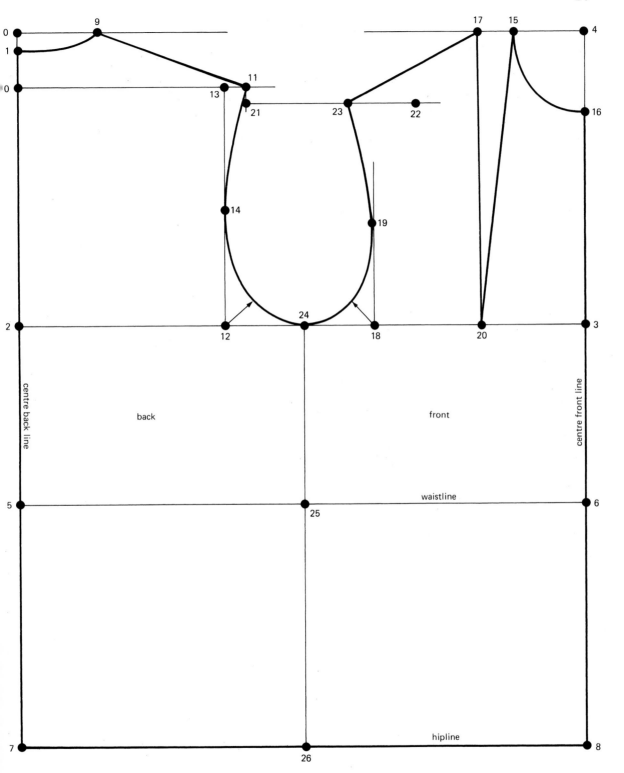

The Tailored Jacket Blocks

For jackets with collars and revers. Close fitting and easy fitting shapes.

MEASUREMENTS REQUIRED TO DRAFT THE BLOCK (example size 12)

Refer to the size chart (page 11) for standard measurements.

bust	88 cm	shoulder	12.25 cm
nape to waist	41 cm	back width	34.4 cm
waist to hip	20.6 cm	dart	7 cm
armscye depth	21 cm	chest	32.4 cm
neck size	37 cm	front shoulder to waist	41 cm

Important Note The easy fitting block has a reduced dart for less bust shaping. Reduce the standard dart measurement by half. The instructions for the easy fitting block are shown in brackets.

Square down from 0; square halfway across the block.

0–1 1.75 cm.

1–2 neck to waist; square across.

1–3 finished length; square across.

2–4 waist to hip; square across.

1–5 armscye depth plus 3 cm (5 cm); square across.

1–6 half the measurement 1–5; square out.

1–7 quarter armscye depth measurement; square out.

5–8 half back width plus 1 cm (3 cm); square up to 9 and 10.

10–11 2 cm; square out.

0–12 one fifth neck size (plus 0.3 cm); draw neck curve.

12–13 shoulder length plus 1.5 cm (3 cm). These measurements include shoulder ease of 0.5 cm.

5–14 half bust plus 8 cm (12 cm); square up, square down to 15 and 16.

14–17 = 0–2 (add 0.3 cm for each size 16, 18 and 20: add a further 0.8 cm for each of the remaining larger sizes.) Example for size 20, 3–4 = 0–2 plus 0.9 cm.

17–18 one fifth neck size plus 1 cm (2 cm).

17–19 one fifth neck size; draw in neck curve. Join point 18 to point 10.

18–20 shoulder measurement plus dart allowance plus 0.5 cm (plus reduced dart allowance plus 2 cm).

18–21 one third shoulder measurement.

21–22 dart measurement (half dart measurement).

14–23 half chest plus half the measurement 21–22 plus 1 cm (3.5 cm). Square up.

23–24 one third the measurement 14–19.

23–25 half the measurement 14–23; square down to 26 and 27 (square up 2 cm for bust point 25). Join 21–25 and 22–25; ensure that the dart lines are the same length. Re-mark point 22.

20–28 2 cm; join 28–22 with a curve.

23–29 half the measurement 8–23; square down to 30 and 31.

Draw armscye as shown in diagram touching points 13, 9, 29, 24, 28; measurement of the curves:

sizes		from 8	from 23
sizes	8–14	2.25 cm (3 cm)	1.75 cm (2.75 cm)
sizes	16–20	2.75 cm (3.5 cm)	2.25 cm (3.25 cm)
sizes	22–26	3.25 cm (4 cm)	2.75 cm (3.75 cm)

Sleeve Draft a two-piece sleeve (page 24).

CLASSIC FRONT EDGE SHAPING

Add required button stand.

Mark points 32 and 33 on waistline and hemline.

33–34 1 cm; join 31–34 with a curve.

32–35 one third the measurement 32–34.

34–36 one fifth the measurement 31–34; draw in front curve.

Shaping the Blocks

The design of the garment will determine the shaping of the block. Two examples are given:

STANDARD SHAPING – fitted designs

2–37 1.5 cm; draw a curved line from 30–37.

37–38 1.5 cm. **3–39** 0.5 cm (1 cm). Draw back seam line 6, 38, 39.

Construct back and front darts as shown; back dart is midway between 5 and 8. (Extend back and front darts to hemline shaping in 2 cm at each hem point.)

Shape back side seam: shape in back waistline 1.5 cm (2 cm); add 1.5 cm to hemline (0.5 cm).

Shape front side seam: shape in front waistline 2 cm (2.5 cm); add 1 cm to hemline (0.5 cm).

SEMI-FITTED SHAPING – 'men's style'

2–37 1.5 cm. **37–38** 1 cm (1.5 cm). **3–39** 0.5 cm (1.5 cm). Draw back seam line 6, 38, 39.

8–40 quarter armscye depth minus 1 cm; square across to 41 on armscye line; square down to 42.

8–43 1.5 cm (2 cm); square down to 44 and 45.

45–46 2.5 cm; draw in back seam line through points 41, 44, 46 (45) and 41, 42, 45 (46).

29–47 one third measurement 23–29; square down to 48 on waistline and 49 12 cm below waistline. Draw in a 1 cm (2 cm) dart on this line.

25–50 3 cm. **27–51** 5 cm. Draw in 1 cm (2 cm) dart on this line (continue the 2 cm shaping to the hemline).

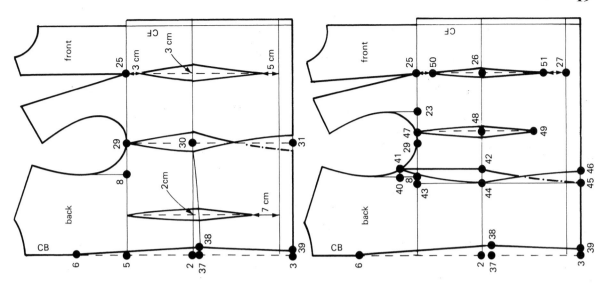

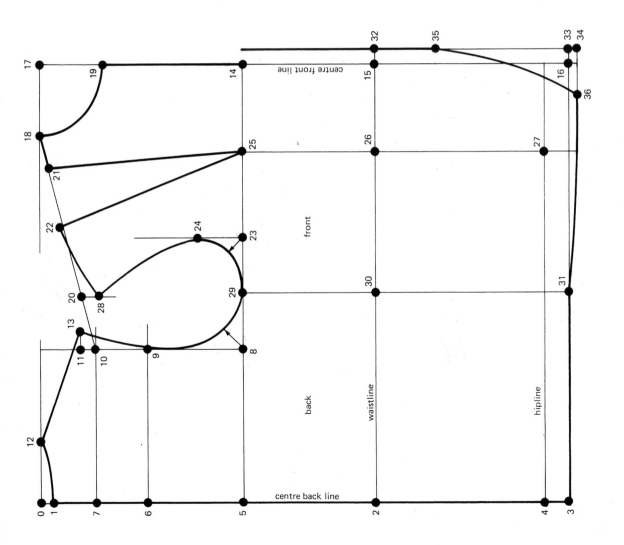

The Classic Coat Blocks

For close fitting coats and easy fitting overgarments.

MEASUREMENTS REQUIRED TO DRAFT THE BLOCK (example size 12)
Refer to the size chart (page 11) for standard measurements.

bust	88 cm	shoulder	12.25 cm
nape to waist	41 cm	back width	34.4 cm
waist to hip	20.6 cm	dart	7 cm
armscye depth	21 cm	chest	32.4 cm
neck size	37 cm	front shoulder to waist	41 cm

Important Note The easy fitting block has a reduced dart for less bust shaping. Reduce the standard dart measurement by half. The instructions for the easy fitting block are shown in brackets.

Square down from 0; square halfway across the block.
0–1 2 cm.
1–2 armscye depth plus 4 cm (6 cm); square across.
2–3 half bust plus 10 cm (15 cm) [i.e. for 88 cm bust; $(88 \div 2) + 10 = 54$ cm]. Square up and down, mark this line the centre front line.
3–4 = 0–2 (add 0.3 cm for each size 16, 18 and 20: add a further 0.8 cm for each of the remaining larger sizes.) Example for size 20, 3–4 = 0–2 plus 0.9 cm.
1–5 nape to waist measurement plus 0.5 cm; square across to 6.
5–7 waist to hip measurement; square across to 8.

Back
0–9 one fifth neck size plus 0.4 cm (0.8 cm); draw in back neck curve 1–9.
2–10 half the measurement 1–2; square out.
1–11 quarter armscye depth measurement; square out.

2–12 half back width plus 1.5 cm (4 cm); square up to 13 and 14.
14–15 2 cm; square out.
9–16 shoulder measurement plus 2 cm (3.5 cm). These measurements include shoulder ease of 0.5 cm.

Front
4–17 one fifth neck size plus 0.2 cm (0.6 cm).
4–18 one fifth neck size plus 0.3 cm; draw in front neck curve 17–18.
17–19 dart measurement (half dart measurement). Joint point 19 to point 14.
19–20 the measurement 9–16 minus 1 cm.
20–21 1.5 cm (1 cm); join 19–21 with a slight curve.
3–22 half chest plus half the measurement 17–19 plus 1 cm (4 cm). Square up.
22–23 one third the measurement 3–18.
22–24 half the measurement 3–22 (square up 3 cm to mark bust point). Join 17–24 and 19–24 to form dart.
22–25 half the measurement 12–22; square down to 26 and 27.
Draw armscye as shown in diagram touching points 16, 13, 25, 23, 21; measurement of the curves:

		from 12	from 22
sizes	8–14	2.75 cm (3.25 cm)	2.25 cm (2.75 cm)
sizes	16–20	3.25 cm (3.75 cm)	2.75 cm (3.25 cm)
sizes	22–26	3.75 cm (4.35 cm)	3.25 cm (3.75 cm)

Note For simple shapes (i.e. kimono block) for mass production, equalize the side seam by making:
2–25 half the measurement 2–3; square down to point 26 on the waistline and 27 on the hipline.

Sleeve Draft the one-piece sleeve (page 22) or a two-piece sleeve (page 24) to fit armscye.

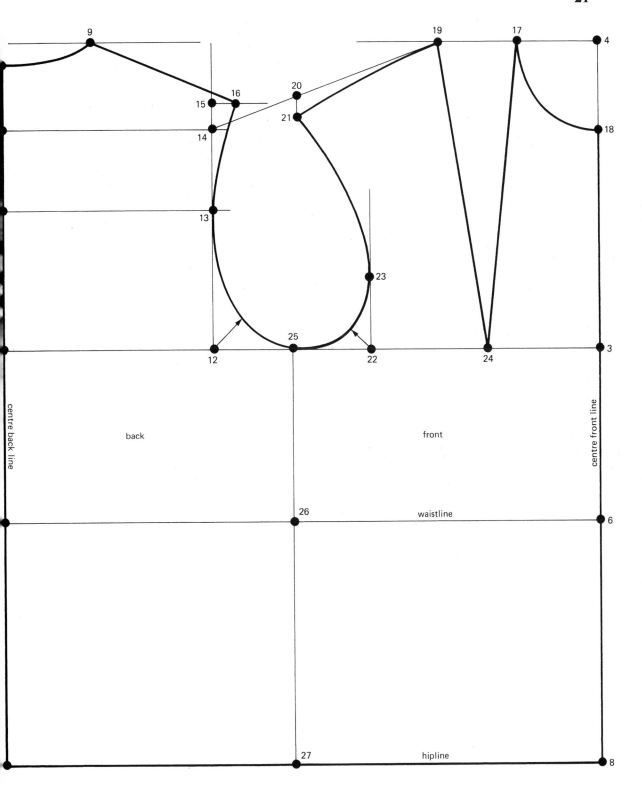

9

19   17   4

20

15   16   18

21

14

13

23

25

12   22   24   3

centre back line

back

front

centre front line

26   waistline   6

27   hipline   8

The One-Piece Sleeve Block

MEASUREMENTS REQUIRED TO DRAFT THE
ONE-PIECE SLEEVE BLOCK (example size 12)
Refer to the size chart (page 11) for standard
measurements.

armscye   measure the armscye
sleeve length   58.5 cm

For coats and easy fitting jackets add 1.5 cm to sleeve
length.

Draw a perpendicular line from the armscye line at 1
touching the front armscye.
1–2 one third armscye measurement (sizes 8–14
minus 0.5 cm, sizes 16–22 minus 0.3 cm); square across.
3 midway between 1 and 2; square across to 4 on the
back scye line; mark balance point; continue line.
1–5 half the measurement 1–3; mark front balance
point as shown. Mark adjacent armscye point 5A
with balance point.
6 front shoulder point.
5–7 the measurement of the curve 5A–6 plus 1 cm
(plus 1.25 cm sizes 16–20; plus 1.5 cm sizes 22–26);
join with a line. Mark top sleeve balance point at 7.
8 back shoulder point.
7–9 the measurement of the curve 4–8 plus 1 cm
(plus 1.25 cm sizes 16–20; plus 1.5 cm sizes 22–26);
join with a line. Mark back sleeve balance point at 9.
10 the underarm point on the side seam; mark with
a balance point.
5–11 the measurement of the curve 5A–10 less 0.3
cm; join with a line.
9–12 the measurement of the curve 4–10 less 0.3 cm;
join with a line.
Square down from 7.

7–13 sleeve length to wrist; square across both ways
for wrist line.
Square down from 11 and 12 to wrist line to marl
points 14 and 15.

Draw in outline of sleeve head:
12–9 hollow the curve 0.75 cm.
9–7 raise the curve 1 cm.
7–5 raise the curve 2 cm at x (one third of distance
7–5).
5–11 hollow the curve 1 cm.

Draw in line of wrist:
14–13 lower the curve 1 cm.
13–15 hollow the curve 1 cm.
For slight sleeve shaping narrow sleeve at wrist
3–5 cm.
The elbow line is on the waistline of the block.

Note It is important that all 'curved measurements'
are measured very accurately along the curved line.
The sleeve is based on the body blocks to ensure a
perfect fit at the armscye.

Ease at the Sleeve Head

The ease in the sleeve head is drafted to give a full
rounded appearance to the sleeve head. For a flatter
insertion reduce the ease allowance in the draft; see
notes 5–7 and 7–9.

Padded Shoulders

All the blocks and sleeves have no allowance included
in the draft for shoulder pads. If pads are required
refer to the section 'Padded Shoulders' (ref. 8 page 48).

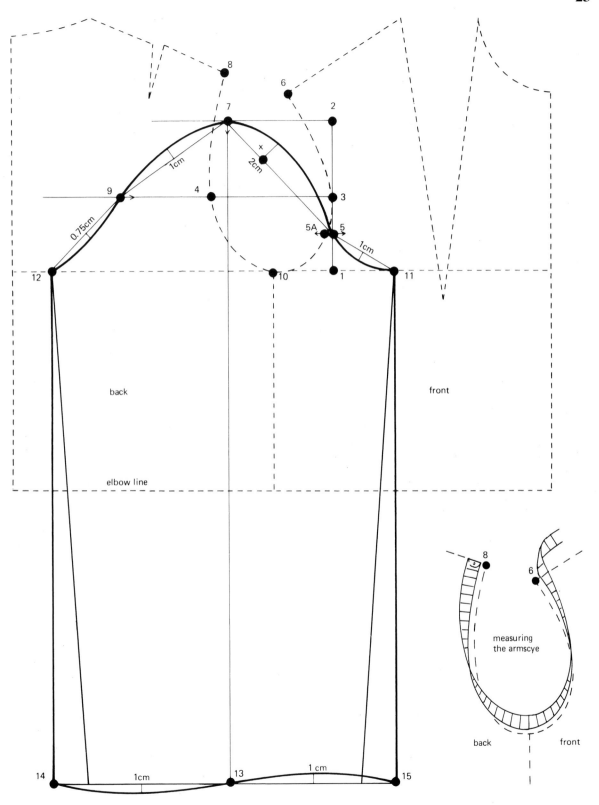

8

6

7

2

+
2cm

1cm

9

4

3

0.75cm

5A

5

1cm

12

10

1

11

back

front

elbow line

8

6

measuring
the armscye

back

front

14

1cm

13

1 cm

15

The Two-Piece Sleeve Block

MEASUREMENTS REQUIRED TO DRAFT THE
TWO-PIECE SLEEVE BLOCK (example size 12)
Refer to the size chart (page 11) for standard
measurements.

armscye	measure the armscye
sleeve length to wrist	58.5 cm
cuff size	13.75 cm

For coats and easy fitting jackets add 1.5 cm to sleeve
length and 1 cm to cuff size.

Mark basic points on body block.
Mark point A at underarm, B and C at shoulder
points.
Mark points D and E at base of lines which are
squared up to touch the armscye curves.

Sleeve
Square up and across from 0.
0–1   one third armscye measurement; square across.
1–2   one third measurement 0–1 plus 1 cm; square
across.
0–3   quarter the measurement 0–1.

On Body Block   E–F equals measurement 0–3 on
sleeve block.
Square out to FP (front pitch point) on armscye.
D–BP (back pitch point) equals the measurement 0–2
on sleeve block.

3–4   the measurement of the curve C–FP plus 1 cm
(plus 1.25 cm sizes 16–22; plus 1.5 cm sizes 24–30).
Join 3–4.
4–5   the measurement of the curve B–BP plus 0.8 cm
(plus 1 cm sizes 16–22; plus 1.2 cm sizes 24–30).
Join 4–5.
0–6   the measurement A–E on body block.

0–7   2 cm; square across both ways.
7–8 and **7–9**   2 cm; square down from 8 and 9.
1–10   sleeve length to wrist; square across to 11 and
12.
10–13   3 cm; square across.
10–14   cuff size for two-piece sleeve; join 10–14 and
10–11.
7–15   half the measurement 7–10; square across
(elbow line). Curve inner sleeve seams inwards 2 cm at
elbow line.
Draw in sleeve head.
5–4   raise the curve 1 cm.
Mark point 16; 4–16 is one third the measurement
4–3.
4–3   raise the curve at 16 2 cm; join 3–8 with a curve.
6–17   the measurement A–BP on body block,
measured straight, plus 0.5 cm.
Join 6–17, draw a curve hollowed 1.5 cm.
Join 6–9 with a slight curve.
Join 17–14 and 5–14.
Mark points 18 and 19 on elbow line.
Curve outer sleeve seams outwards 2.3 cm (2.5 cm
sizes 16–20; 2.7 cm sizes 22–26) at 18 and 19.

Note   It is important that all 'curved measurements'
are measured very accurately along the curved lines
with the tape upright (see diagram).

Ease at the Sleeve Head
The ease in the sleeve head is drafted to give a full
rounded appearance to the sleeve head. For a flatter
insertion reduce the ease allowance in the draft; see
notes 3–4 and 4–5.

Padded Shoulders
All the blocks and sleeves have no allowance included
in the draft for shoulder pads. If pads are required
refer to the section 'Padded Shoulders' (ref. 8 page
48).

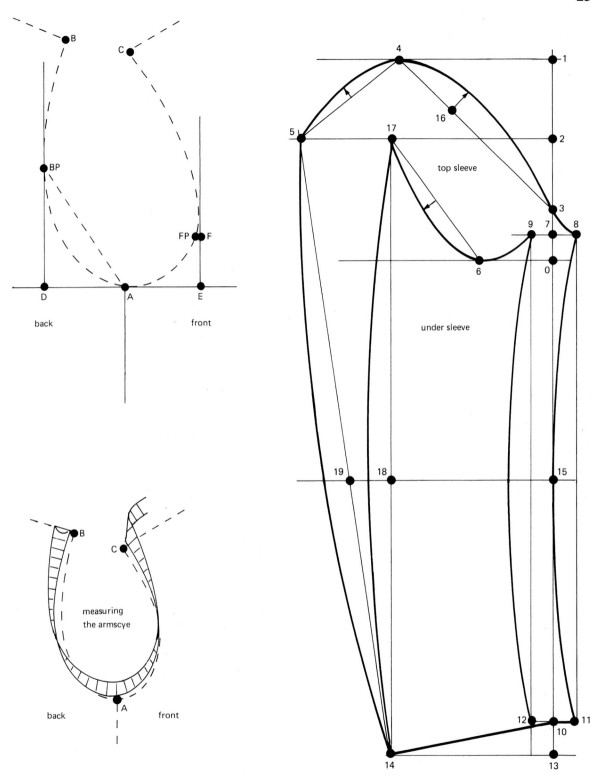

back

front

BP

FP F

D   A   E

back   front

measuring
the armscye

back   front

top sleeve

under sleeve

The Sleeveless Blocks

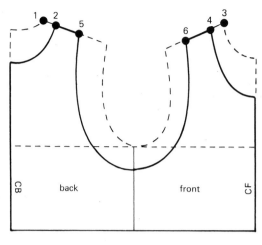

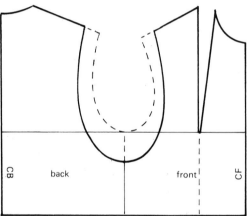

It is a simple matter to draw new armscye shapes onto a block or adapted pattern. If a wider finished shape is required, open the underarm seam the required amount before starting the armscye adaptation.

1 SIMPLE SINGLET SHAPES

Use the dartless block adaptation shown below for woven fabrics, the knitwear or tee shirt blocks for jersey fabrics.
Make 1–2 and 3–4 the same measurement; draw in neck.
Make 2–5 and 4–6 the same measurement; draw in armscye.

2 DART TRANSFER

Trace block required with reduced bust darting.
If lowered armscye is required draw in armscye shape.
Drop a vertical line from base of bust dart.
Cut up line; close bust dart. Mark points 1, 2, 3, 4.
2–5 is the measurement 3–4. Draw new side seam 1–5.

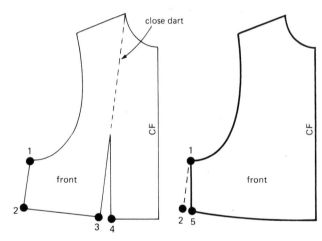

3 THE CLOSE FITTING SLEEVELESS BLOCK

Trace the close fitting bodice block. Mark points 16 and 31. Mark side seam 1–2.
Draw new side seam lines 1.5 cm each side of 1–2. Cut round bodice pieces; rejoin the side seam 1–2.

Draw new armscye depth line 1 cm above original line.
Mark points 3 and 4 1 cm in from shoulder edge. Mark points 5 and 6 1 cm in and 1 cm up from 16 and 31.
1–7 1 cm. Draw new armscye using points 3, 5, 7, 6, 4.

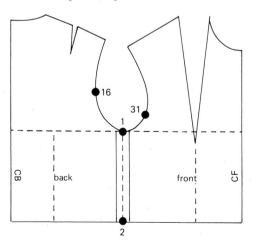

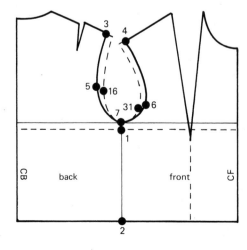

Shaping the Waist

All waisted garments require front waist dropped 1 cm (1.5 cm–2 cm large sizes); join to back with curved line.

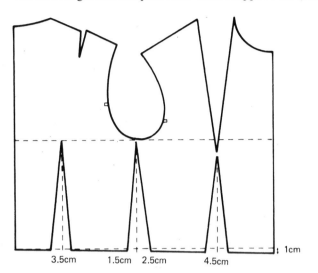

3.5cm 1.5cm 2.5cm 4.5cm 1cm

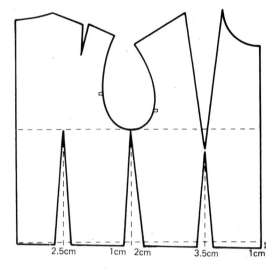

2.5cm 1cm 2cm 3.5cm 1cm

CLASSIC WAIST SHAPING

Shaping the waist of the close fitting block requires half the waist measurement plus 3 cm ease. This means 12 cm shaping (all sizes). Shape block on the dotted lines: 3.5 cm at back dart, 1.5 cm at back side seam, 2.5 cm at front side seam, 4.5 cm at front dart.

THE CLOSE FITTING SLEEVELESS BLOCK

The sleeveless block has already been reduced by 3 cm. This means 9 cm shaping (all sizes). For classic waist shaping follow the dotted lines: 2.5 cm at back dart, 1 cm at back side seam, 2 cm at front side seam, 3.5 cm at front dart.

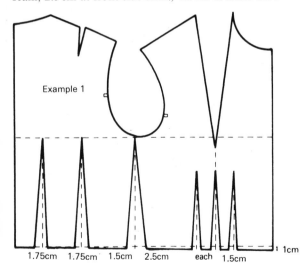

Example 1

1.75cm 1.75cm 1.5cm 2.5cm each 1.5cm 1cm

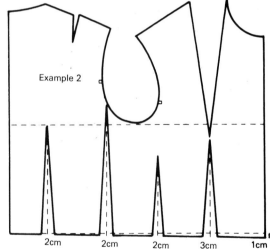

Example 2

2cm 2cm 2cm 3cm 1cm

EXAMPLES OF ALTERNATIVE WAIST SHAPING

The waist shaping can be distributed in different ways depending on the design or block used.

The shaping can be reduced if less fitted styles are required.

Example 1 A design showing the shaping of 12 cm distributed into more darts.

Example 2 Design showing the elimination of the side seam and an easy fitting shape. Waist reduced only 9 cm.

The Dress Blocks

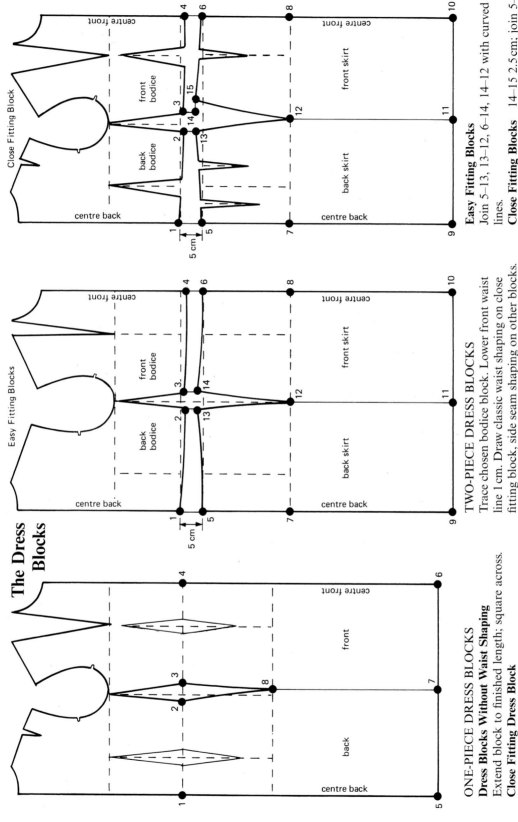

Close Fitting Block

Easy Fitting Blocks

5 cm

front bodice

back bodice

centre back

centre front

front skirt

back skirt

5 cm

front bodice

back bodice

centre back

centre front

front skirt

back skirt

front

back

centre back

centre front

ONE-PIECE DRESS BLOCKS

Dress Blocks Without Waist Shaping
Extend block to finished length; square across.

Close Fitting Dress Block
Trace close fitting bodice block to hipline; draw classic waist shaping. Mark 1, 2, 3, 4.
Square down from 1 and 4 to 5 and 6. Square across. 7 is midway 5–6; square up to 8.
Join 3–8 and 2–8 with curved lines.
Extend back and front darts 13cm.

TWO-PIECE DRESS BLOCKS

Trace chosen bodice block. Lower front waist line 1 cm. Draw classic waist shaping on close fitting block, side seam shaping on other blocks. Mark 1, 2, 3, 4; square down from 1 and 4.
1–5 5cm; square across to 6.
5–7 waist to hip; square across to 8.
5–9 finished length; square across to 10. 11 is midway 9–10; square up to 12. 13 and 14 are below 2 and 3 and 1.25cm up from line 5–6.

Easy Fitting Blocks
Join 5–13, 13–12, 6–14, 14–12 with curved lines.

Close Fitting Blocks 14–15 2.5 cm; join 5–13, 13–12, 6–15, 15–12 with curved lines.
Back darts: construct two darts 1.75cm wide, 12cm and 14cm long. Place darts each side of bodice dart squared down from line 5–13.
Front dart: construct a dart 2cm wide and 10cm long directly below bodice dart.

Part One: Classic Form Cutting
2   FROM BLOCK TO PATTERN

From Block to Pattern

DRESS STANDS AND TOILES

It is possible to cut out patterns without a dress stand. Many people who sew for pleasure do not have one.

However, they are a very valuable piece of equipment. Students should combine flat pattern cutting with work on the dress stand. Design ideas that look acceptable on a flat piece of paper can look ugly and distorted on the rounded form of the body or the dress stand. If a dress stand is not available, you can use the figure of a colleague or your own body. The making of calico toiles is essential when designing advanced styles. A design toile is the pattern cut out in calico and made up to check and perfect the design. Drapes and intricate cuts can be worked on the stand before the toile is sewn.

When the toile is made up, it should be seen on a moving figure to consider the proportions and to ensure the correct amount of ease has been allowed.

THE PATTERN

Three different types of pattern are used by designers when drafting patterns. It is necessary to know the difference.

The Block Pattern . . . is the basic pattern that is used as a basis for all adaptations. The block pattern is traced or 'wheeled' onto pattern paper to produce the working pattern.

The Working Pattern . . . is used for marking out the basic style lines and design features (e.g. pockets, collars, buttonhole placings). Pattern sections are traced off and may be further adapted. Complicated styles may need a number of trials at this stage.

The Final Pattern . . . is the pattern from which the garment will be cut. It must be clearly marked with all the information required for making up the garment.

Before commencing any adaptation the following points should be considered:
1. Choose the correct blocks (e.g. if a baggy trouser style is required use an easy fitting trouser block).
2. Decide the length; lengthen or shorten the block.
3. Decide if any easy fitting armscye is required (see lowered armscye ref. 23 page 54).

GOOD LINES AND CURVES

Refer to the diagrams on the page opposite.

When drafting patterns it is essential that lines and curves are smooth, as any uneven lines will show as unsightly bumps on the finished garment.

1   When a curved line meets a straight line it must run into it smoothly.

2   Neck and armscye curves must be perfect. Make sure all design curves are beautifully shaped, especially where they meet a fold line. French curves are very useful for drawing curved lines.

3   Pattern pieces that are 'cut and spread' can give an uneven outline. Draw it as a smooth even line.

4   When a dart is machined the base of the dart is drawn upwards; this creates a 'V' shape. Compensate for this by shaping the base of the dart downwards on the seam (4).

CLOSE FITTING BODICE – DARTS AND SEAMS

When the working pattern is completed the darts and seams of a close fitting bodice can be shaped to give a better fit. However, in most mass production patterns, the seam and dart lines remain straight.

5   To avoid sharp points at the bust shorten the length of the bust dart and front waist dart by 2 cm.

6 and 7   To achieve a fitted shape around the diaphragm, curve the side seam slightly inwards (6) and the bust and waist darts slightly outwards (7 and 8). This method can be used on the side seam of the sleeve (8).

Do not use this method on skirt darts.

Do not overshape (maximum 0.3 cm darts, 0.5 cm side and sleeve seams).

PRINCIPLES OF PATTERN MAKING

The following chapters cover pattern adaptations, manipulating the block to make different designs. Basic principles are common to many pattern pieces; these should be considered before one begins.

Seam Lines . . . a pattern piece can be cut across vertically, horizontally, diagonally, with curved lines etc.; when the sections are joined the pattern piece will have a seam, but the basic shape remains the same. Dart shaping can be moved to seam lines so that the shaping remains but the dart disappears (ref. 2 page 80).

Shape . . . a garment can fit closely to the figure, be semi-fitting or easy fitting in shape. This is achieved by using the blocks with or without shaping. Some examples of changes of pattern shape are:
widening the outline . . . . . . inserting extra body ease;
hidden shapes . . . . . . adding pleats and godets;
puff and bell shapes . . . . . . adding width to the design by tucks or gathers;
cone shapes . . . . . . widening the hem line only.

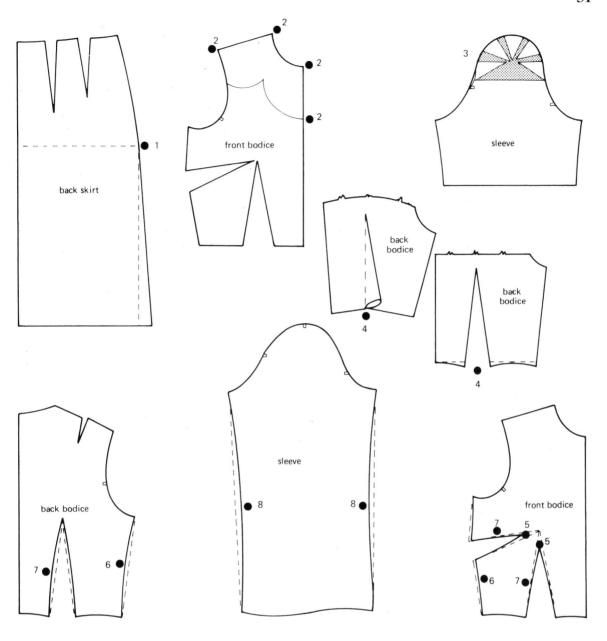

back skirt

front bodice

sleeve

back bodice

back bodice

sleeve

back bodice

front bodice

Adding Pieces . . . when adding pockets, peplums, panels, flaps, etc. consider carefully the balance of the design.

Body Movement . . . in more advanced pattern cutting parts of bodices are added to sleeves. When working these designs always be aware that the body must be able to move. It is only on wide full garments that very simple shapes can be used.

Beautiful Shapes . . . it is always necessary to have good lines and shapes. When cutting intricate patterns small amounts of the basic block may be lost or small parts added. How much one can do this depends on one's skill and experience. That is why it is so difficult to cut the subtle shapes achieved by our top designers.

Cutting individual garments gives designers much more freedom; they are not restricted by the price limits and the fabrics used in mass production.

Seam Allowances

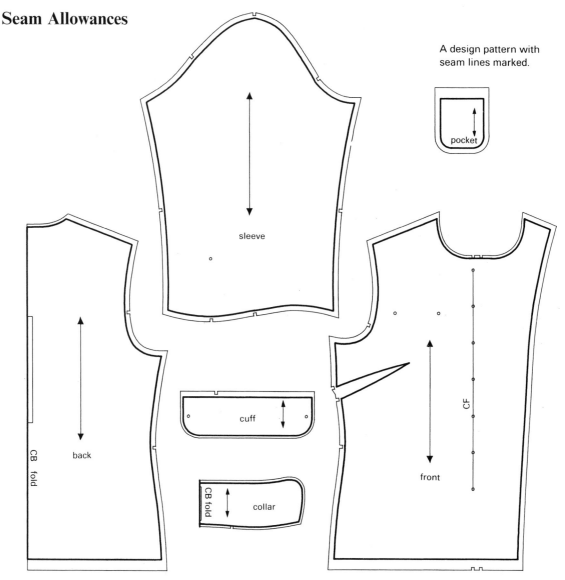

A design pattern with seam lines marked.

Manufacturers require finished patterns to have seam allowances added. Some require their designers to adapt patterns from blocks that already include the seam allowance. This is a difficult task for a beginner. It is better for students to work with nett patterns (those without seam allowance); especially when drafting complicated styles. The seam allowance can be added afterwards.

Seam allowance widths vary with the type of manufacture and garment. The following examples are a general guide.

Basic Seams   e.g. side seams, style seams . . . 1 to 1.5 cm.

Enclosed Seams   e.g. collars, cuffs . . . 0.5 cm.

Hems   depth depends on shape and finish . . . 1 to 5 cm. Decorative seams usually require more seam allowance.

Fabrics that fray easily will require wider turnings especially around facings and collars.

The width of the seam allowance must be marked on the pattern by lines or notches.

No seam allowance is required on a fold line.

It is important that seam allowances added to the pattern are accurate and clearly marked.

TOILE PATTERNS
It is not necessary to add seam allowances at this stage, they can be marked directly on the calico.

INDUSTRIAL PATTERNS
The seam lines are not marked on these patterns. The seam allowance is usually stated in the making up specification and only varying seam allowances will be marked by notches.

Pattern Instructions

A production pattern, seam lines are not marked.

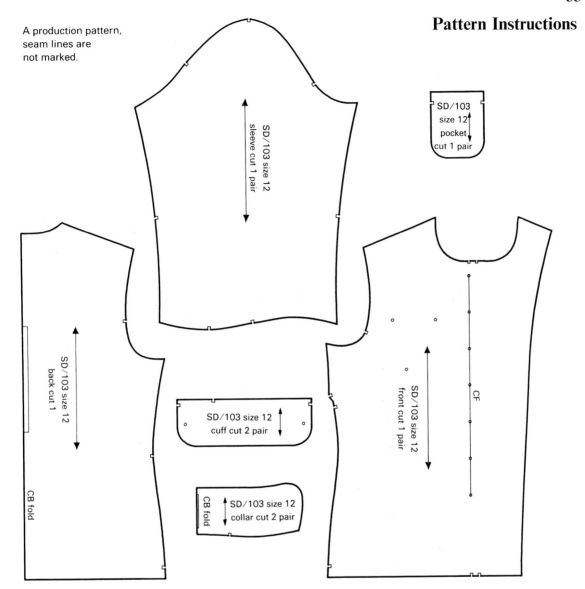

SD/103 size 12 sleeve cut 1 pair

SD/103 size 12 pocket cut 1 pair

SD/103 size 12 back cut 1

CB fold

SD/103 size 12 cuff cut 2 pair

CB fold SD/103 size 12 collar cut 2 pair

SD/103 size 12 front cut 1 pair

CF

To enable the garment to be made up correctly the following instructions must be marked on the pattern:

1. The name of each piece.
2. Centre back and centre front.
3. The number of pieces to be cut.
4. Folds.
5. Balance marks . . . these are used to make sure pattern pieces are sewn together at the correct points.
6. Seam allowances . . . these can be marked by lines round the pattern or notches at each end of the seam. If a pattern is nett (has no seam allowance), mark this clearly on the pattern.
7. Construction lines . . . these include darts, buttonholes, pocket placings, tucks, pleat lines, decorative stitch lines. These lines are marked on the pattern or shown by punch holes.
8. Grain lines . . . to achieve the effect you require, you must understand the principle of placing a pattern on the correct grain of the fabric (see over page). Mark the grain line with an arrow. Mark the grain lines on the working pattern before it is cut up into sections. Once in pieces it can be difficult to find the correct grain on complicated pattern sections.
9. Pattern size.
10. Style no., e.g. SD/103.

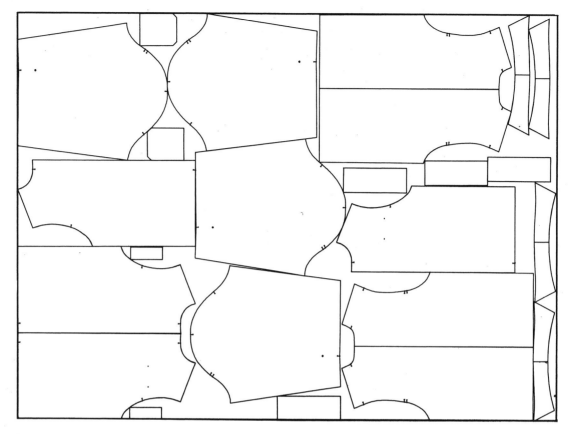

A computer-generated cost lay plan with 84% efficiency.

Fabric Grain

All woven fabrics have warp threads and weft threads. The warp threads run parallel to the selvedge of the fabric and are the strongest; the weft threads run across the fabric and are weaker.

It is good practice to have the vertical lines of the pattern running parallel to the warp threads. Pattern pieces can be cut on the cross for the following reasons:
Design Features . . . stripes and checks cut at different angles can produce interesting designs.
Natural Stretch . . . fabric cut on the cross has natural stretch characteristics; this allows the pattern to be cut with less ease. The design then fits the figure closely but remains comfortable.
Drape . . . folds, drapes and softly flaring skirts hang better when cut on the cross. The effects of cutting on the cross are increased by the choice of fabrics, i.e. crepes, satins and soft woollens.

Once the grain has been decided and marked on the pattern, always check that you have laid it on the fabric correctly before cutting out, or a distorted garment will be produced.

Lays

Cost is very important, therefore economical lays are required by manufacturers. A 'lay' (or marker) is the plan of the pattern pieces as they are placed on the fabric. Fabrics that have to be cut in one direction are usually very uneconomical; fabrics that allow the pieces to be laid in both directions will reduce fabric costs. The practice of saving fabric by laying pattern pieces across the fabric or 'off the grain' should not be attempted by a beginner as this practice can ruin a garment.

When a designer submits a sample, a cost lay plan is made, usually of two garments, so that an accurate costing can be produced. This may be done in varying widths of fabric.

If more than one fabric is used in a garment, more than one lay plan will be made. The collection of pattern pieces required for each lay is known as a 'model'. Lay planning and marker making by computer are increasing rapidly as the cost of systems is reducing. This method increases efficiency, that is the percentage area of fabric used by the pattern. Most manufacturers aim for 80% utilization of the fabric.

Part One: Classic Form Cutting
3 BASIC ADAPTATIONS OF THE BODICE BLOCKS

Positions of bust and shoulder darts

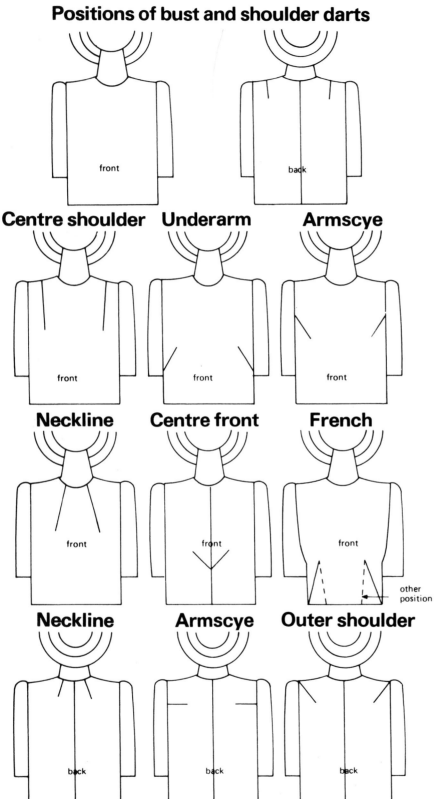

Centre shoulder **Underarm** **Armscye**

front · front · front

Neckline **Centre front** **French**

front · front · front · other position

Neckline **Armscye** **Outer shoulder**

back · back · back

DARTING THE BODICE TO GIVE SHAPE FOR THE BUST AND SHOULDER BLADES

It is necessary to consider the shape of the body when designing a bodice. At this stage do not be concerned with waist darts, they are used to shape the waist only.

Experiment with the bust and shoulder darts which provide the shaping for bust and shoulder blades.

Their positions on the bodice block are shown on the drawings.

These positions can be moved around the body as long as the point of the dart remains at the point of the bust or shoulder blades. See diagram opposite. Try swinging the darts to new positions.

Bust Dart

Centre Shoulder trace round from bodice block. Draw a line from centre shoulder to the point of the bust. Cut up the line. Close original dart and secure with tape. The bust dart is now in cèntre shoulder position. By the same method transfer bust dart to: *Underarm – Armscye – Neckline* and *Centre Front*.

French Dart this dart combines bust dart and front waist dart. Trace round front bodice block, draw in the waist shaping. Draw a line from a point at waist side seam to bust point. Cut up the line. Close bust dart and front waist dart to make a very large dart at base of side seam. This large dart can be placed at the waist position.

Note When the bust dart is in the final position for the design, shorten it by 2 cm.

Back Shoulder Dart

Neck trace round back bodice block. Draw a line from neck to base of shoulder dart. Cut up the line. Close shoulder dart. By the same method transfer shoulder dart to: *Armscye – Outer Shoulder Point.*

Other positions of bust and shoulder darts

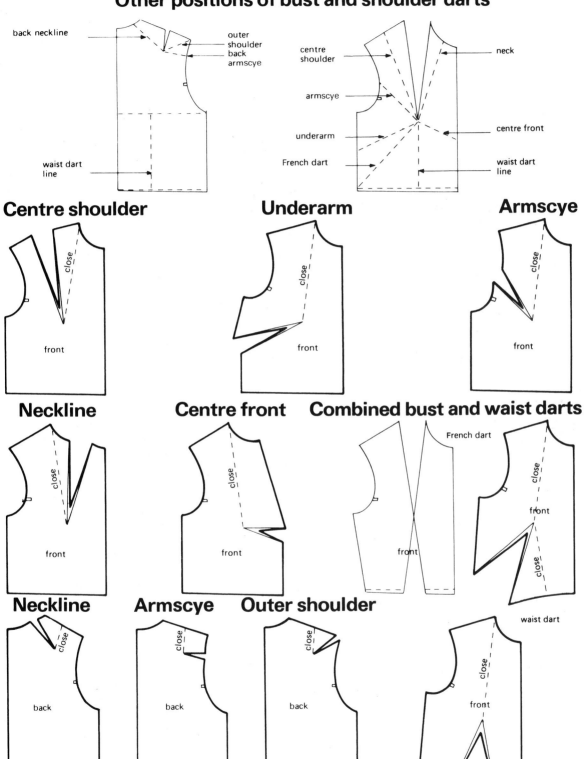

back neckline

outer
shoulder
back
armscye

waist dart
line

centre
shoulder

neck

armscye

underarm

centre front

French dart

waist dart
line

Centre shoulder

close

front

Underarm

close

front

Armscye

close

front

Neckline

close

front

Centre front

close

front

Combined bust and waist darts

French dart

front

close

front

close

waist dart

Neckline

close

back

Armscye

close

back

Outer shoulder

close

back

close

front

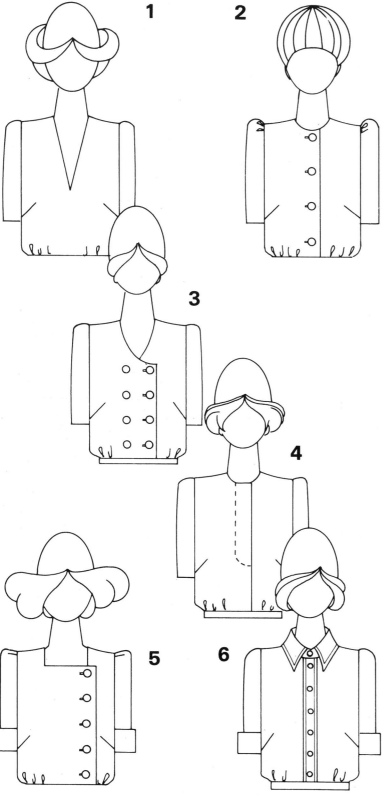

Openings

1   LOW CUT FRONTS
Low cut necks can gape at front. To correct, move bust dart to underarm position. Draw neckline. Make small dart approx. 0.6 cm wide from neckline to bust point. Close dart. Correct slightly distorted neckline.

2   STANDARD BUTTONED FRONT
Mark buttonholes on centre front line (buttonholes overlap this line by 0.2 cm); add buttonstand approx. 2.5 cm; this varies with size of button. Fold outer line, wheel through the outline and facing line to make extended facing.

3   DOUBLE BREASTED FRONT
Alter neckline to shape required. Draw in two button lines, equal distance each side of centre front. Mark buttonholes (as standard front). Add buttonstand. Wheel through separate facing.

4   FLY FRONT
Right Front   Add buttonstand to centre front. Draw in finished stitch line. Add an extension to front edge 5 cm below stitch line and 2.5 cm wider than width of stitching. Wheel through a facing with the same extension. Mark vertical buttonholes on centre front line of facing.
Left Front   Construct left front as a standard buttoned front.

5   ASYMMETRICAL FRONT
Trace complete front of bodice, mark button line, mark buttonholes, add buttonstand. Draw in neckline. Make a separate facing.
Trace left front to button line, add buttonstand and extend facing.

6   SHIRT FRONT
Right Front   add buttonstand 1.5 cm wide. Draw a line 1.5 cm in from centre front. Wheel through front strap. Mark in vertical button holes on centre front line.
Left Front   Add buttonstand and an extended facing 3 cm wide.

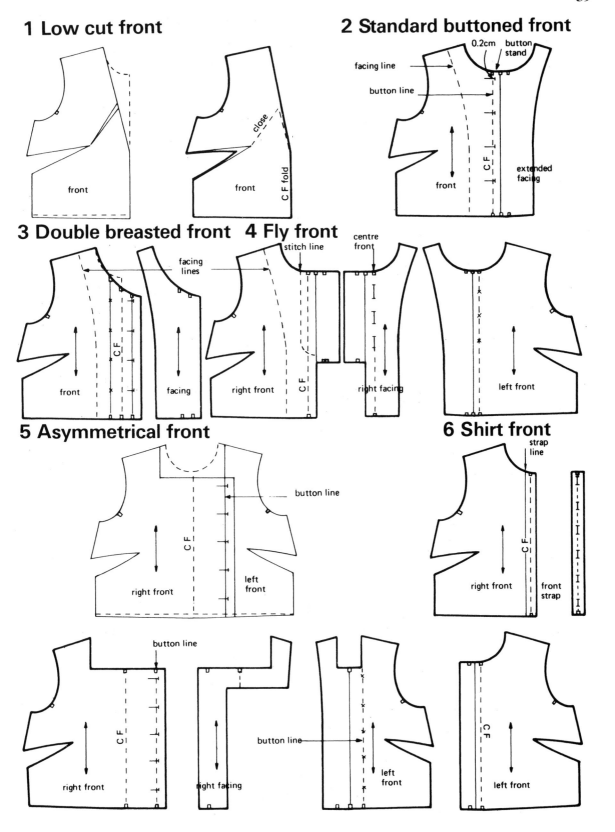

1 Low cut front

front

close

front

CF fold

2 Standard buttoned front

0.2cm button stand

facing line

button line

CF

front

extended facing

3 Double breasted front

4 Fly front

facing lines

stitch line

centre front

front

CF

facing

right front

CF

right facing

left front

5 Asymmetrical front

button line

CF

right front

left front

6 Shirt front

strap line

CF

right front

front strap

button line

CF

right front

right facing

button line

left front

CF

left front

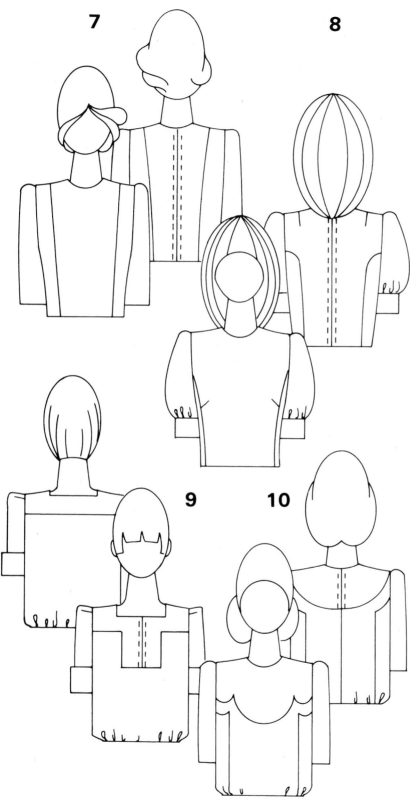

7

8

9

10

DARTS IN SEAMS

Darts can be placed in seams if the seam goes through the bust point. If seam is away from the bust point a small dart or ease will still be required to give shape to the bust, e.g. 8.

7 BUST DART IN VERTICAL SEAMS

Trace round bodice block required. Draw a line from back shoulder dart to top of waist dart. Transfer bust dart to centre shoulder. Cut out panel sections and trace round.
Curve panel and side seams as shown. Shape waistline at base of panels.

8 BUST DART IN CURVED VERTICAL SEAMS

Trace round bodice block required. Draw in fitted side seam and curved panel lines; draw in required amount of waist shaping on these lines. Draw a line from front panel to the base of bust dart.
Cut out panel sections, trace round. Close bust dart to transfer it to panel line. Shape seams, shape waistline at base of panels.

9 BUST DART IN HORIZONTAL SEAMS

Trace round bodice block required.
Back Yoke Draw in back yoke line, slope it down 1 cm to armscye edge from base of shoulder dart. Cut away yoke; close shoulder dart. Draw in square neckline.
Back Draw panel line, points 1–2. Draw slight waist shaping. Cut up panel. Trace round back pattern.
Front Transfer bust dart to side panel line. Draw in square neckline and front yoke line. Cut away yoke and trace round. Close bust dart.

10 BUST DART IN CURVED SEAMS

Trace round bodice block required. Draw in panel lines on block. Cut into sections. Trace round lower sections.
Back Yoke Extend back dart to edge of yoke. Close dart.
Front Yoke Close bust dart.

7 The bust dart in vertical seams

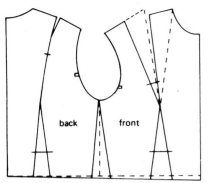

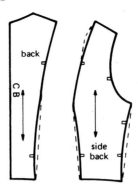

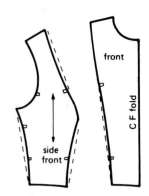

back

C B

side back

side front

front

C F fold

8 The bust dart in curved vertical seams

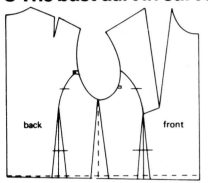

back

front

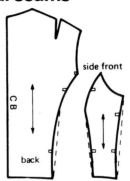

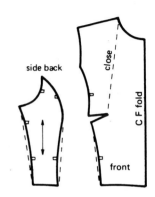

C B

back

side front

side back

close

C F fold

front

9 The bust dart in horizontal seams

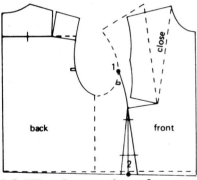

back

front

close

front

1

2

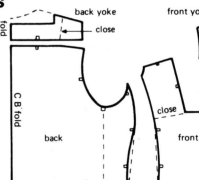

fold

back yoke

close

front yoke

C B fold

back

close

front

C F fold

C F

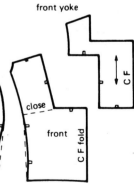

10 The bust dart in curved seams

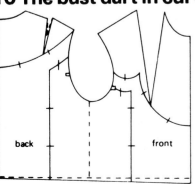

back

front

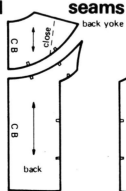

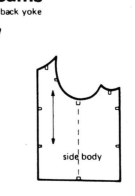

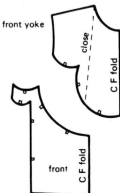

C B

close

back yoke

front yoke

close

C F fold

C B

back

side body

front

C F fold

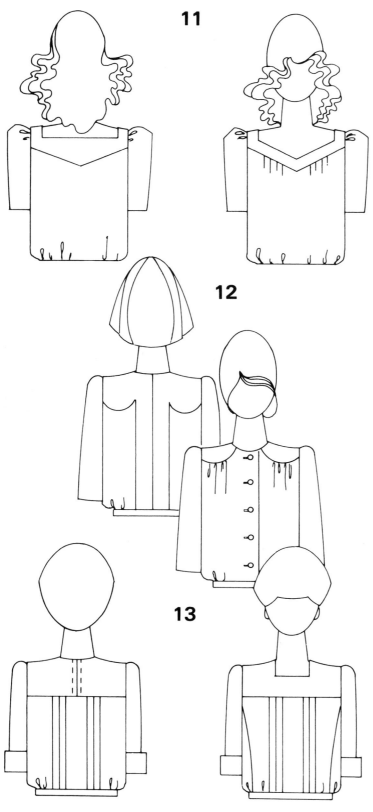

11

12

13

DARTS IN FULLNESS
Darts can be placed in fullness, e.g. tucks, gathers and pleats.

11   BUST DART IN TUCKS
Trace round bodice block required. Transfer bust dart to underarm (cut down side seam to top of dart).
Yokes   Draw in yoke lines, cut away, close back dart. Draw in neckline. For wide necklines narrow shoulder at armscye of back and front yokes.
Back   Trace round back section.
Front   Draw vertical line through bust point; cut up this line. Close underarm dart. Trace round front sections allowing 2 cm gap between vertical lines. Mark four tucks on the top line of front. Size of tuck is the distance 1–2 divided by 4.

12   BUST DART IN GATHERS
Draw round bodice block required. Cut up side seam.
Back   Draw in back panel. Cut up lines. Trace round panels. Close dart.
Front   Transfer bust dart to underarm. Draw in yoke line; mark balance points. Drop a vertical line from yoke through bust point. Cut away yoke. Cut up vertical line, open 3 cm. Close underarm dart, trace round pattern. Mark buttonholes. Add buttonstand and facing to centre front.

13   BUST DART IN PLEATS
Trace round bodice block required. Draw in front panel line. Cut up panel line. Transfer bust dart to panel seam. Draw in back yoke line, slope down 1 cm at armscye from base of shoulder dart. Draw in front yoke line. Cut away yokes and trace round. Close back dart. Draw in front neckline.
Bodice Sections   Draw in pleat lines (2 cm wide) on both bodices cut up pleat lines. Insert 4 cm between the pleat lines. Trace round new patterns, close underarm dart. Fold pleats, cut out patterns.
Note   Pleats on front bodice can be stitched down to bust line.

11 The bust dart in tucks

12 The bust dart in gathers

13 The bust dart in pleats

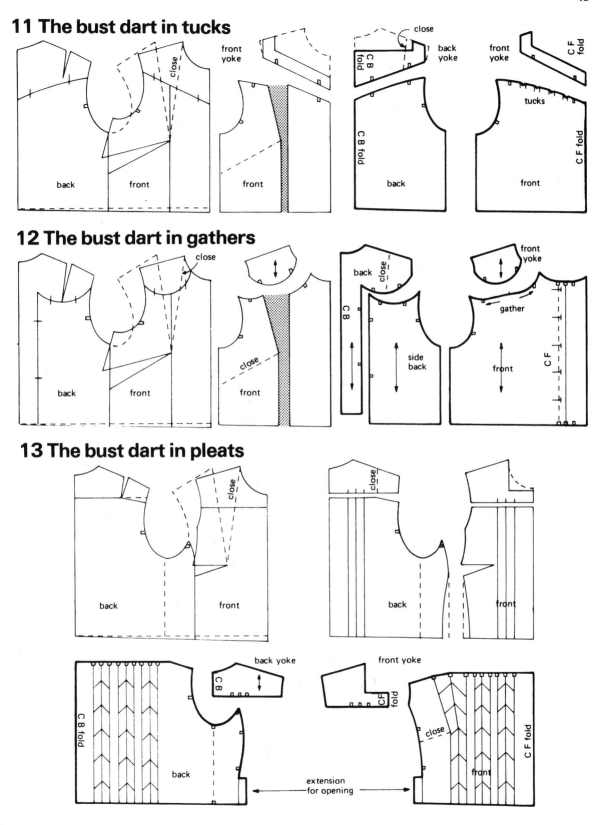

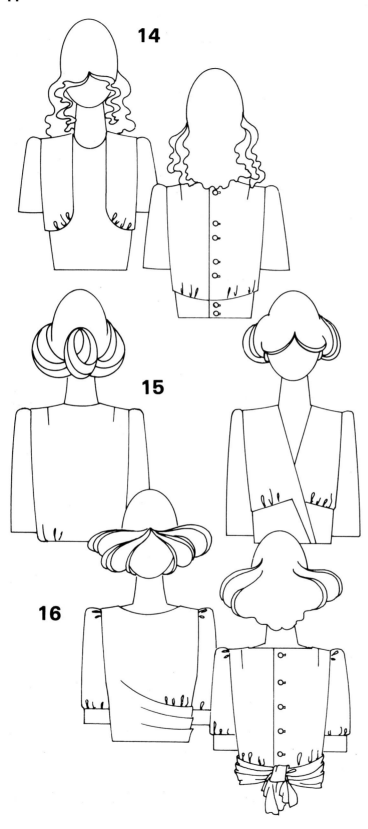

14 GATHERED BUST SEAM

Trace round fitted bodice block. Transfer bust dart to armscye, draw in shaped bust seam and extend across back. Mark balance points for position of gathers. Draw a line from front armscye to shaped bust seam as shown.

Shaped Front Panel Cut away lower sections and place together as shown, overlap 2.5 cm at top of side seam. Trace round making a smooth line along top edge. Mark buttonholes and add buttonstand, at centre back.

Side Front Close bust dart. Cut up drawn line, open 2 cm at bottom for extra fullness. Trace round pattern.

Back Straighten side seam. Mark buttonholes, add buttonstand. Make a combined facing for back and lower panel.

15 WRAP OVER FRONT

Trace round fitted bodice block (both sides of front). Transfer dart to armscye. Draw in wrap over front and midriff line. Mark balance points for positions of gathers. Make a small dart in neckline (ref. Low Cut Front, page 38).

Front Cut up side seams and cut away lower section. Close armscye and neck darts on upper section, trace round, straighten neckline. Close dart on lower section, trace round.

Back Trace round back pattern, rub out waist dart.

16 DRAPED FRONT

Trace round bodice block required (both sides of front). Mark drape lines across front bodice. Cut up side seam.

Back Trace round back pattern, lower neckline, mark buttonholes, add buttonstand and extended facing, rub out dart.

Front Cut along drape lines, close waist darts. Close both bust darts. Open drape lines approx. 4 cm. Trace round pattern. Lower neckline. Extend lower section to length required for tie. Trace tie piece for facing and back tie pattern.

14 Gathered bust seam

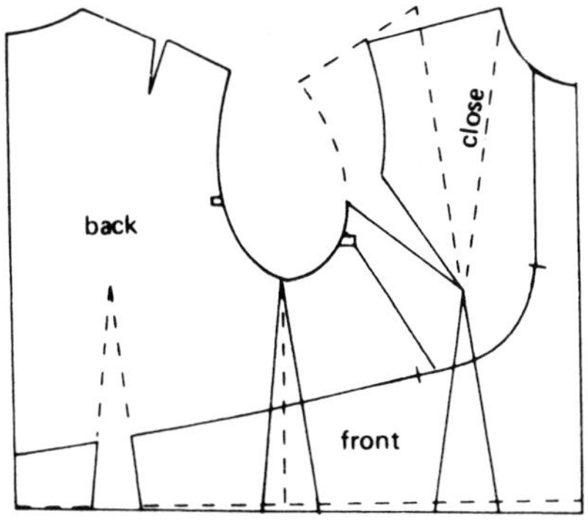

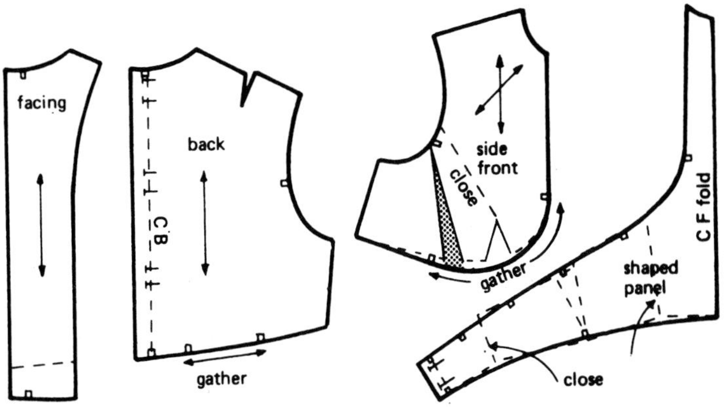

back

close

front

facing

back

C B

gather

side front

close

gather

C F fold

shaped panel

close

15 Wrap over front

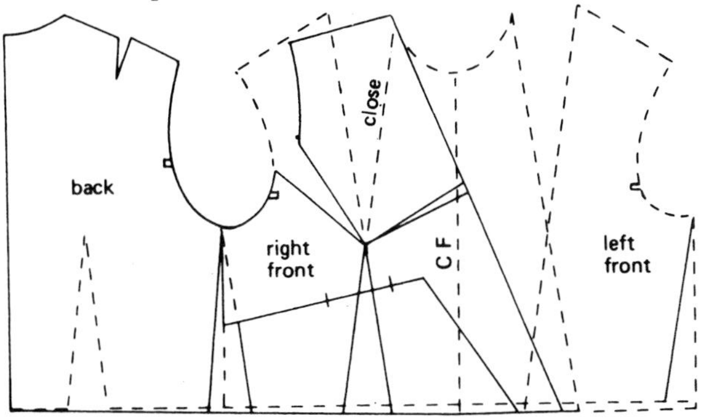

back

close

right front

C F

left front

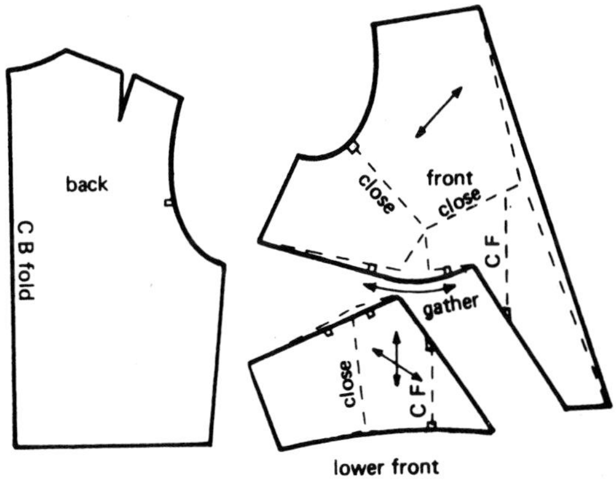

back

C B fold

close

front

close

C F

gather

close

C F

lower front

16 Draped front

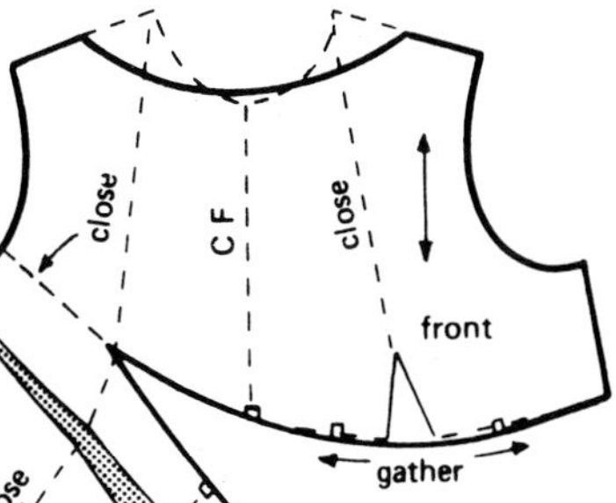

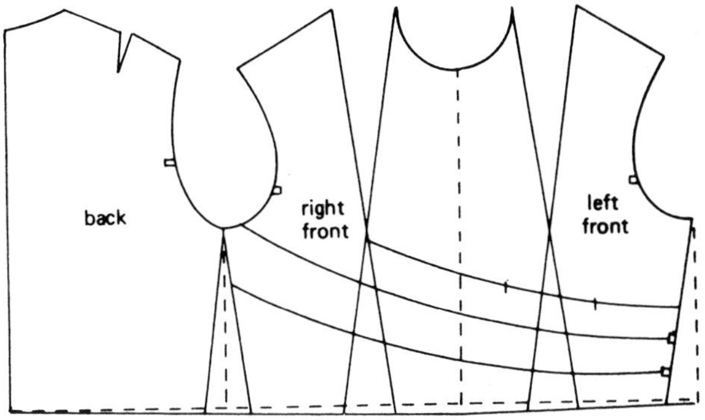

close

C F

close

front

gather

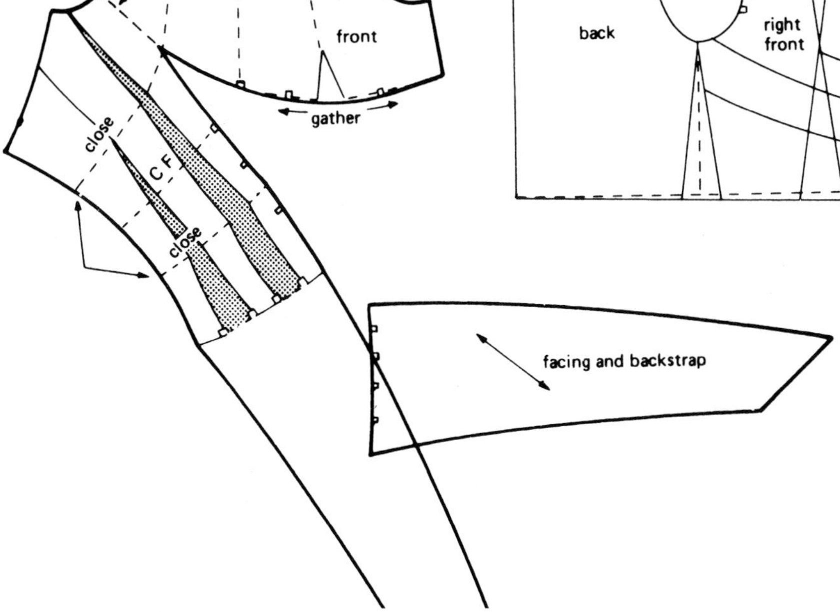

close

C F

close

back

right front

left front

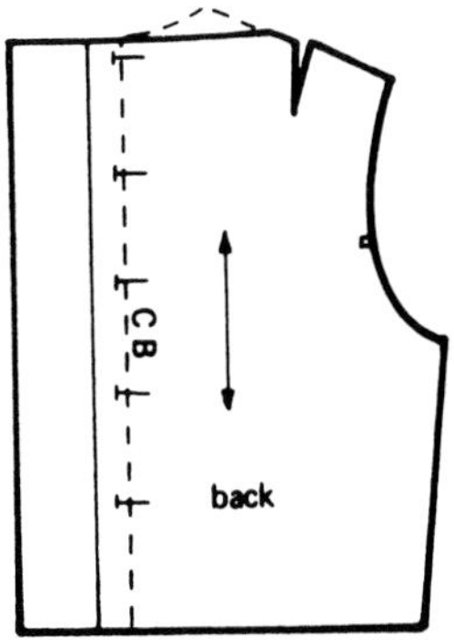

facing and backstrap

C B

back

17 Classic blouse

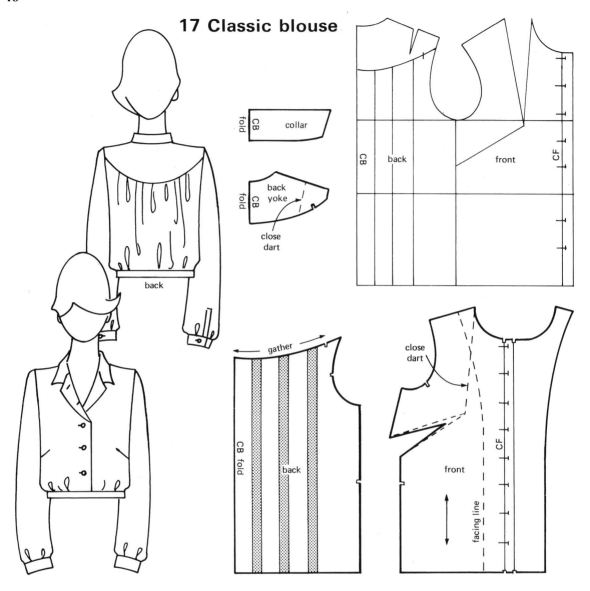

CLASSIC BLOUSE SHAPES

The design illustrates the procedure and order for the simple adaptation of a blouse shape with a set in sleeve.

The basic shape is suitable for styles that require the retention of bust shaping and therefore require a block with a bust dart. Select the close fitting block for full bust shaping, the easy fitting for an easier fit.

Note   If a classic shirt style without bust darting is required select the basic shirt block on page 134.

17   CLASSIC BLOUSE

Trace round bodice block required to hipline. Draw in buttonholes; add buttonstand. Place any shoulder ease into 0.5 cm dart. Draw back yoke line; divide the line into four sections; square down. Cut up side seam.

Back   Cut away yoke, extend dart to yoke line; close dart. Cut up lines on back section, open approx. 2 cm. Redraw yoke line curve.

Front   Transfer dart to underarm; shorten dart. Draw in facing line; construct an extended facing (ref. 2 page 38).

Sleeve   Shirt sleeve (ref. 2 page 48 or ref. 24 page 54).

Collar   Convertible collar (ref. 8 page 70).

Part One: Classic Form Cutting
4 SLEEVE ADAPTATIONS

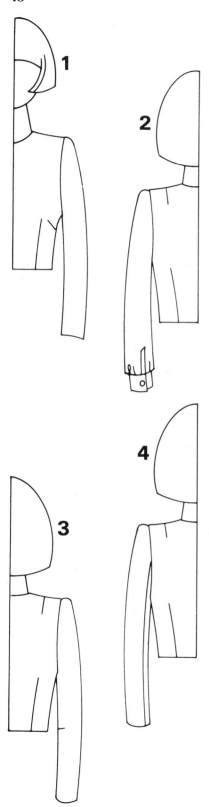

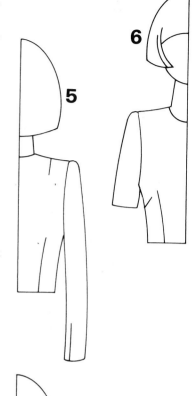

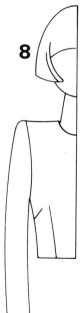

1 STRAIGHT SLEEVE

Trace basic sleeve block, hollow side seams 0.5 cm. Short sleeve line is midway between armscye and elbow. Three quarter line is midway between elbow and wrist.

2 SHIRT SLEEVE

Shorten straight sleeve by depth of cuff. Mark back opening midway between centre line and side seam. Narrow at wrist 2.5 cm.

3 SEMI-FITTED SLEEVE

Trace straight sleeve. Narrow sleeve at wrist by 3 cm. Shape seam. Cut from back elbow line to point 1 and from point 1 to wrist line. Pivot this section forward 4 cm, to make a dart at elbow line. Halve the length of dart less 1 cm. Mark in new centre line from 1 to centre of wrist.

4 SLEEVE WITH BACK SEAM

Trace semi-fitted sleeve. Draw line from back balance point through dart point to wrist ($^1/_4$ wrist measurement). Place side seams together at underarm and wrist. Close dart.

5 CLOSE FITTING SLEEVE

Trace semi-fitted sleeve. Take 1.25 cm off each side seam. Cut up centre seam, overlap 1 cm. Drop line from point of dart to wrist. Cut line, close elbow dart. Shorten dart. Make wrist opening. Raise armscye 1.5 cm. Cut sleeve on the cross in woven fabrics.

6 SHORT SLEEVE

Trace straight sleeve pattern to short sleeve line. Shape in 1.5 cm at the bottom of each side seam.

7 FITTED SHORT SLEEVE

Draw 1 cm dart on centre line. Close dart. Trace round pattern.

8 PADDED SHOULDERS

Trace bodice and sleeve blocks. Slash from armscye to neck of bodice. Open depth of pad. Cut across sleeve head and up centre line. Open out the same amount inserted in armscye.

1 Straight sleeve

2 Shirt sleeve

3 Semi-fitted sleeve

4 Sleeve with a back seam

5 Close fitting sleeve

6 Short sleeve

7 Fitted short sleeve

8 Padded shoulders

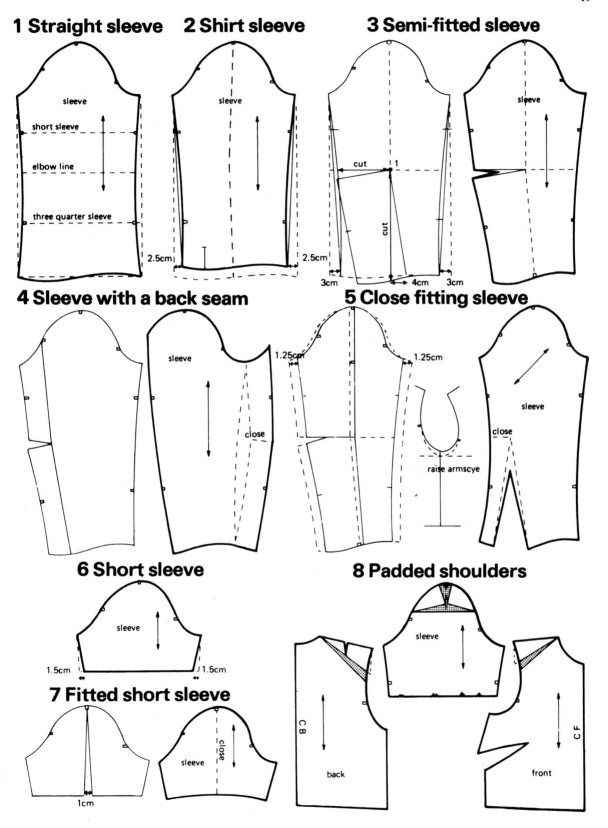

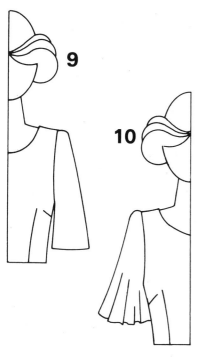

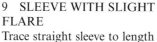

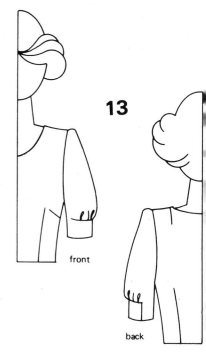

9 SLEEVE WITH SLIGHT FLARE

Trace straight sleeve to length required. Divide into six sections. Cut up lines, open approx. 1 cm. Grain line is in centre of middle opening.

10 VERY FLARED SLEEVE

The sleeve is shown with more flare inserted between the sections.

11 GATHERED INTO A CUFF

The very flared sleeve can be gathered into a cuff constructed to fit the top arm measurement.

12 SLEEVE WITH FLARED SECTION

Trace straight sleeve to length required. Shape in 1 cm. Draw in curved shape. Divide lower sleeve into six sections. Cut away lower sleeve. Cut up lines, open for required amount of flare. Trace round pattern.

13 SLEEVE WITH MOCK CUFF

Trace short sleeve, lengthen 4 cm. Draw in 'cuff' shape. Drop five vertical lines from sleeve head as shown. Cut along 'cuff' line and up lines. Open to give required amount of flare. Trace round pattern. Fold paper along 'cuff' hemline, wheel through to trace 'cuff' facing. Cut out pattern.

14 BISHOP SLEEVE

Trace straight sleeve. Divide into six sections. Cut out, cut up lines. Draw a vertical grain line on a new piece of paper. Open centre line of sleeve evenly each side of line (e.g. 8 cm). Open the two back lines 8 cm, front lines 4 cm. After reducing cuff depth measurement, add extra length, twice as much at centre back.

15 LANTERN SLEEVE

Trace straight sleeve to length required, draw in seam. Divide into six sections. Cut out top and bottom sleeve. Cut up lines of upper section, open for required amount of flare. Open sections of lower sleeve at the top the same amount, overlap slightly at lower edge.

front

back

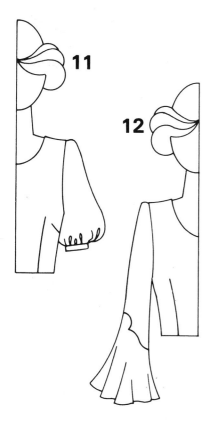

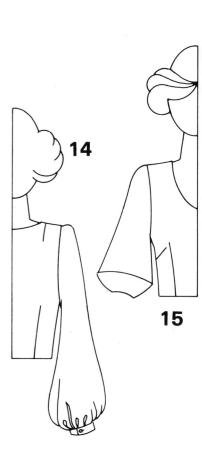

9 Sleeve with slight flare

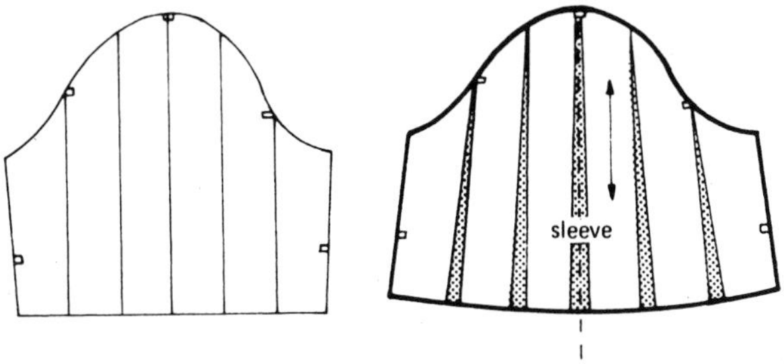

10 Very flared sleeve

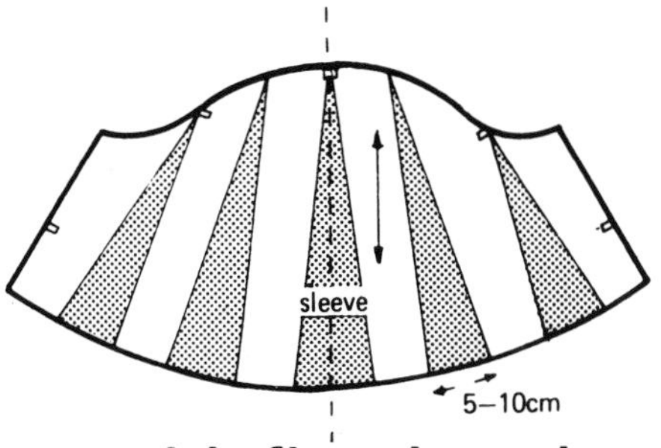

sleeve

sleeve

5—10cm

11 Gathered into a cuff

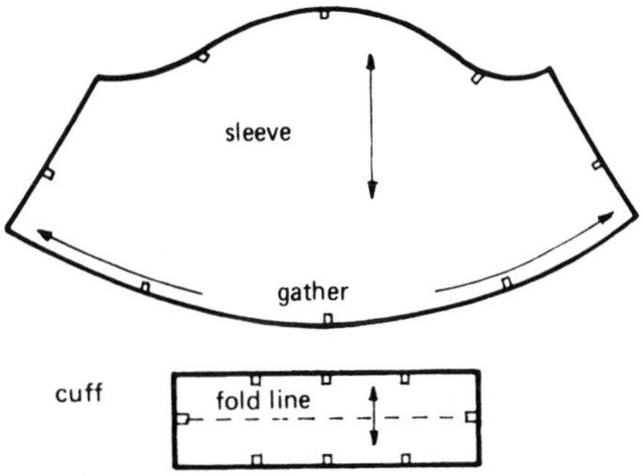

sleeve

gather

cuff

fold line

12 Sleeve with flared section

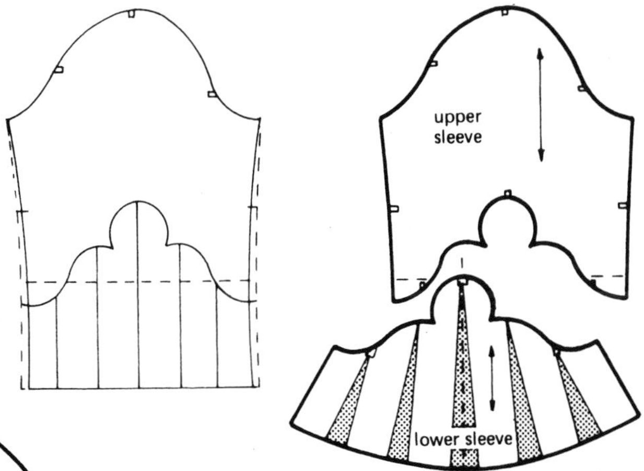

upper sleeve

lower sleeve

13 Sleeve with mock cuff

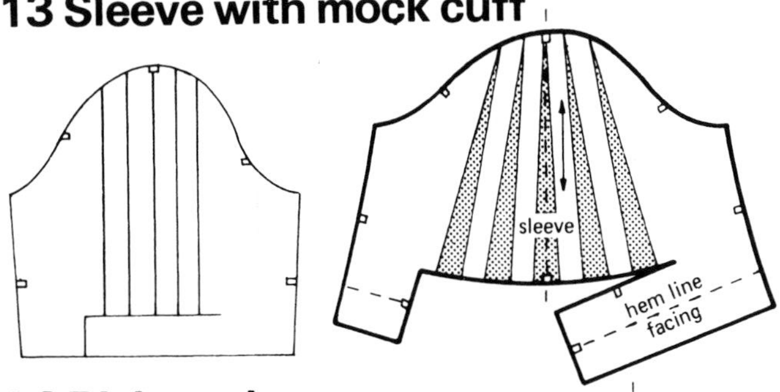

sleeve

sleeve

hem line
facing

15 Lantern sleeve

upper sleeve

lower sleeve

overlap

14 Bishop sleeve

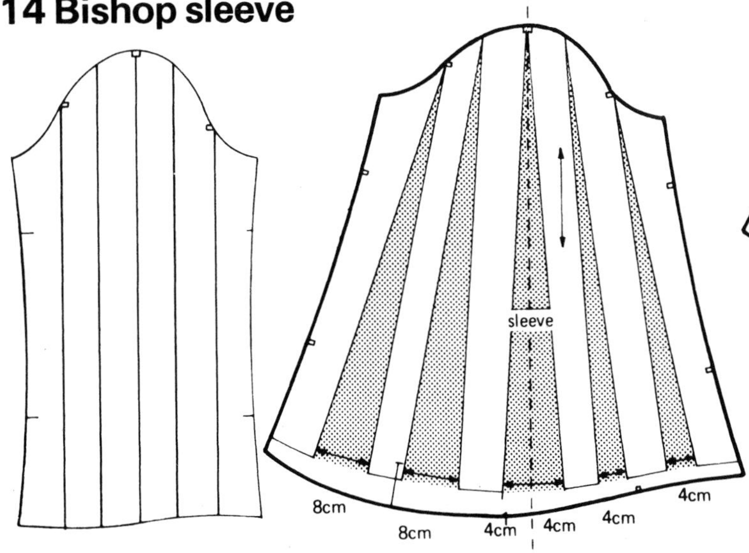

sleeve

8cm

8cm

4cm

4cm

4cm

4cm

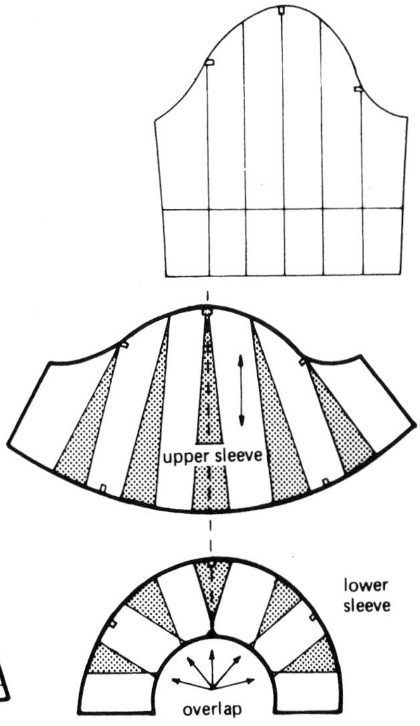

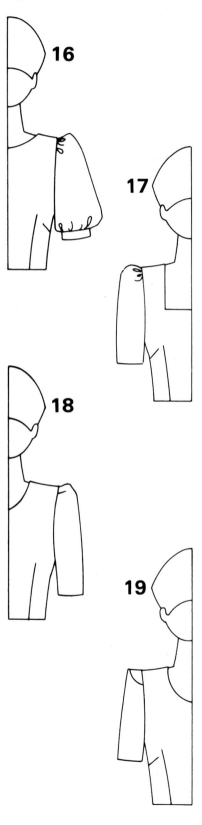

16

17

18

19

ADAPTING THE BODICE AND SLEEVE

Raised sleeve heads give a wide-shouldered look. If not required take 1 cm off shoulder edges as shown, add 1 cm to sleeve head.

16   PUFF SLEEVE

Trace short sleeve. Divide into six sections. Cut out, open sections amount required. Add extra depth to sleeve head and hem as shown.

17   GATHERED HEAD

Trace short sleeve. Divide sleeve head into five sections above back balance point. Mark balance points for gathers at top of sections 1 and 5. Cut up sections, open out.

18   DARTED HEAD

Proceed as for gathered head, using four sections. Draw in darts. Trace round pattern shaping dart edges.

19   SEAMED HEAD

Trace short sleeve. Drop three vertical lines from sleeve head. Draw in seam line 4 cm down. Wheel through top piece, cut out, open each section 1.5 cm, trace round. Cut out *complete* sleeve, open out 0.75 cm, to fit inset.

20   INSET CAP SLEEVE

Trace short sleeve. Lower sleeve head 2 cm. Draw in depth of cap. Divide into sections, cut out and open till lower line is straight.

21   STRAPPED HEAD

Trace short sleeve. Draw strap approx. 3 cm wide, divide into four sections. Take 2 cm ease from sleeve head. Cut up strap lines and centre line, open out as shown. Raise sleeve head 4 cm.

22   RAISED SEAM

Trace semi-fitted sleeve with a strapped head. From strap, drop lines to quarter elbow line, then to quarter wrist line. Cut out, cut up lines. Trace centre section. Close back dart. Join outer sections of sleeve at underarm and wrist. Shape in front seam 1 cm.

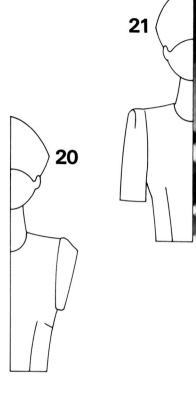

21

20

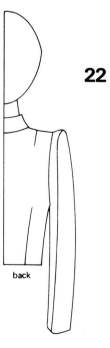

22

back

front

53

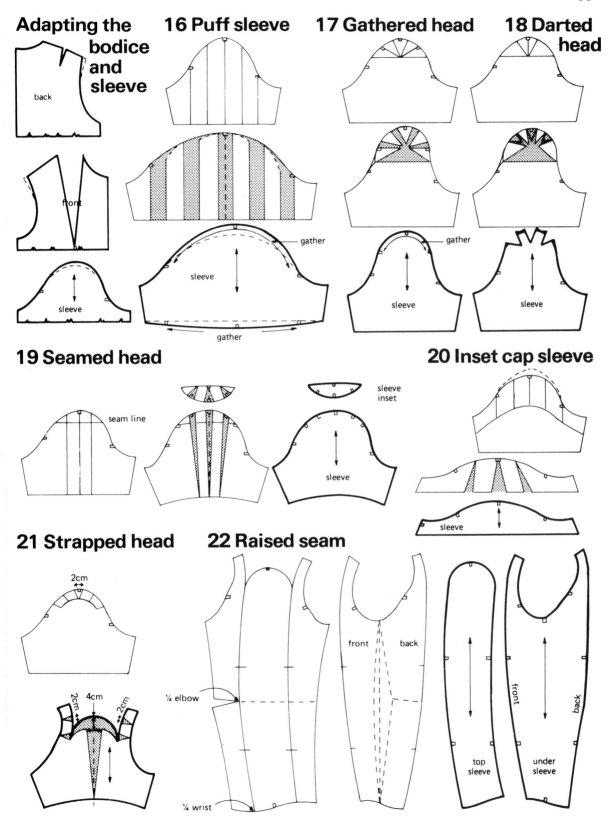

Adapting the bodice and sleeve

back

front

sleeve

16 Puff sleeve

sleeve

gather

gather

17 Gathered head

gather

sleeve

18 Darted head

sleeve

19 Seamed head

seam line

sleeve inset

sleeve

20 Inset cap sleeve

sleeve

21 Strapped head

2cm

2cm   4cm   2cm

22 Raised seam

¼ elbow

¼ wrist

front   back

front

back

top sleeve

under sleeve

23

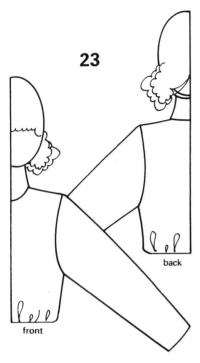

front

back

23   LOWERED ARMSCYE

For an easy fitting body and armscye shape, complete this adaptation for the lowered armscye before continuing with any further adaptation.

Body Section   Trace body section of block required; cut up side seam, open 4cm; draw new side seam down centre. Lower scye depth line 2.5cm.

Mark 1 and 2 on each scye depth line and 3 and 4 at sleeve pitch points.

Draw in new armscye shape as shown.

Sleeve   Trace one-piece sleeve block. Draw a parallel line below armscye depth, the distance is half the measurement 1–2. Mark points 5 and 6 at front and back pitch points.

Draw the curve 5–7 to new armscye depth line, the curve should equal the measurement of the curve 3–2.

Draw the curve 6–8 to equal curve 4–2.

Draw underarm seam, narrow at wrist if required.

Note   The amount the block is widened and the armscye lowered can be varied, but proportions must remain constant.

24   EASY FITTING 'SHIRT' ARMSCYE

Complete adaptation for lowered armscye. Mark points 2, 3, 4, 5, 6.

Body Section   Extend the shoulder approx. 2.5cm, raise shoulder 0.5cm. 3–9 and 4–10 half the measurement of the shoulder extension.

Draw new shoulder and armscye shape.

Sleeve   Mark point 11 at sleeve head.

11–12 amount shoulder is extended.

5–13 half the measurement 3–9.

6–14 half the measurement 4–10.

Draw in new sleeve head from 13–14.

25   DROPPED SHOULDER WITH LOWERED ARMSCYE

Construct as for shirt armscye. If the shoulder extends more than 2.5cm it is usually necessary to widen the sleeve.

Mark points 15 and 16 at shoulders.

13–12 should equal 9–15 plus 0.5cm.

14–12 should equal 10–16 plus 0.5cm.

If sleeve requires widening, cut up centre line and open required amount. It is possible to open the sleeve at the sleeve head only.

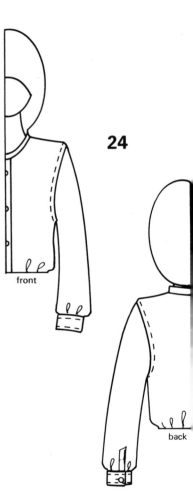

24

front

back

25

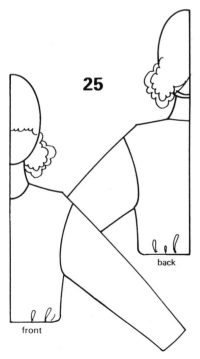

front

back

23 Lowered armscye

24 Easy fitting 'shirt' armscye

25 Dropped shoulder with lowered armscye

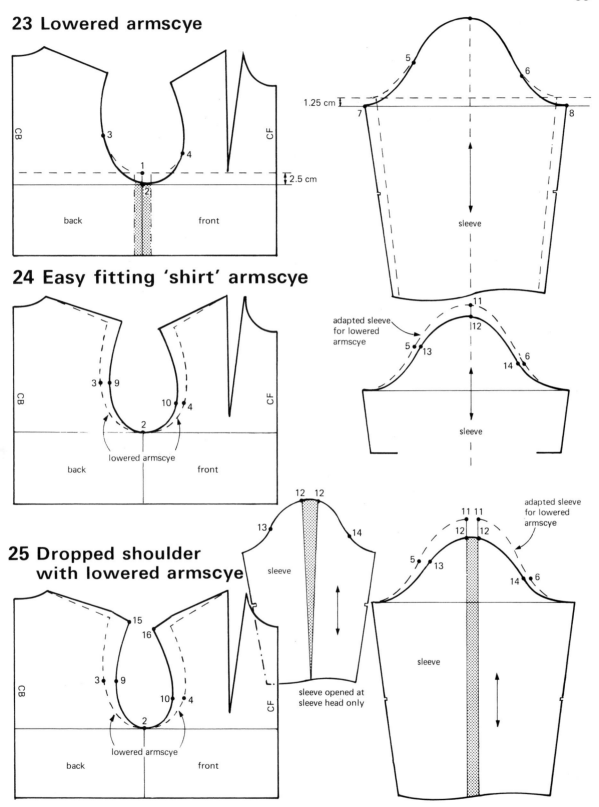

CB

CF

3

1

4

2

back

front

2.5 cm

5

6

7

8

1.25 cm

sleeve

adapted sleeve for lowered armscye

11

12

5

13

14

6

sleeve

lowered armscye

3 9

10 4

2

12 12

13

14

sleeve

sleeve opened at sleeve head only

adapted sleeve for lowered armscye

11 11

12 12

5

13

14

6

sleeve

15

16

3 9

10 4

2

lowered armscye

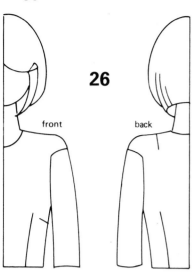

26

front   back

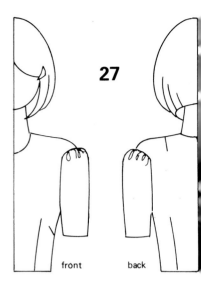

27

front   back

26 DROPPED SHOULDER

Trace bodice and sleeve blocks. Mark balance points 1, 2, 3, 4. Extend shoulder to shape required. Mark balance points 5 and 6. Make 7–3 equal the distance 1–5. Make 8–4 equal the distance 2–6. 9 is down from the sleeve head, the amount shoulder is extended. Draw sleeve head 7, 9, 8.

Widened Raise outer shoulders 1 cm. Widen centre sleeve 2 cm. Check the fit of the sleeve head.

27 DROPPED SHOULDER WITH PUFF SLEEVE

Trace round bodice and short sleeve block. Adapt for a dropped shoulder. Divide sleeve into four sections and open required amount. Overlap each section 0.5 cm at bottom. Raise sleeve head for extra fullness.

28 EXTENDED SLEEVE

Trace round bodice and straight sleeve block to required length. Rub out back shoulder dart and remove 1 cm from back shoulder at armscye edge. Draw in neckline. Draw in shoulder strips 2.5 cm wide on back and front. Mark centre line of sleeve, extend it at the top. Place back and front shoulder strips to this line. Trace round, cut out.

29 FLARED EXTENDED SLEEVE

Diagram shows flared sleeve.

30 EXTENDED SLEEVE WITH YOKE

Trace round bodice and short sleeve block. Cut up centre line of sleeve. Draw neck. Draw yoke lines (maximum 12 cm from top of block), drop back yoke line 1 cm from dart to armscye. Raise shoulder 1.5 cm at armscye edges. Place sleeves to bodices, match balance points, sleeve heads touching yoke line, and 1 cm from new shoulder points. Trace round yoke and sleeve combined. Cut out, close back dart. Trace round lower bodices.

One-Piece Sleeve Draw vertical line, place sleeves together at vertical line, to make shoulder dart.

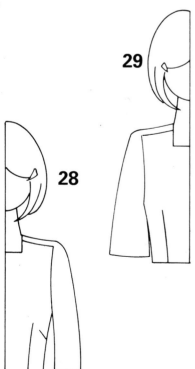

28

29

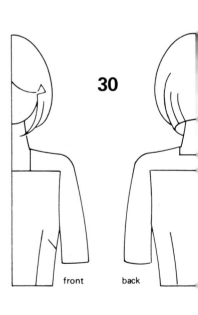

30

front   back

26 Dropped shoulder

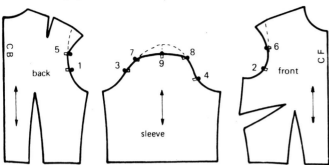

27 Dropped shoulder with puff sleeve

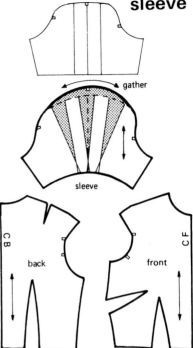

Widened

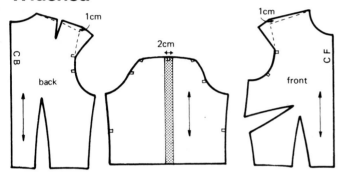

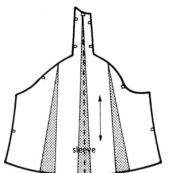

28 Extended sleeve

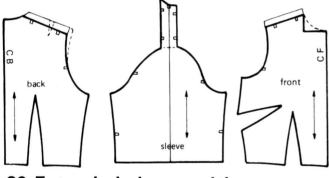

29 Flared extended sleeve

30 Extended sleeve with yoke

One-piece sleeve

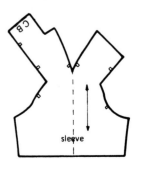

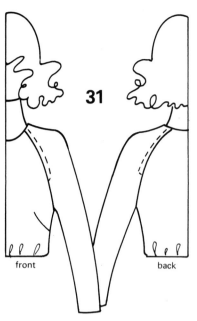

31

front

back

31 BASIC RAGLAN SLEEVE

Trace round bodice block required and one-piece sleeve block. Take 1 cm off front shoulder line; add 1 cm to back shoulder line. Mark points 1 and 2, 3 cm in from new shoulder points. Place any back shoulder ease into dart. Move front balance points forward 3 cm. Mark balance points 3 and 4. Join 1–3 and 2–4 with a curved line. Cut away sections.

One-Piece Sleeve Draw centre line of sleeve 1 cm forward. Mark point 5, 2 cm down from sleeve head. Place sections to sleeve matching balance points, place shoulder points to sleeve head. Close back dart. Trace round making a slightly shaped shoulder line to point 5.

Two-Piece Sleeve Divide sleeve at centre line, add 1 cm to each centre line; curve in to point 5.

32 FLARED RAGLAN SLEEVE

Divide one-piece sleeve into four sections. Cut, open required amount.

33 DEEP RAGLAN SLEEVE

Trace round bodice block required and one-piece sleeve block. Place any back shoulder ease into a dart. Add 2 cm to each bodice side seam. Mark 4 at original front pitch point. Use directions for classic raglan, but curve raglan lines below armscye line. Mark points 6, 7, 8, 9.

Sleeve Place sections to sleeve as above, note the way the underarm pieces lay on the sleeve, match balance points. Draw a line below armscye line half the distance the bodice armscye has been lowered. 6–10 = 6–8, 7–11 = 7–9. Join with curved lines. Cut out. Draw straight lines from midway between 6–10 and 7–11 to 4 cm below underarm point. Cut up the lines and open out 4 cm. Trace round.

For two-piece sleeve follow directions for basic raglan two-piece sleeve.

34 RAGLAN WITH SQUARE SHOULDER

Draw lines from shoulder notch to raglan lines; open approx. 1.5 cm. Raise shoulder approx. 1 cm.

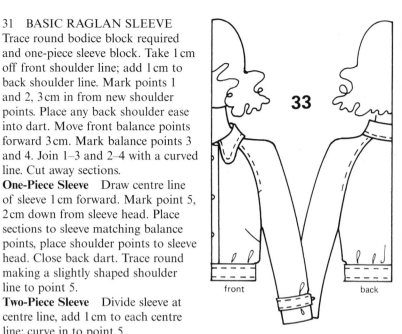

33

front

back

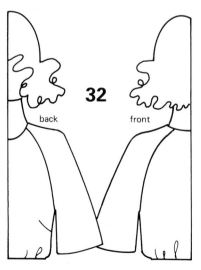

32

back

front

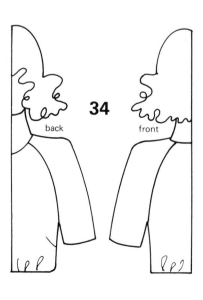

34

back

front

31 Basic raglan sleeve

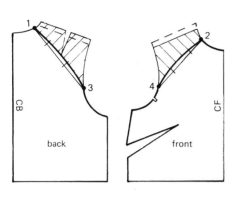

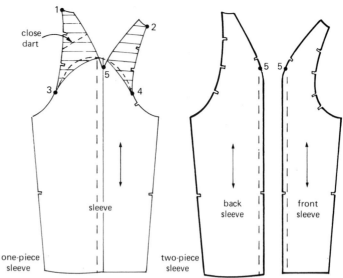

one-piece sleeve

two-piece sleeve

33 Deep raglan sleeve

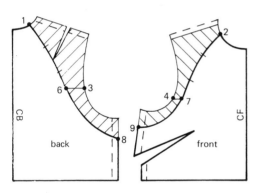

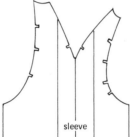

32 Flared raglan

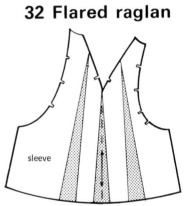

34 Raglan with square shoulder

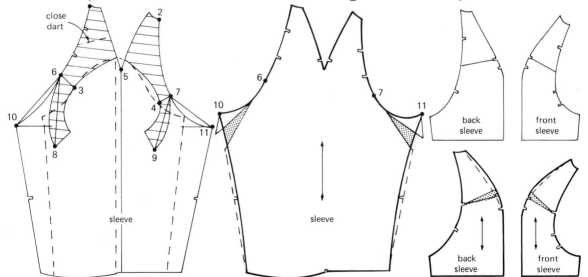

The Shaped Kimono Blocks

KIMONO SLEEVES

Kimono blocks can be used for designs that vary from close fitting shapes to easier fitting shaped garments. The kimono adaptations in this chapter demonstrate designs that still retain the bust dart, using the close fitting block, the easy fitting block or the overgarment blocks.

For kimono designs based on a simple shape without darting see page 136 which demonstrates kimono shapes created by flat cutting with no bust dart shaping.

35 BASIC KIMONO BLOCK

Trace round back and front sections of easy fitting bodice block or overgarment block as required.
Trace sleeve block, narrow underarm seam at wrist if required.

Back   Mark points 0 and 1 on side seam; square out.

1–2 3.5 cm; square up to 3.

Mark 4 at shoulder point, 5 at neck point.

Divide the sleeve block down the centre line.

Place back sleeve head to touch shoulder point 4 and underarm of sleeve to touch line 2–3. Mark point 6.

0–7 one third the measurement 0–1 minus 0.5 cm. Join 7 to wrist point 8.

7–9 6 cm.

7–10 6 cm; join 9–10 with a curve.

4–11 1.5 cm; join 5–11 and 11–12 at wrist point.

Front   Transfer bust dart from shoulder to waistline.
Mark points 13 and 14 on side seam.

13–15 3.5 cm.

14–16 3.5 cm; join 15–16.

Mark point 17 at shoulder point, 18 at neck point.

16–19 the measurement 3–6 on back section. Place underarm of front sleeve to point 19 and the sleeve head to shoulder (it will rise above shoulder point).

14–20 the measurement 0–7; join 20 to wrist point 21.

20–22 6 cm.

20–23 6 cm; join 22–23 with a curve.

17–24 1.5 cm; join 18–24 and 24–25 at wrist point. Transfer bust dart to position required.

36 CLOSE FITTING KIMONO BLOCK

Trace round close fitting bodice block and one-piece sleeve block. Divide sleeve down centre line.
Construct as basic kimono block with the following alterations: 0–7 and 14–20 quarter measurement 0–1 minus 0.5 cm. Draw a line 8 cm long from centre of underarm (directed towards the neck).

Gusset   Draw a horizontal line; mark points 1 and 2, 13 cm apart. Draw a vertical line midway between 1 and 2, draw lines from 1 and 2, 8 cm long, to touch the vertical line above and below. When the block is completed transfer bust dart to required position. For waist shaping refer to page 27.

37 EASY FITTING KIMONO BLOCK

Use the easy fitting bodice block or overgarment block.
Construct as for basic kimono block with the following minor alterations.
Add 2.5 cm to the side seam and mark points 0 and 1 and 13 and 14 on the new side seams.
Make 0–7 one third the measurement 0–1 plus 1.5 cm.

SHOULDER ADAPTATION

The shoulder line can be brought forward to give a good line at shoulder. For this adaptation the basic block is adapted before drafting a kimono block.

Body Section   Take 1 cm off front shoulder line; add 1 cm to back shoulder line.

Sleeve   Draw centre line of sleeve 1 cm forward.

35 Basic kimono block

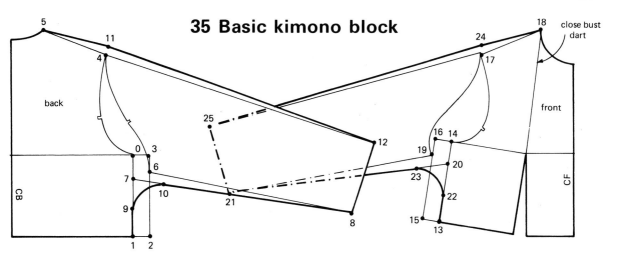

36 Close fitting kimono block

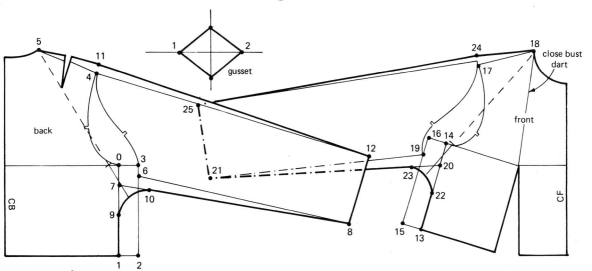

Shoulder adaptation

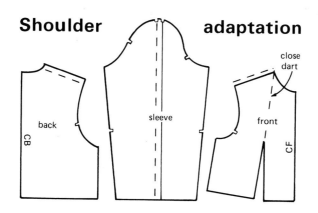

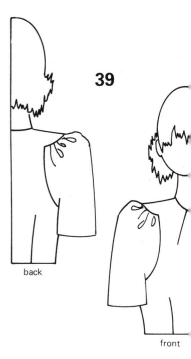

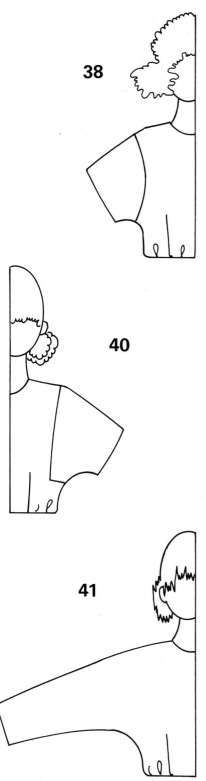

38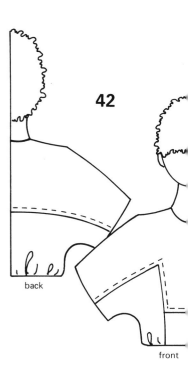

38 DOLMAN SLEEVE

Trace round kimono block required; mark points 10 and 23.

Draw in armscye shape to centre of underarm curve (the distance from shoulder notch should be the same on back and front sections).

Remove shaped sections (1.5 cm wide) two thirds length of front armscye, three quarters length of back armscye. Mark balance points at centre of sections. Draw lines from balance points to points 10 and 23.

Cut off sleeve sections, join at centre.

Cut up gusset lines and open 4 cm.

Trace sleeve, raise sleeve head 0.5 cm.

39 SHAPED SLEEVE

Example shows adapted dolman sleeve based on close fitting kimono block.

Construct dolman sleeve with shaped armscye required.

Divide top edge of sleeve into four sections and open amount required.

Raise sleeve head approx. 1.5 cm.

Direct back shoulder dart to armscye shaping, close dart.

40 SQUARE ARMSCYE

Trace round kimono block required.

Draw in square armscye to centre of underarm curve. Remove shaped sections from armscye as for dolman sleeve. Draw lines from balance points to centre of underarm curve.

Complete sleeve as for dolman sleeve.

41 BATWING

Trace kimono block required. Draw line from centre of underarm curve to neck.

Cut along line, open required amount.

Redraw underarm curve.

42 KIMONO STYLE WITH YOKE

Trace round kimono block required.

Draw yoke lines, extend down sleeves.

Draw in lines from underarm to yokes (directed towards neck point).

Trace round each pattern piece.

Insert 4 cm gusset shape at underarm.

Note Designs with extra body fullness or those based on the wide kimono block do not require a gusset insert.

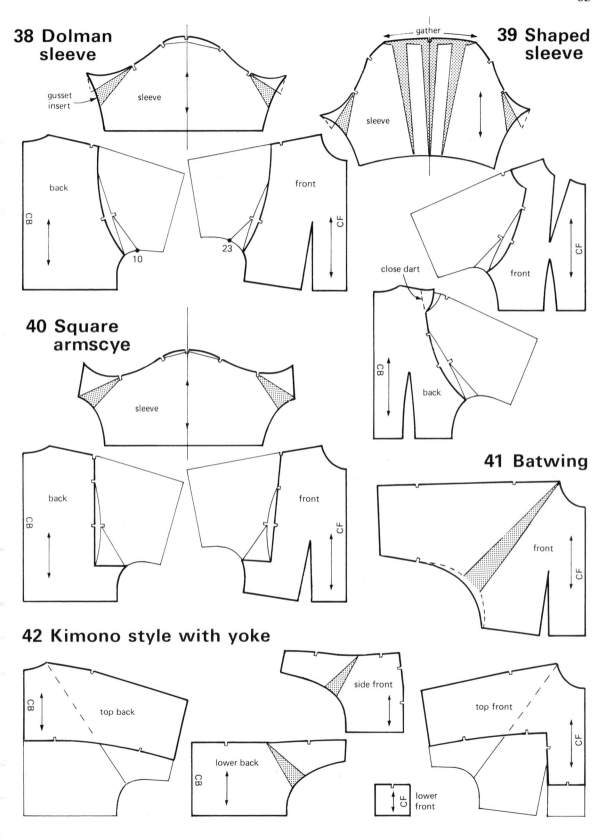

38 Dolman sleeve

gusset insert

sleeve

back

CB

10

front

CF

23

39 Shaped sleeve

gather

sleeve

close dart

front

CF

CB

back

CF

40 Square armscye

sleeve

back

CB

front

CF

41 Batwing

front

CF

42 Kimono style with yoke

CB

top back

side front

top front

CF

lower back

CB

CF

lower front

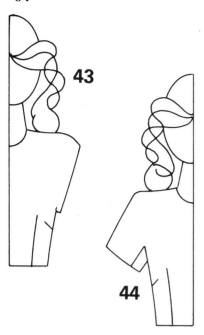

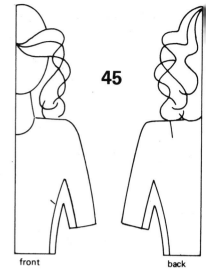

43 CAP SLEEVE

Trace block required, raise shoulder 1 cm. Mark balance points 3 cm below armscye. Extend shoulder to width required. Draw in outer edge of cap with a smooth line.

44 CAP SLEEVE WITH GUSSET

Trace kimono block required with short sleeve (shoulder length approx. 32 cm), without curve at underarm. Widen sleeves 1 cm. Draw a line from underarms (directed at centre shoulders), mark points 1 and 2, 7 cm along line. Mark points 3 and 4, 4.5 cm in from sleeve underarm seam. Cut out sections.

Gusset Draw vertical line, place underarm seams of sections to this line. Join 1 to 2. Construct a triangle shape equal to the one formed above the line. Cut out.

45 CAP SLEEVE WITH PANEL

Construct 'cap sleeve with gusset' pattern (no waist darts). Transfer bust dart to neckline. Draw in panel lines. Draw waist darts on them. Cut away the four sections. Close neck dart, cut out bodice patterns.

Panel with Gusset Draw round gusset. Place sections 1, 2, 3, 4 round gusset as shown. Trace round.

46 FLARED CAPE

Trace kimono block required. Transfer bust dart to neckline. Draw in cape. Mark front strap line and cut away. Drop vertical lines from back neck and shoulder; from front shoulder and bust point. Cut out. Cut up lines. Close bust dart, open other lines to make the same amount of flare. Trace round.

47 FITTED CAPE

Draft a kimono pattern from block required, make sleeve overlap side seam 2.5 cm. Draw in panel lines. Draw in cape. Divide cape sleeve head into sections. Cut off panels. Cut up sleeve head sections. Draw vertical grain line. Place centre sleeve lines to this line, raise head sections as shown. Trace round.

43 Cap sleeve

44 Cap sleeve with gusset

45 Cap sleeve with panel

46 Flared cape

47 Fitted cape

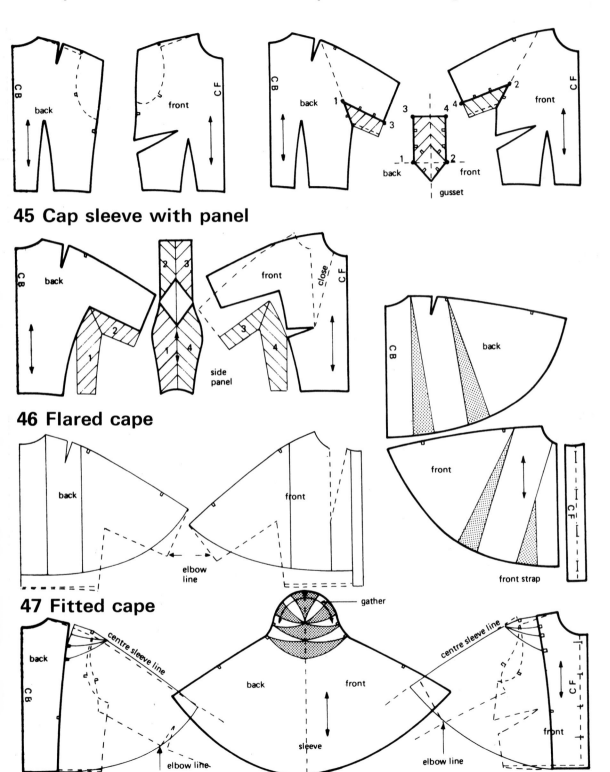

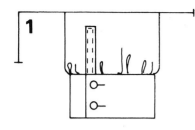

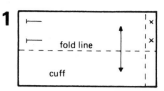

CUFFS

Shirt Cuff

Draw rectangle twice the depth of finished cuff, width = wrist measurement plus 5cm, plus 1.5cm underwrap for buttons. Mark buttonholes and button points.

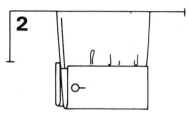

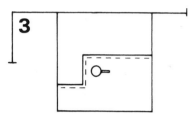

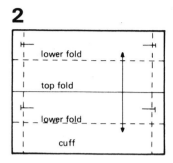

Double Shirt Cuff

Draw cuff with buttonstand at both ends. Mark buttonholes. This cuff is drawn four times the depth of the finished cuff. Mark fold lines as shown.

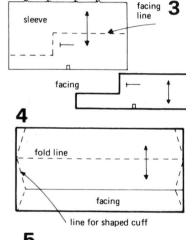

Sleeve Facing

Trace round lower edge of sleeve. Lower edge of sleeve must be even. Draw in line of facing on sleeve. Wheel through onto new paper. Cut out and mark buttonhole.

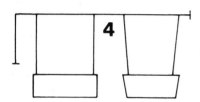

Straight Cuff with Facing

Draw a rectangle, width of sleeve bottom and twice the depth of finished cuff. Add a facing to lower edge (depth approx. 3cm).

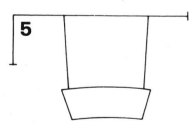

Shaped Cuff

Draw a rectangle 1–2 = depth of finished cuff, 2–3 = width of bottom of sleeve. Divide into six sections. Cut out, open out at top edge to width required at top of cuff. Trace round, cut out.

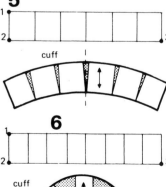

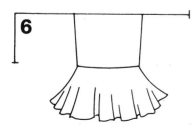

Frilled Cuff

Draw a rectangle, 1–2 = depth of finished cuff; 2–3 = width at the bottom of sleeve. Divide into eight sections. Open out the sections until they make a complete circle. Trace round, cut out.

Part One: Classic Form Cutting
5 CONSTRUCTING COLLARS

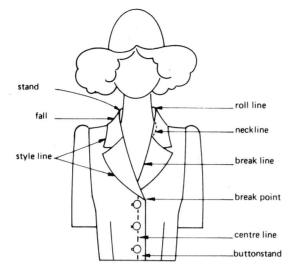

stand

fall

style line

roll line

neckline

break line

break point

centre line

buttonstand

Collars – General Principles

TERMS   used when constructing collars.
Neckline the line where collar is joined to neck.
Style Line outer edge of collar or rever.
Roll Line the line where collar rolls over.
Stand rise of the collar from neckline to roll line.
Fall depth of collar from roll line to style line.
Break Point where the rever turns back to form lapel.
Break Line line along which lapel rolls back.
Before Drafting a Collar   lower neckline if required, mark buttonline, buttonholes, buttonstand.
After Drafting a Collar   add 0.25 cm to outer edge of top collar and from point 1–2 as shown in diagram. This ensures that seam line of outer edge of collar will not show when made up, and the back neck of collar will sit properly. Add 0.5 cm for thick fabrics.
Special Note   diagram opposite shows a principle that applies to the making of all collars. When drawing the style line, allow for depth of collar stand. Experiment on a dress stand or figure for final effects.
Collar Types   collars fall into four basic groups: *Flat collars* sit flat (or almost) around shoulders.
Standing collars stand up around the neck or stand, roll over, then fall.
Collars cut in one with the garment
Collars with revers, separate collar and rever.

Flat Collars

1   PETER PAN (FLAT) COLLAR
Place shoulder of back bodice to shoulder of front bodice, neck points touching, outer shoulders overlapping by 2 cm. Draw in collar shape. Wheel off collar.

2   ETON COLLAR
Construct a Peter Pan collar. Divide collar into six sections. Cut out, cut up lines, overlap at outer edge 0.75 cm. Trace round collar with a smooth line.

3   FLAT COLLAR WITH LOW NECKLINE AND SLIGHT STAND
Trace round front bodice, draw in neckline. Take a 0.6 cm dart out of neckline (ref. Low Revers, page 72). Place back shoulder to front shoulder, neck points touching. Draw in collar. Wheel off collar. Divide into five sections, cut up lines, overlap 1 cm at outer edge of collar. Trace round collar.

4   SAILOR COLLAR
Place back bodice to front bodice as for Peter Pan collar. Draw in 'V' neckline. Draw in collar as shown. Wheel off pattern and cut out.

front

back

If the outer edge of a flat collar is reduced
it sits higher in the neck, increasing the stand

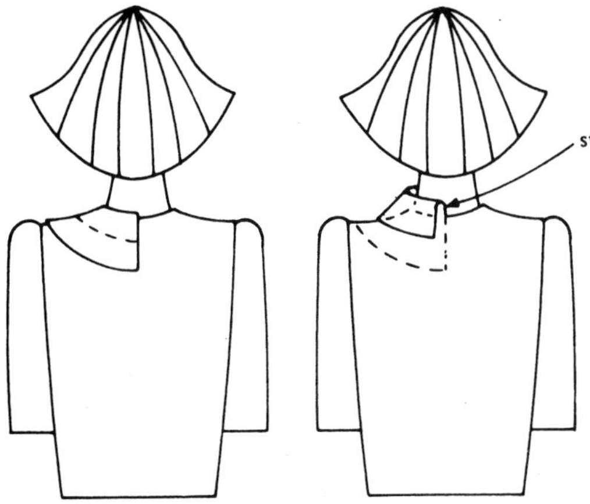

If the outer edge of a standing collar is widened
it sits lower at the neck, reducing the stand

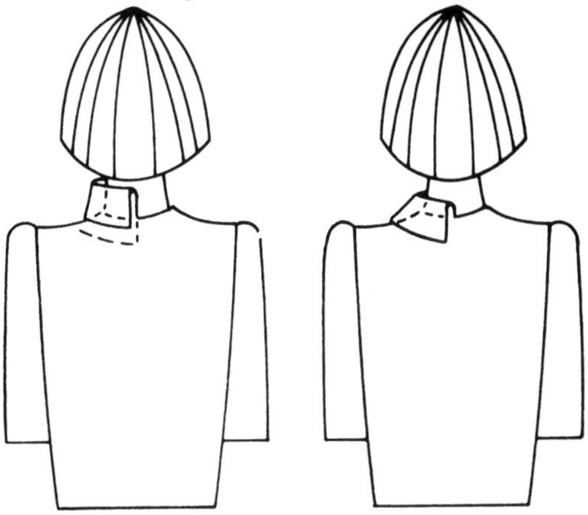

stand

Top Collars

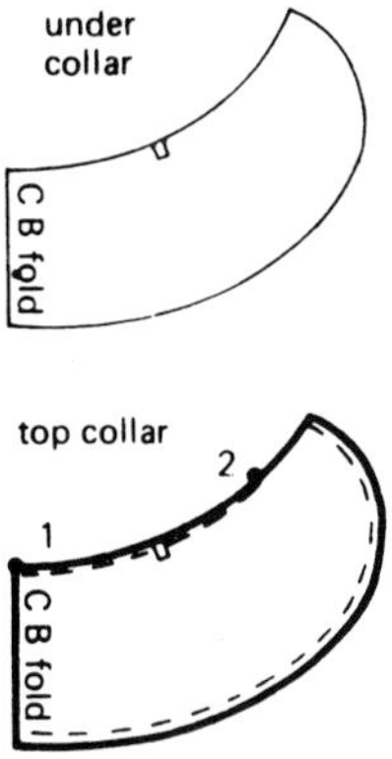

under collar

C B fold

top collar

C B fold

1

2

1 Peter Pan collar

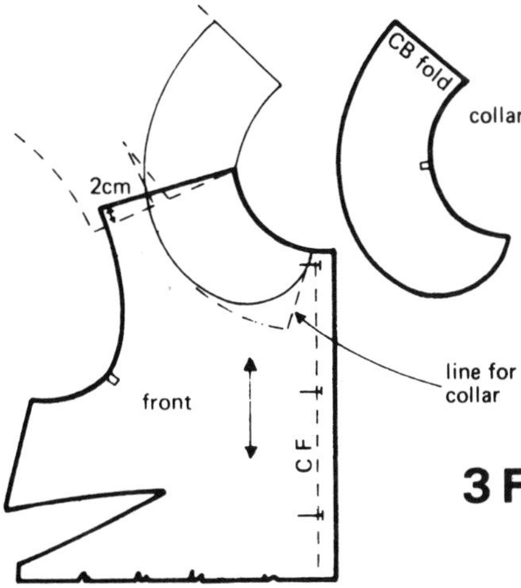

CB fold

collar

2cm

front

C F

line for Eton collar

2 Eton collar

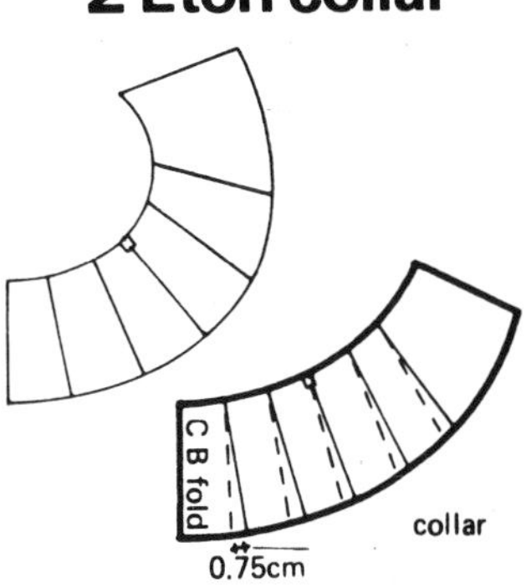

C B fold

collar

0.75cm

3 Flat collar — low neck

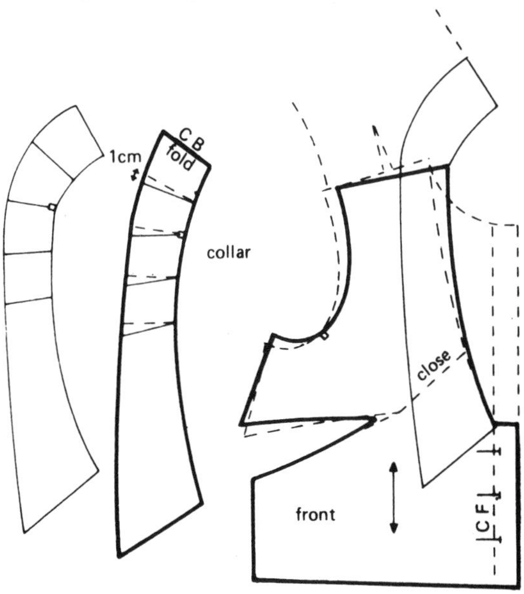

4 Sailor collar

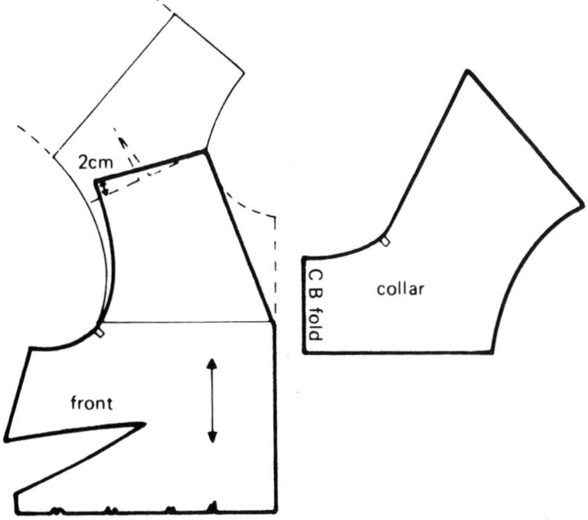

2cm

C B fold

collar

front

1cm

CB fold

collar

close

front

C F

Standing Collars

Measure the Neck
If neckline requires lowering, complete this, then measure neckline. Standing collars must be measured accurately with tape upright (see diagram). Place back to front with shoulders touching; measure from centre back to centre front for half neck measurement.

5   MANDARIN COLLAR
1–2 full neck measurement, 2–3 approx. 4 cm. Draw rectangle. Curve outer edges. Mark centre back. Divide into six sections, cut out. Cut up four outer lines, overlap 0.5 cm. Trace round.

6   STANDING STRAIGHT COLLAR
Lower neckline approx. 1 cm at centre back and shoulders and 2.5 cm at centre front. Measure new neckline.
Square both ways from 1. 1–2 half neckline measurement.
2–3 buttonstand; square up. 1–4 collar depth; square across to 5. 3–6 = 1 cm; 5–7 = 1.5 cm; join 6–7.
7–8 = measurement 2–3; join 2–8.
1–9 = half measurement 1–3; join 6–9 with a curve.

7   POLO COLLAR
1–2 full neck measurement, 2–3 four times finished depth of fall. Draw rectangle. Mark centre front, fold line, roll lines. Cut collar on cross in woven fabrics.

8   CONVERTIBLE COLLAR
Construct rectangle 1–2 half neck measurement, 1–4

= collar depth approx. 9 cm. 3 is three quarters distance 1–2. Shape neckline 0.5 cm up to 5. Shape to outer edge.
Changing the Style Line   Square up from 3 to 6. The style line can be changed from 6 as shown in diagram.
Shaped Collar – Concealed Stand   Construct convertible collar. 1–7 = 3.5 cm, draw curved line from 7 to 3. Divide 1–3 into four sections. Cut out collar and stand. Cut up lines. Overlap stand at outer edge 0.2 cm on each line. Open outer edge of collar 0.4 cm. Cut 0.6 cm from centre back of collar. Trace collar and stand.

9   SHIRT COLLAR
Lower front neckline 0.5 cm (not shirt block).
1–2 = half neck measurement; square up.
1–3 = collar stand and depth measurement; square across.
1–4 = three quarters measurement 1–2; 2–5 = 0.5 cm.
1–6 = half measurement 1–3 minus 1 cm; square across to 7.
7–8 = 0.75 cm; draw in collar outline from 3–8.
5–9 = buttonstand; join 8–9 and 4–9 with curves. Mark buttonhole.
Separate Stand   Trace shirt collar. 6–10 = 0.75 cm. Shape line from 10 to line from 3. Trace collar and stand.
Shaped Shirt Collar   Trace shirt collar and stand. Divide, shape them as for convertible collar and stand.

10   WING COLLAR
Construct the rectangle and stand for a basic shirt collar. Mark points 1, 2, 3, 4. 5 = half 1–4. Square up from 3–6. Draw in collar shape as shown.

Measure the neck

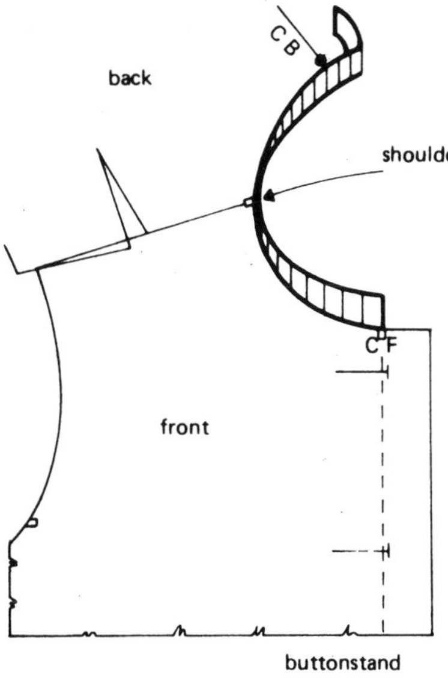

back

C B

shoulder notch

shoulder seam
notch

C F

front

buttonstand

5 Mandarin collar

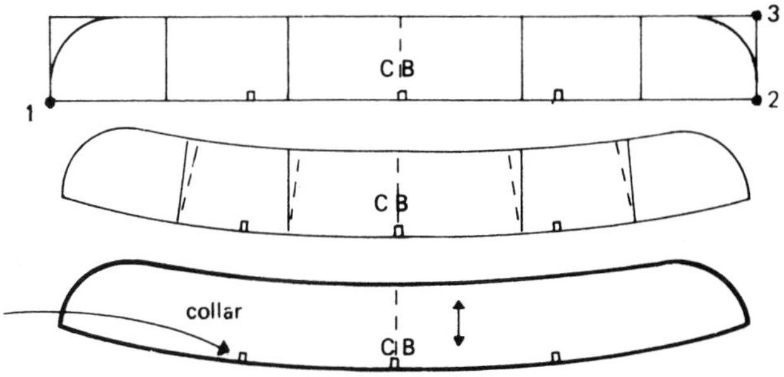

C B

1

3

2

C B

shoulder seam
notch

collar

C B

6 Standing straight collar

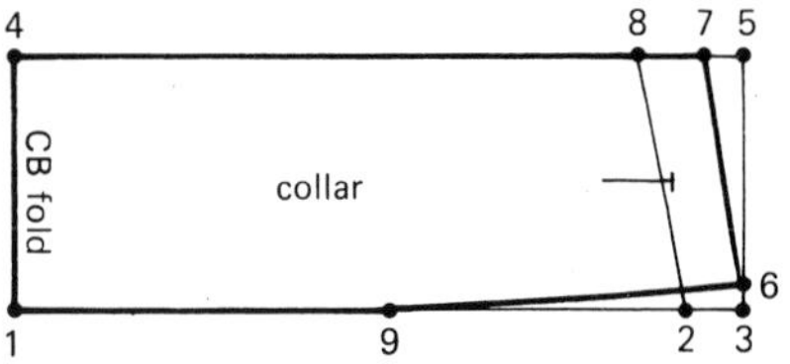

4

8 7 5

CB fold

collar

6

1

9

2 3

7 Polo collar

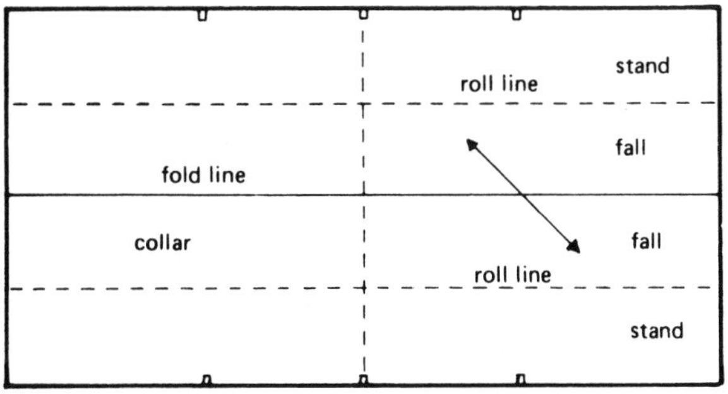

stand

roll line

fold line

fall

collar

fall

roll line

stand

8 Convertible collar

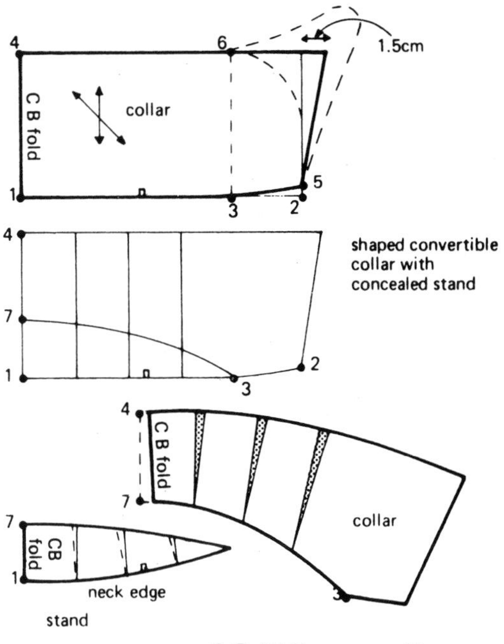

4

6

1.5cm

C B fold

collar

1

3

2

5

shaped convertible
collar with
concealed stand

4

7

1

3

2

4

C B fold

collar

7

1

neck edge

stand

3

9 Shirt collar

3

collar

C B fold

6

8 7

4

9

1

2

shirt collar
with separate
stand

lower
front
neckline

front

C F

C B fold

collar

10

6

C B fold

stand

4

shaped
shirt collar

3

C B fold

stand

C B fold

neck edge

collar

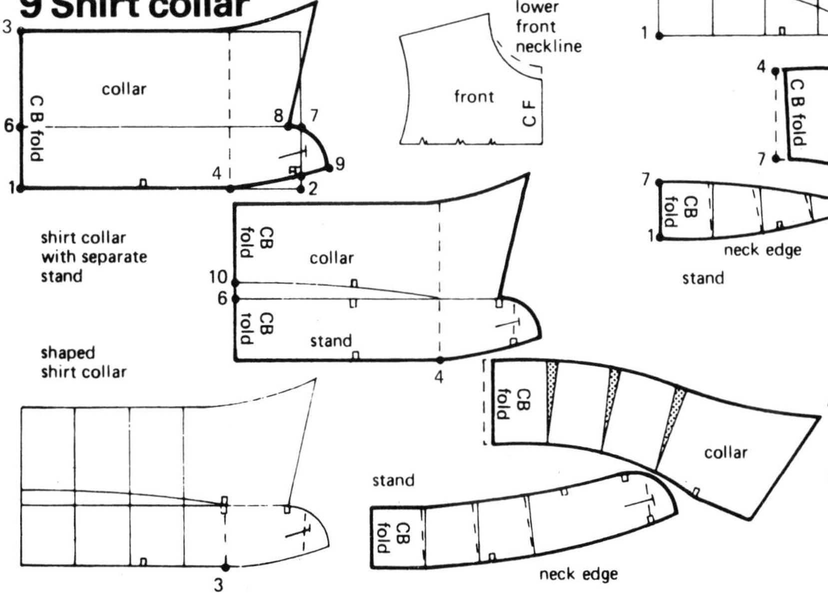

10 Wing collar

4

6

5

C B fold

collar

1

3

2

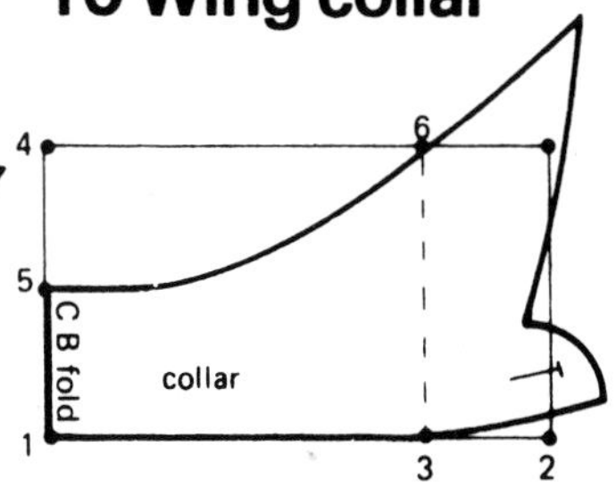

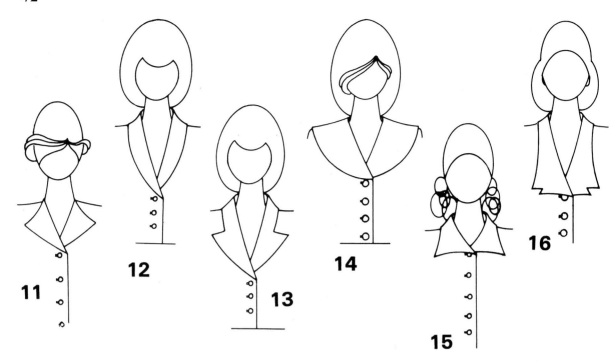

Collars Cut in One with the Garment

Before drafting close fitting collars with low revers, make 0.6 cm neck dart, transfer this to bust dart.

11   REVER FRONT
Trace round front bodice, mark buttonholes, add buttonstand. Mark break point level with top buttonhole. Draw line from neck point to break point. Draw rever shape on bodice. Fold along break line. Wheel through rever shape. Unfold, trace round pattern, cut out. Trace off facing. Add 0.25–0.5 cm to outer edge of rever facing.

12   CLASSIC ROLL COLLAR
Trace round front bodice (low revers – dart neck). Mark buttonholes, add buttonstand. Mark point 1 at break point, mark neck point 2. Extend front shoulder line. Place reversed back bodice to front bodice at neck point. Swing back so that the outer shoulder edge overlaps extended line by 8.5 cm. Mark back neck point 3. 2–4 = 2 cm, 3–5 = 3 cm, 5–6 = 6 cm, 6–7 = 0.5 cm. Draw in roll line 5–4 and break line 4–1. Draw in style line from 7–1.
Facing   Trace off facing. Allow 0.25–0.5 cm round outer edge of collar. Draw line across facing below rever. This allows the facing to be cut in two parts, lower half on the straight grain of fabric, top half can have centre back line placed to a fold of the fabric to avoid a back seam.

13   CHANGING THE STYLE LINE
The outer line of the roll collar can be changed in many different ways to produce new designs.

14   SHAWL COLLAR
Collars that are wide around the shoulders and back must have smaller swing (e.g. 3 cm) so that the outer edge becomes wider. Continue as for roll collar.
Shawl Collar with Seam   Draw a line from neck point to centre of overlap at collar edge. Separate back collar. Shape shoulder seam of front and back collar.

15   HIGH SHAPED COLLAR
Trace round front bodice, mark buttonholes and buttonstand. Mark break point 1 level with top button. Mark 2 at neck point, 2–3 = 1.5 cm. Draw dart parallel to break line as shown. Draft roll collar, use point 3 as neck point. Draw in back of collar and shaped style line. Trace off facing and complete as for roll collar.

16   HOLLOWED NECKLINE
Construct a classic roll collar draft. Draw in style line, example shows design with notch. Draw line from point 2 at neck to centre line 5 cm above top buttonhole. Draw in 1.5 cm dart on this line. Trace off facing including dart, complete as for roll collar.

Low revers

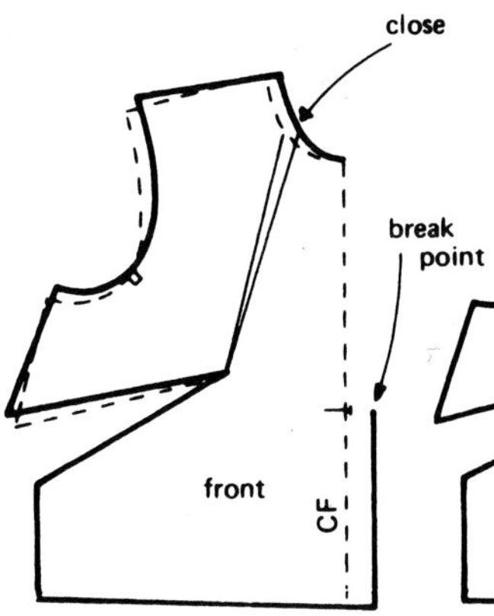

close

facing line

11 Rever front

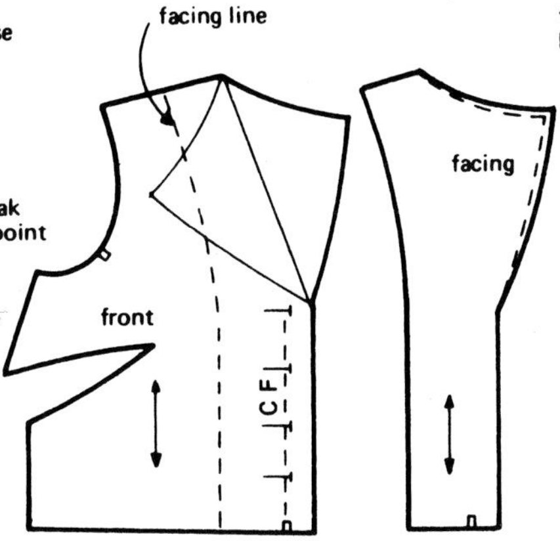

facing

front

CF

break point

front

CF

12 Classic roll collar

6 7 5 3

facing line

2 4 8.5cm

close

front

CF

1

C B fold

seam

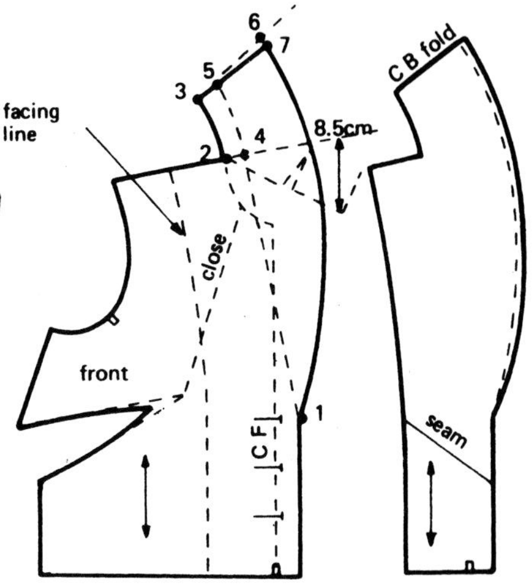

13 Changing the style line

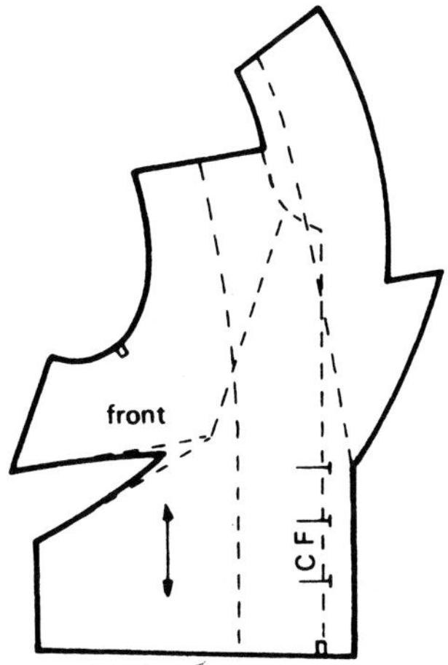

front

CF

14 Shawl collar

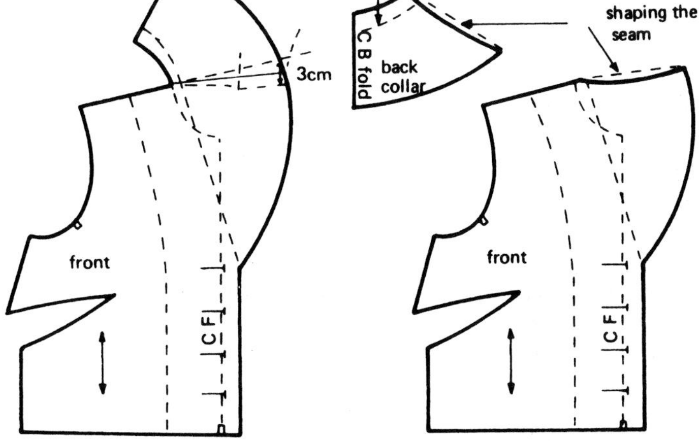

3cm

front

CF

roll line

C B fold

back collar

shawl collar with shoulder seam

shaping the seam

front

CF

15 High shaped collar

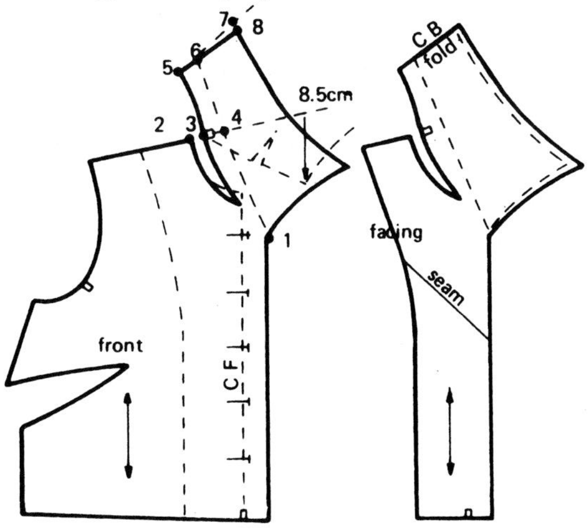

7 8 5 6 2 3 4

8.5cm

front

CF

C B fold

facing

seam

16 Hollowed neckline

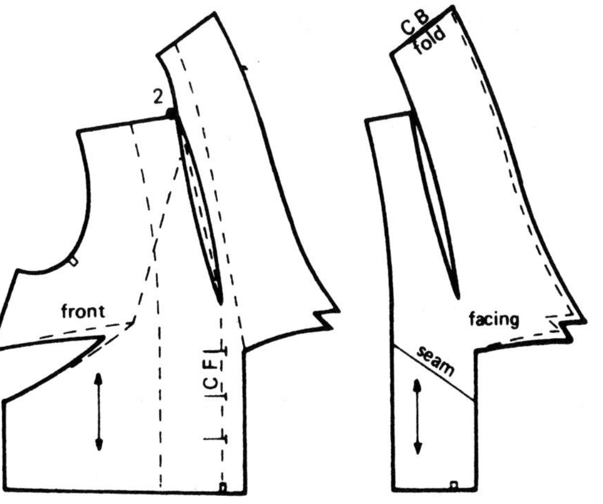

2

front

CF

C B fold

facing

seam

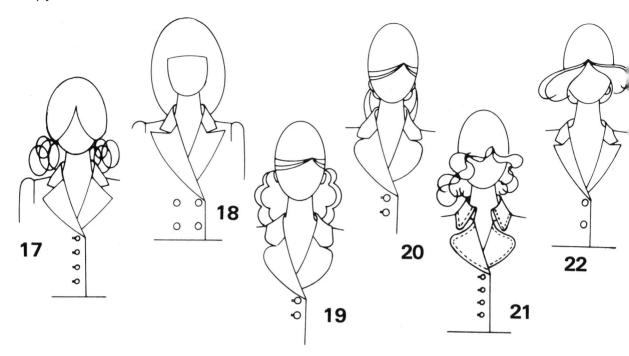

Collars with Revers

For low revers make 0.6 cm neck dart (page 72).

17 CLASSIC GENTS COLLAR (TAILORED)

Trace round front bodice. Raise front neck 0.5 cm.
Mark point 1, square across, rub out existing
neckline. Mark in buttonhole, add buttonstand.
Extend shoulder line. 2–3 = 2 cm along the line. 4 =
break point. Join 4 to 3 with a dotted line, extend line,
3–5 = back neck measurement plus 1 cm. 5–6 = 2 cm
(6–3 is same measurement as 5–3); square a line
across at right angles to the line 6–3. 6–7 = 3 cm, 6–8
= 5 cm. Draw a line from shoulder point parallel to
break line. 9 = 1.5 cm up from the line from 1.
Draw in neckline 2, 9, 1 and outline of rever as shown
(check shape by folding back along break line).
Draw in collar 1, 9, 7, 8 and outer style line. Draw in
roll line from 6 to break line. Mark balance points on
neck and collar.
Top Collars and Facings Because under collars on
tailored garments are cut on the cross and shaped
with the iron, cut top collars from shaped under
collar, add the extra amounts to outer edges (page
68). Add 0.5 cm to rever on facing from break point
to collar point.

18 CLASSIC REEFER COLLAR (TAILORED – DOUBLE BREASTED)

The construction is the same as for a gents collar.
Note the different shape at the top of the revers.

19 STANDARD REVER

Construct as for gents collar, but use existing neckline
of block and join 7 to 1 in curve as shown.
Collar with Lower Stand Mark point 1 on roll line.
Divide collar between centre back and point 1 into
four sections, cut out, cut up lines, open 0.5 cm (extra
for wider collars). Trace round pattern.

20 STANDARD REVER WITH CONCEALED STAND

Construct standard rever pattern, with collar. Draw in
concealed stand midway between shoulder balance
point and roll line. Proceed as for shaped convertible
collar (ref. 8 page 70).

21 COLLAR AND REVER WITH COMPLETE STAND

Construct a standard rever pattern with collar, but
measurement 2–3 = 3 cm (or depth of stand required).
Collar must meet rever at break line point 1.
Collar and Stand Trace collar, join 6 to 1 with straight
line, shape neck edge to point 9, 2.5 cm down from 1.
Proceed as for shaped shirt collar (ref. 9 page 70).

22 COLLAR SET AWAY FROM NECK

Trace round front bodice, lower neckline required
amount on front and back pattern. Construct
standard rever on new neckline, with new back neck
measurement.

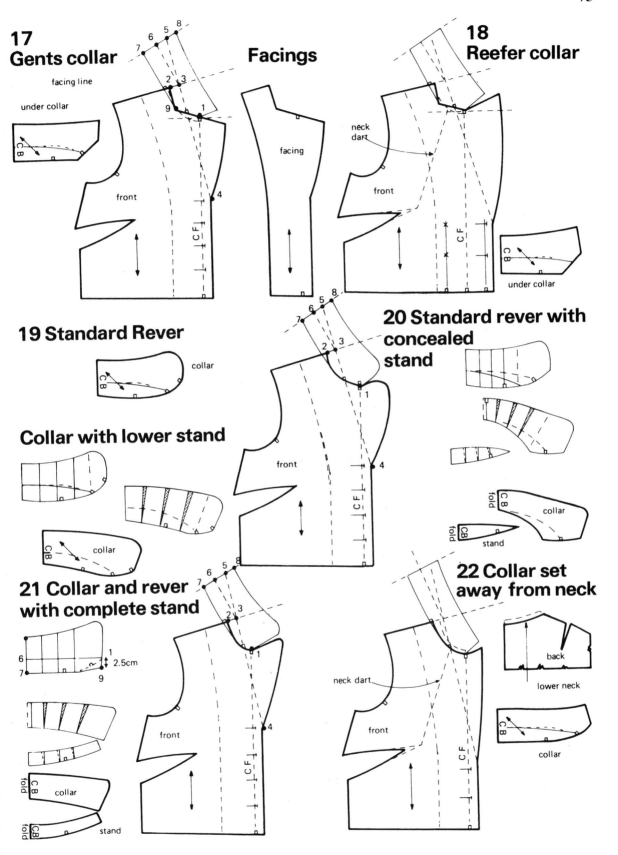

17 Gents collar

facing line

under collar

CB

front

CF

4

6 5 8
7
2 3
9 1

Facings

facing

18 Reefer collar

neck dart

front

CF

under collar

CB

19 Standard Rever

collar

CB

20 Standard rever with concealed stand

front

CF

4

6 5 8
7
2 3
1

fold CB collar

fold CB stand

Collar with lower stand

CB collar

21 Collar and rever with complete stand

6 1
2.5cm
7
9

front

CF

4

6 5
7
2 3
1

fold CB collar

fold CB stand

22 Collar set away from neck

neck dart

front

CF

back

lower neck

CB collar

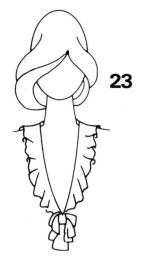

23

23 FRILLED COLLAR
Construct a flat collar of required shape (ref. 1 page 68). Divide into seven sections. Cut out. Cut up lines and open till neck makes almost a full circle. Trace round collar making a smooth line. This makes only half a collar so collar requires a back seam.

24 FRILLED REVER
Trace round bodice block, construct a collar and rever based on the method of making a gents collar (ref. 17 page 74). Cut off rever, divide into sections, cut up lines and open out 6cm as shown. Trace round pattern.

25 SIMPLE COWL COLLAR
Lower neckline approx. 3cm at the shoulders, 1.5cm at centre back, 3.5cm at centre front.
Mark new neckline points 1, 2, 3, 4. Square up and across from 5. 5–6 = 3cm.
6–7 = the measurement 1–2 (measured in a curve) minus 1cm; square up. Draw a parallel line 2cm below line from 5.
7–8 = the measurement 3–4 (measured in a curve) minus 0.6cm; square up.
7–9 one third the measurement 6–7.
7–10 one third the measurement 7–8.
Curve the neckline 0.5cm on each section as shown.
5–11 is the depth of collar (example is 17cm); square across to 12.
Fold along the line 11–12, cut out pattern with paper folded to repeat the shape.

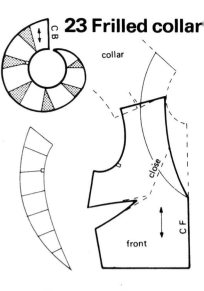

23 Frilled collar

24 Frilled rever

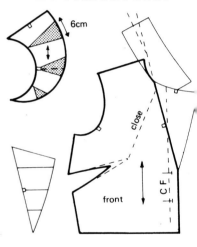

24

25

25 Simple cowl collar

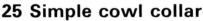

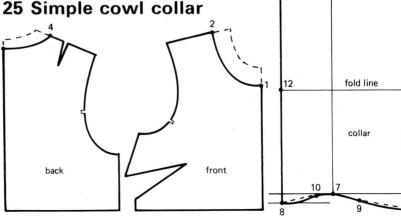

Part One: Classic Form Cutting
6 THE BASIC FITTED SKIRT BLOCK AND ADAPTATIONS

The Tailored Skirt Block

The tailored skirt block is used when the skirt is *not* required to be attached to a bodice. Less ease has been added to the hips of the skirt and this gives a closer fit. The side seam is moved forward.

Note There is 1 cm ease in the waistline of the skirt. The waistline of a skirt should always be eased onto the skirt waistband or petersham.

MEASUREMENTS REQUIRED TO DRAFT THE TAILORED SKIRT BLOCK (example size 12)

Refer to the size chart (page 11) for standard measurements.

waist	70 cm
hips	94 cm
waist to hip	20.6 cm
skirt length (affected by fashion)	

Square down and across from 1.

1–2 half the hip measurement plus 1.5 cm, square down; this line is the centre front line.
1–3 skirt length, square across to 4 on the centre front line.
1–5 waist to hip measurement, square across to 6 on the centre front line.

Back

5–7 quarter the hip measurement plus 1.5 cm ease, square down to 8 on the hemline.
1–9 quarter waist measurement plus 4.25 cm.

9–10 1.25 cm; join 10 to points 1 and 7 with dotted lines.
Divide the line 1–10 into three parts, mark points 11 and 12.
Using the line 1–10, square down from points 11 and 12 with dotted lines.
11–13 14 cm.
12–14 12.5 cm.
Construct two darts on these lines, each 2 cm wide.
Draw in the waistline with a slight curve; draw in the side seam curving it outwards 0.5 cm.

Front

2–15 quarter the waist measurement plus 2.25 cm.
15–16 1.25 cm, join 16 to points 2 and 7 with dotted lines.
16–17 is one third the distance 2–16; using the line 2–16, square down from 17 with a dotted line.
17–18 10 cm.
Construct a dart on this line 2 cm wide.
Draw in the waistline with a slight curve, draw in the side seam curving outwards 0.5 cm.

Special Note for Individual Figures

If the waist is small in proportion to the hip size of the standard block, increase the width of the darts to 2.5 cm. This will require you to draft:
1–9 quarter waist plus 5.25 cm.
2–15 quarter waist plus 2.75 cm.
This ensures a more even suppression around the waistline.

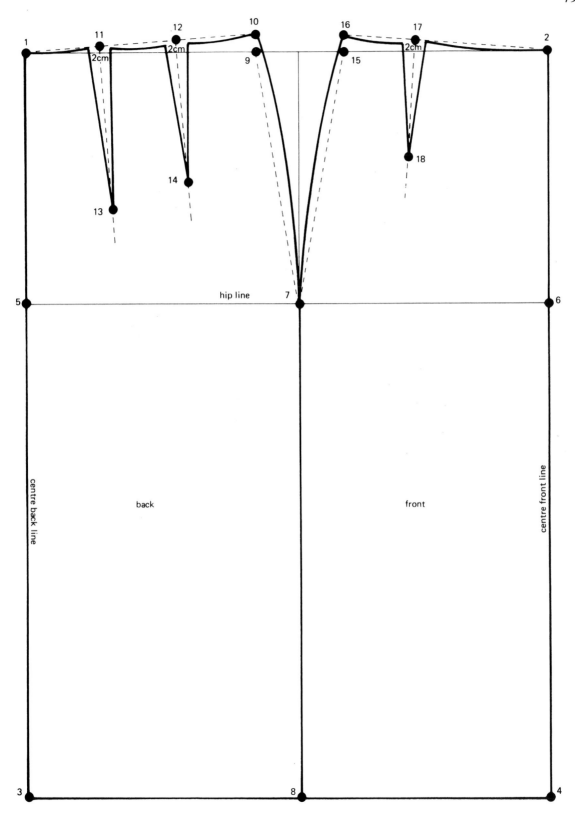

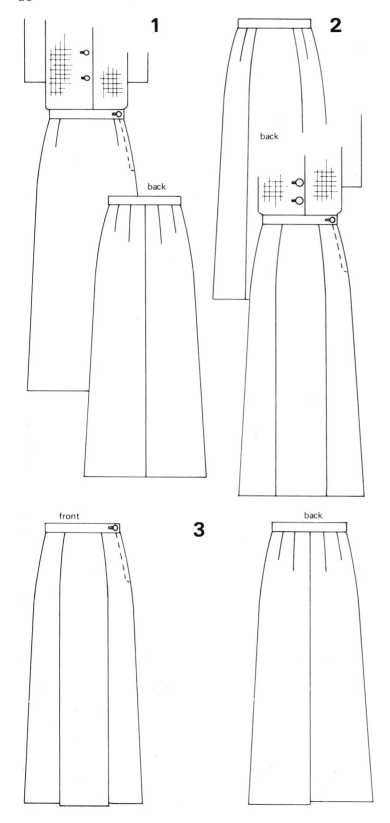

1

2

back

back

back

3

front

back

Skirt Patterns – Examples

Choose the correct skirt block. If the skirt is a separate garment use the tailored skirt block. If the skirt is to be attached to a bodice use the skirt of the two-piece dress block.

Waist Darts All waist darts can have their positions moved, but the darting must be evenly distributed.

1 STRAIGHT SKIRT

Trace round skirt block.
Mark points 1 and 2 on centre back line. 2–3 = 1 cm. Join 1 to 3. This becomes new centre back line; it gives a slight swing to the back skirt to prevent seating. *Use this swing on straight skirts only.*
Add 2.5 cm flare to side seams at hem. Mark point 4. Join 4 to hip point.
Note A completely straight skirt can be cut without swing or flare.

2 PANEL SKIRT

Trace the straight skirt pattern. Draw panel lines on front and back. Transfer front and one back dart onto these lines. Cut up panel lines and along dart shaping to separate the pieces. Trace round new pattern sections.

3 STRAIGHT SKIRT WITH VENT PLEAT – BOX PLEAT

Trace the straight skirt pattern.
Back Mark centre back line.
Pleat Stitch Line Add a pleat to this line 8 cm wide. Fold pattern on pleat stitch line and cut out.
Front Mark pleat line, transfer dart to this line. Separate panels. On a new piece of paper draw three parallel lines 8 cm between. Place panels to the outer lines as in the diagram; trace round panels. Fold pattern along pleat lines so that pleat folds towards centre front. Cut out pattern.

1 Straight skirts

completely straight

slightly flared

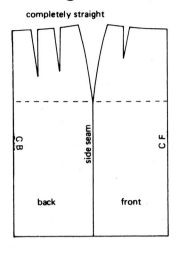

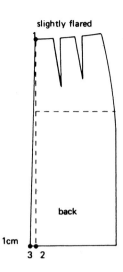

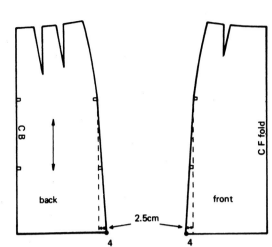

C B

side seam

C F

back

front

back

1cm

3 2

C B

back

2.5cm

4

C F fold

front

4

2 Panel skirt

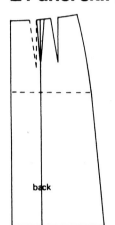

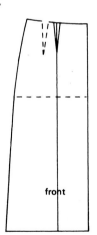

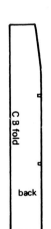

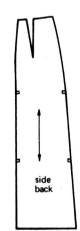

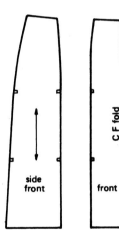

back

front

C B fold

back

side back

side front

front

C F fold

3 Straight skirt with vent pleat — box pleat

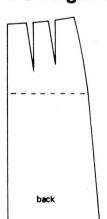

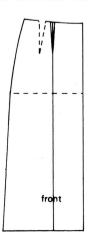

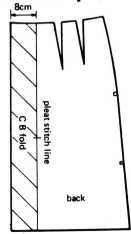

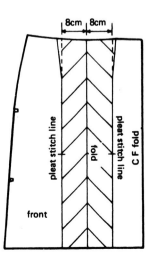

back

front

8cm

C B fold

pleat stitch line

back

8cm 8cm

pleat stitch line

fold

pleat stitch line

C F fold

front

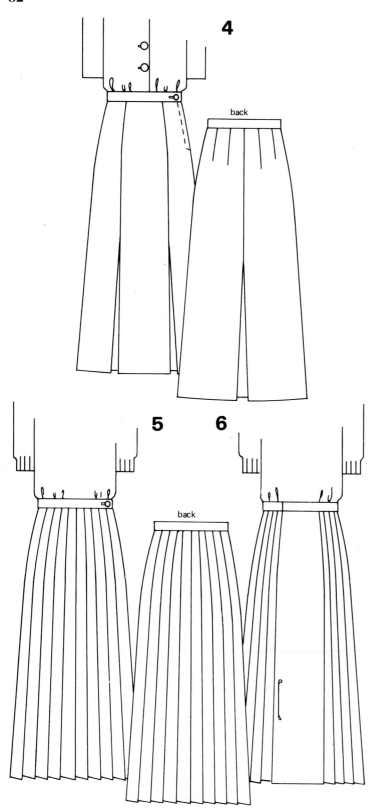

4

back

5   **6**

back

4 STRAIGHT SKIRT – INVERTED PLEATS

Trace straight skirt pattern.

Back On a new piece of paper draw three parallel lines 8 cm between. Place back skirt pattern to inner line and trace around. Fold pattern along the pleat line so that pleat falls towards side seam. Cut out pattern.

Front Mark pleat line, transfer dart to this line, separate panels. On a new piece of paper draw five parallel lines 8 cm between. Place panels to outer lines as in diagram; trace round panels. Fold the pattern so that pleat 1 folds towards side seam, and pleat 2 folds towards centre front. Cut out pattern.

Note If a tight lay is required the centre panels of the pleat can be cut as a separate panel *or* the pleat can be finished at the line 1–2.

5 SKIRT WITH ALL-ROUND PLEATS – WORK DIRECTLY ONTO CLOTH

Decide pleat width; work out the number of pleats required to make up the hip measurement plus approx. 2 cm ease.

Work directly onto the cloth. Cut a piece of fabric; depth = skirt length plus hem and seam allowance; width = three times (hips + ease) plus seam allowance. The fabric will have to be seamed to obtain this width. Mark pleats with pins as shown in diagram. Fold pleats and tack to hip line. To shape waist take the edge of each pleat and lap it over the required amount to obtain correct waist measurement.

6 KILT – WORK DIRECTLY ONTO CLOTH

The pleats are made as above. Eight pleats less are required for a kilt. Allow 10 cm each side of centre front for top wrap; allow same amount for underwrap.

4 Straight skirt — inverted pleats

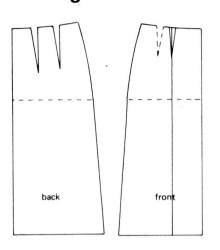

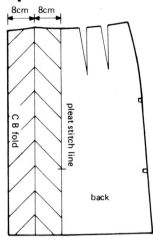

8cm 8cm

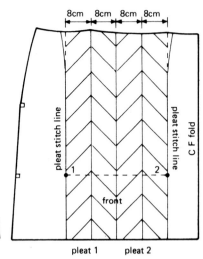

8cm 8cm 8cm 8cm

back

front

C B fold

pleat stitch line

back

pleat stitch line

pleat stitch line

C F fold

front

1 2

pleat 1 pleat 2

5 Skirt with all-round pleats

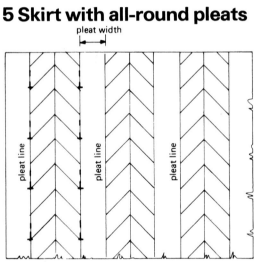

pleat width

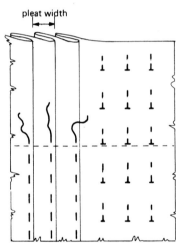

pleat width

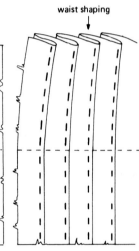

waist shaping

pleat line

pleat line

pleat line

6 Kilt

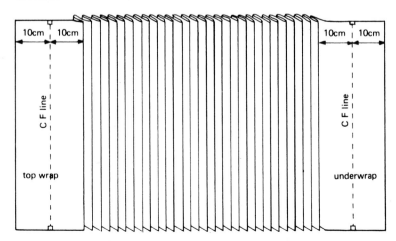

10cm 10cm

10cm 10cm

kilt before the
waist is shaped

C F line

C F line

top wrap

underwrap

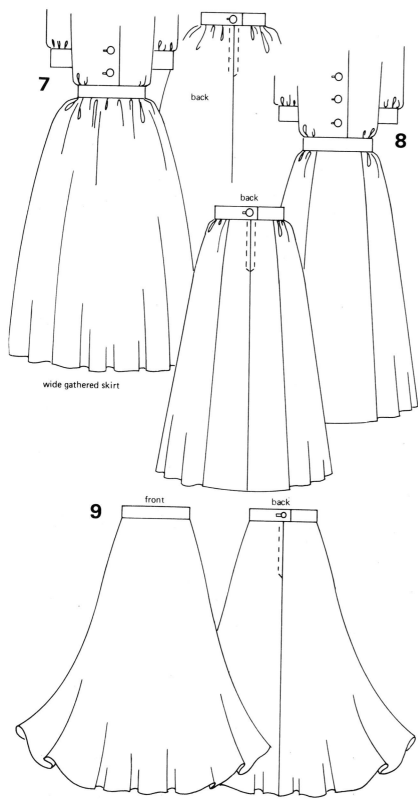

7

back

8

back

wide gathered skirt

9   front   back

7   GATHERED SKIRT

Slightly Gathered   Cut two rectangles depth = skirt length, width = one quarter hips + 15 cm. Curve the waistline 1.5 cm higher at the side seam.

Very Gathered   Cut directly in cloth. Cut a piece of fabric; depth = skirt length plus hem and seam allowance, width = approx. three times hip size. The fabric will have to be seamed to obtain the width. (Place waistline to selvedge on suitable fabrics only.) Fold fabric. Place centre front to fold. Mark side seams at half the distance.

8   GATHERED SKIRT WITH PANELS

Trace round basic block.

Draw in panel lines. Transfer front dart and one back dart to these lines, rub out the other back dart. Divide back and front side panels in half with a dotted line; mark B1 and B2, F1 and F2. Cut out.

Centre Front – Centre Back Panels
Trace round panels, add approx. 5 cm flare at hem of panel seam.

Side Panels   Trace round panel 1, add approx. 5 cm flare at hem of panel seam. Draw a line parallel to the dotted line, width 12 cm. Place panel 2 to this line and trace round. Add approx. 5 cm flare at hem of the side seam.

Note   When adding flare take flare line to hipline.

9   CIRCULAR SKIRT

The construction of a circular skirt is based on the circle. Make the waist measurement the circumference. Calculate the radius (see Appendix, page 197). Square both ways from 1. 1–2 = the radius. 1–3 = the radius. Draw a quarter circle from 2–3. 2–4 = skirt length. With a metre stick mark out the edge of circle as shown.

Half Circular Skirt   Construct the pattern as for the circular skirt but make the following alteration:
1–2 = twice the radius.
1–3 = twice the radius.

7 Gathered skirts

slightly gathered

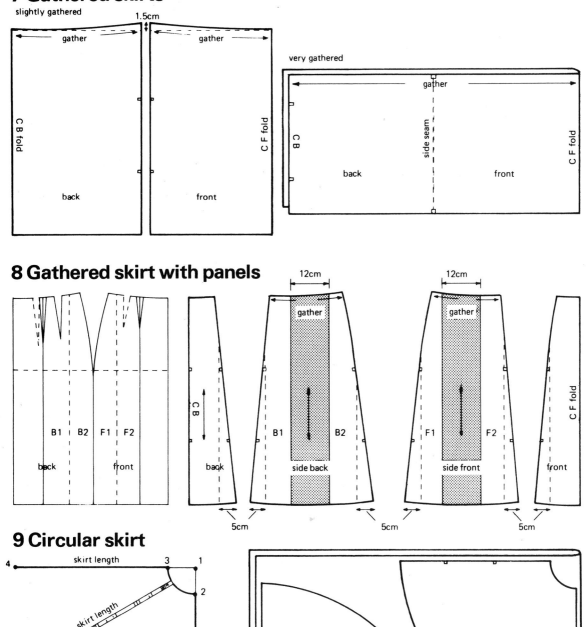

very gathered

8 Gathered skirt with panels

9 Circular skirt

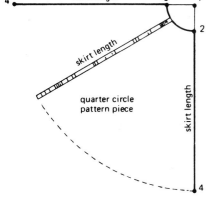

quarter circle pattern piece

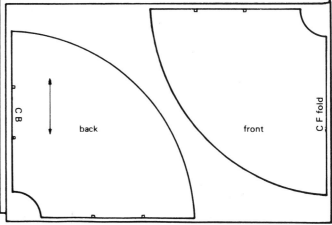

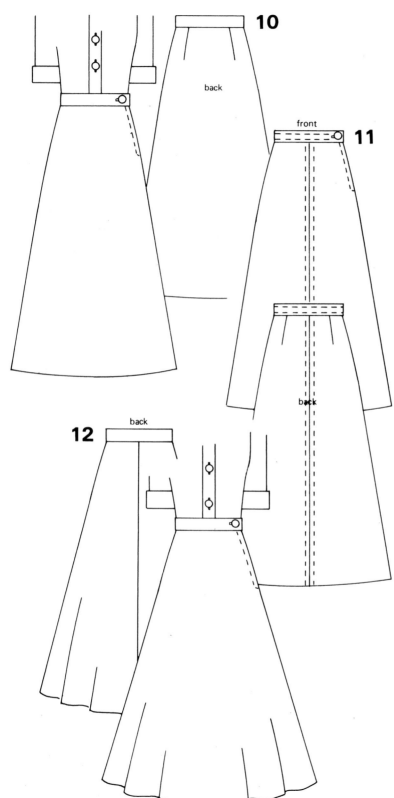

10 BASIC 'A' LINE SKIRT

Trace round basic block.

Front Change the 2 cm front dart into two 1 cm darts placed at points where waistline is divided into three. From the base of the darts draw vertical lines to hem. Cut out pattern and cut up vertical lines. Close up darts.

Place on a new piece of paper, trace round new outline. Make sure the flare openings at hem are equal. Add 2.5 cm flare to hem at side seam.

Back Reduce the two waist darts to 1 cm and draw in a new 2 cm dart midway between. From original darts drop vertical lines to hem. Close the two outer 1 cm darts, then proceed as for the front pattern. The flare openings at the hem can be made equal to the front pattern if required. Add 2.5 cm flare to hem at side seam.

11 FOUR GORED SKIRT

A four gored 'A' line skirt with the grain in the centre of the panel will have a better 'hang'.

Back Mark in hipline; mark points 1 and 2, 3 is midway between 1 and 2. Mark in original side seam of basic block; mark points 4 and 5 on hemline, 6 is midway between 4 and 5. Join 3 to 6. This line is the grain line.

Front Proceed as for back.

Note This skirt can be cut on the straight or cross.

12 SKIRT WITH EXTRA FLARE

Trace round basic block.

Drop vertical lines from all darts and a point midway between front dart and centre front. Cut out block and cut up vertical lines. Close darts to give flare at hemline, open vertical line on front pattern to give an equal amount of flare.

Trace round new outlines on a new piece of paper. Add 2.5 cm flare to hem at side seams.

10 Basic 'A' line skirt

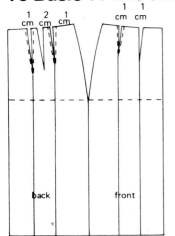

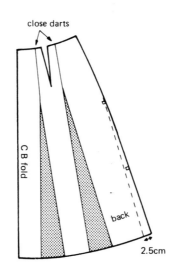

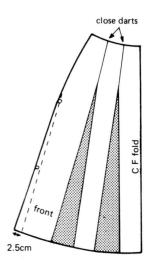

close darts

close darts

C B fold

back

C F fold

front

2.5cm

2.5cm

11 Four gored skirt

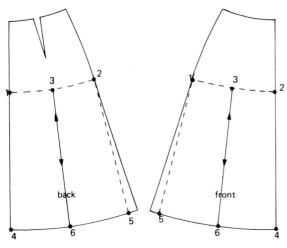

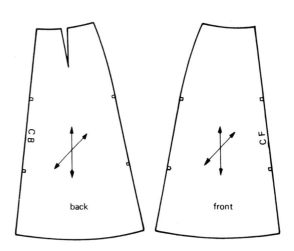

back

front

C B

back

C F

front

12 Skirt with extra flare

close darts

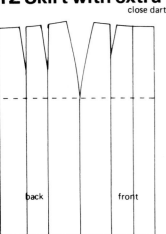

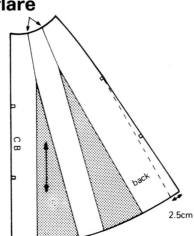

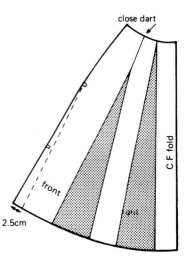

close darts

close dart

back

front

C B

back

C F fold

front

2.5cm

2.5cm

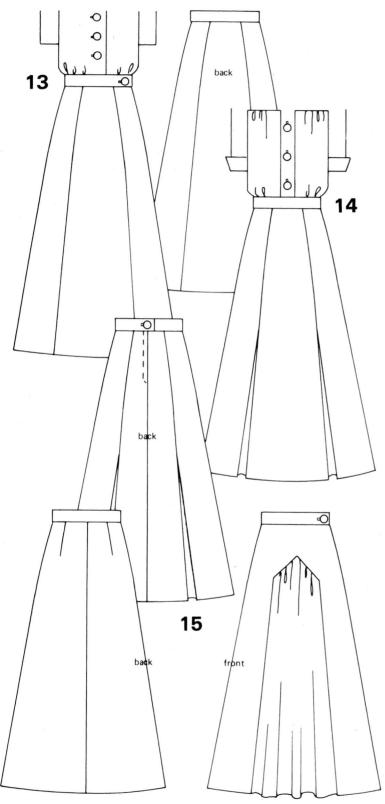

13 GORED 'A' LINE SKIRT

Trace round 'A' line skirt pattern.

Back Draw in hipline and original side seam. Mark points 1, 2, 3, 4, on hip and hemline. 1–5 is one third 1–2. 1–6 is one third 3–4. Draw in panel line, transfer the back dart onto this line. 7 is midway 5–2. 8 is midway 6–4. This is the grain line for side panel. Cut up panel line and dart shaping. Trace round new pattern pieces.

Front Proceed as for back, there is no dart in front pattern.

Note When skirt is not evenly divided by panel line, square down from hipline on side panel to find grain.

14 GORED AND PLEATED 'A' LINE SKIRT

Trace round gored skirt pattern.

Back Extend pleat stitch line to waist by ruling a straight line (leave shaping at the waist marked). Mark points 1 at waistline and 2 at hemline. 1–3 = 6cm. 2–4 = 9cm. Join 3 to 4. Fold along pleat line and cut out pattern.

Side Back Extend pleat stitch line to waist and make pleat for side back as described above.

Pleat Backing Draw a vertical line. Mark points 5 and 6; 5–6 = length of the pleat stitch line. 5–7 and 5–8 = 6cm. 6–9 and 6–10 = 9cm. Join 7 to 9 and 8 to 10.

Cut out backing piece.

Front Patterns Proceed as for back patterns, there is no waist shaping in the front.

15 'A' LINE SKIRT – GATHERED INSET

Trace round 'A' line skirt pattern.

Back Basic 'A' line pattern.

Front Draw in the design of inset on front pattern. Divide inset into three equal parts. Cut out inset from front pattern. Cut up the vertical lines. Place onto new paper; open out the sections, inserting 4cm at top for gathers and 7cm at bottom for flare. (More can be inserted if required.) Trace round new outline of inset.

13 Gored 'A' line skirt

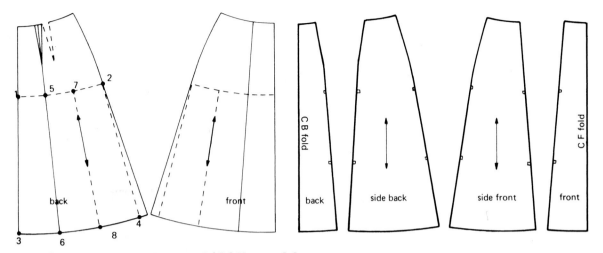

14 Gored and pleated 'A' line skirt

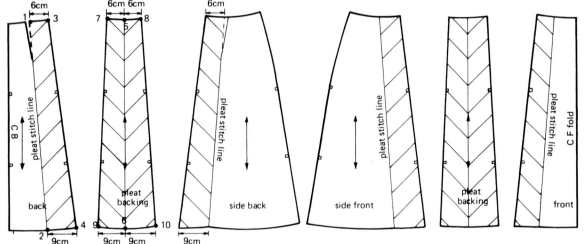

15 'A' line skirt — gathered inset

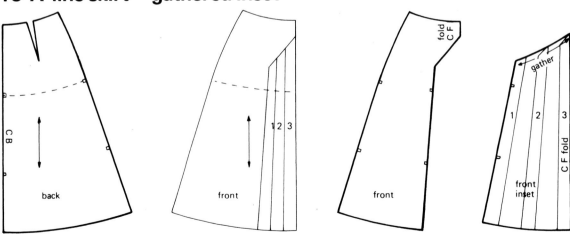

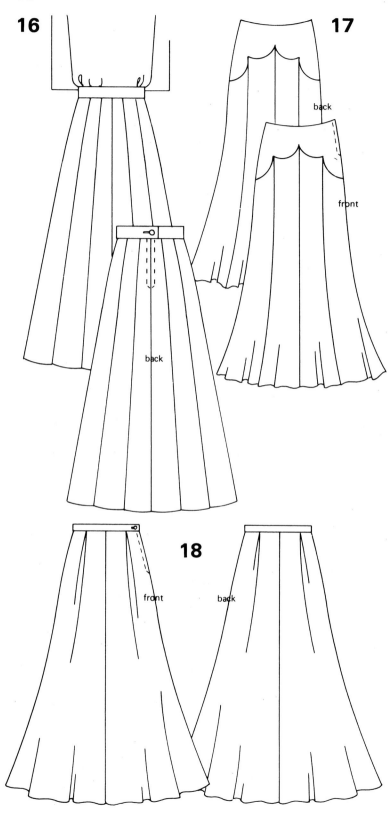

16   **17**

18

16 GORED SKIRT

(If using the tailored skirt block, transfer complete side seam to centre of block.) Rub out waist darts. Divide front and back skirt into six equal sections on hipline. Square up and down.

New Darting   Darts to touch a dotted line 14 cm down from waistline. Add 1 cm to waistline at front and back side seam. Make two 2.5 cm darts on back panel lines and two 1.5 cm darts on front panel lines. Add 3 cm flare to hem of all panel seams.

17 GORED SKIRT WITH LOW FLARE

Trace round basic skirt block. Draw in shaped yoke and drop vertical lines from the shaped points. Mark balance points halfway down the length of the skirt. Extend waist darts to yoke line.

Yokes   Cut yokes from pattern, close darts and trace round new outline on new piece of paper.

Gores   Cut out skirt and cut up vertical lines. Trace round the four gores. Add 7 cm flare at hem, join to low balance points.

Note   Skirt can be cut on the cross.

18 FLARED SKIRT – UNPRESSED PLEATS

Trace round basic block.

Back   Draw in pleat line, move inner dart onto this line. Cut out pattern and cut up pleat line. On a new piece of paper draw vertical lines 1–2. 1–3 and 3–4 = 5 cm; 2–5 and 5–6 = 7 cm. Join lines 3–5 and 4–6.

Place the pieces of back each side of lines 4–6 and trace round. Add 5 cm flare to hemline at centre back and 7.5 cm to hemline at side seam. Fold pattern on pleat lines, one pleat folded towards centre back, the other towards side seam. Cut out pattern.

Front   Draw in pleat line. Transfer front dart to this line, proceed as for the back.

Note   Skirt can be cut on the cross.

16 Gored skirt

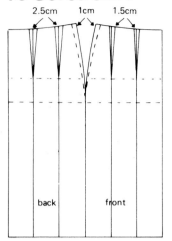

2.5cm   1cm   1.5cm

back   front

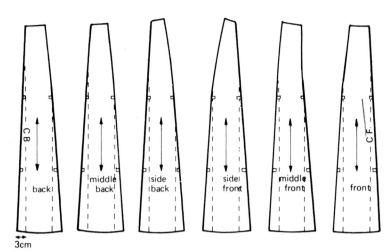

C B

back   middle back   side back   side front   middle front   front

C.F.

3cm

17 Gored skirt with low flare

back   front

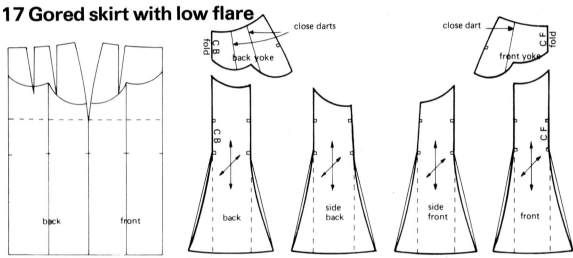

close darts

fold   C B   back yoke

close dart

C F fold   front yoke

C B   back   side back   side front   front   C F

7cm

18 Flared skirt — unpressed pleats

back   front

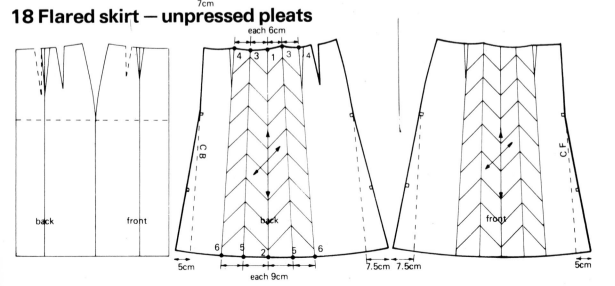

each 6cm

4 3 1 3 4

C B   back   C F   front

6 5 2 5 6

5cm   7.5cm 7.5cm   5cm

each 9cm

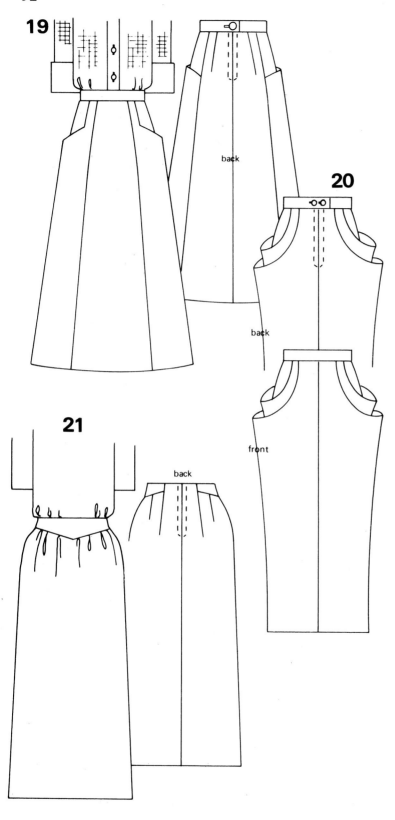

19 SKIRT WITH HIP POCKET

Trace round basic skirt block.
Draw in front and back panel lines.
Transfer front dart and one back dart onto these lines. Draw in pocket line. Mark depth of pocket bag. Cut up panel lines.

Back and Front Trace round back and front sections, add 5 cm flare to outer edge of panel at the hem.

Lower Side Panel Trace round side panel; cut away along pocket line. Add 5 cm flare to side seam at hem.

Top Side Panel Trace round side panel to depth of pocket bag line. Add flare.

Pocket Facing Trace round top side panel; cut away along pocket line.

20 COWL SKIRT

Trace round basic skirt block.
Mark point 1 midway between front dart and centre front. Decide the depth of the cowl lines, draw the cowl lines from the base of the darts and point 1. Cut up side seams and along cowl lines.

On a new piece of paper draw a horizontal line. Place side seams of skirt to this line and allow hem of side seams to touch. This opens the cowl lines.

Trace round pattern and make a good curve at the hem.

21 SKIRT WITH GATHERED FRONT

Trace round straight skirt pattern.
Draw in yoke line, number sections 1, 2, 3, 4. Divide front skirt into three sections 5, 6, 7.

Yoke Cut yoke from block, close darts; trace round pattern with good curves.

Back Cut out and trace back section.

Front Cut out front; cut up section lines. Open sections at waist only (approx. 4 cm), trace round pattern.

19 Skirt with hip pocket

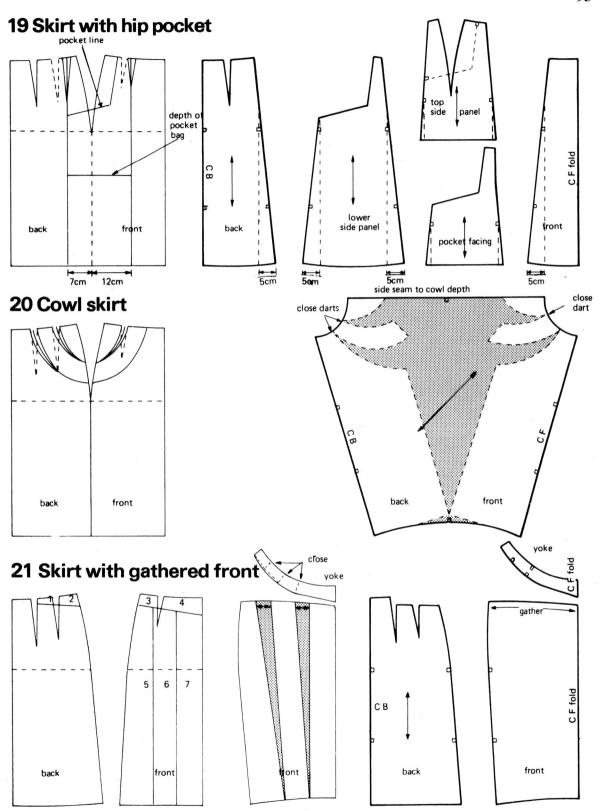

pocket line

depth of pocket bag

back   front

7cm   12cm

C B

back

5cm

lower side panel

5cm   5cm

top side panel

pocket facing

C F fold

front

5cm

20 Cowl skirt

back   front

side seam to cowl depth

close darts   close dart

C B   C F

back   front

21 Skirt with gathered front

close

yoke

1 2   3 4

5 6 7

front

back   front

yoke

C F fold

gather

C B

back

C F fold

front

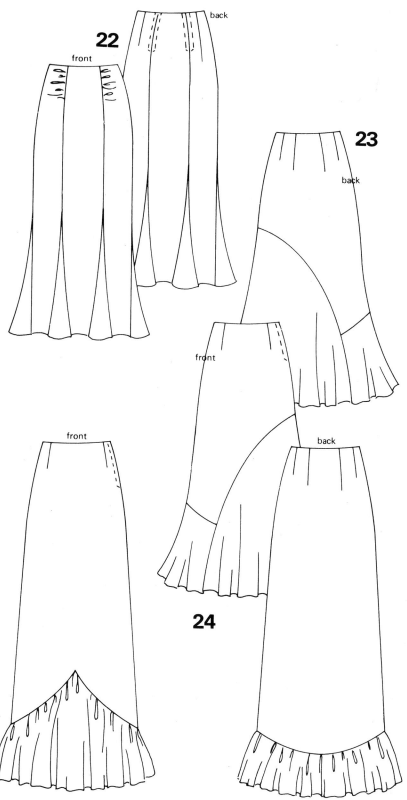

22   SKIRT WITH GODETS
Trace round basic skirt block.
Draw in panel lines, transfer front dart
to front panel line; mark godet points.
Cut out block and cut up panel lines.
Back Panels   Trace round back and
side back panels.
Front   Trace round front panel.
Side Front   Divide side panel into five
sections to hipline. Cut along these
lines, open each section approx. 2 cm a
inner edge.
Trace round pattern.
Godet   Draw a vertical line; mark
points 1–2 the godet length. Decide
width of godet, divide the width evenly
each side of line, mark points 3 and 4.
Square up from these points. Mark
points 5 and 6 on these lines. 1–5 and
1–6 are the length of the godet; join
points 5, 2, 6, with a curve.

23   ASYMMETRICAL SKIRT
Trace round basic skirt block (double
sections).
Draw in lower panel lines, divide lower
panels into sections. Cut away lower
panels, cut up sections.
Large Side Flounce   On a new piece
of paper draw a vertical line. Place side
seams of lower panel to the line. Open
out each section equally at the hem the
amount required for flare. Trace round
pattern.
Small Side Flounce   Repeat the
instructions to create small flounce.

24   SKIRT WITH A FLOUNCE
Trace round straight skirt pattern.
Draw in the lower panel lines; divide
lower panels into sections. Cut away
lower panels; cut up sections, on a new
piece of paper open sections approx.
4 cm at the top and 7 cm at the bottom.
Trace round new pattern making good
curves.
Note   It is necessary to ensure that
when curved pattern pieces are opened
at the top, each section is laid on a line
squared out from the line of the
previous section (e.g. line 1–2).

22 Skirt with godets

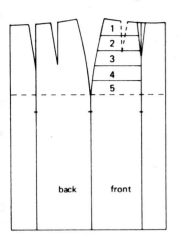

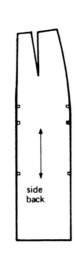
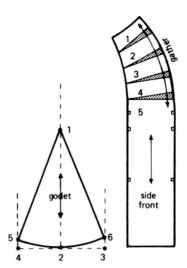
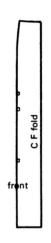

1
2
3
4
5

back   front

C B fold
back

side
back

godet

1
2
3
4
5

5   1   6
4   2   3

gather

1
2
3
4
5

side
front

C F fold

front

23 Asymmetrical skirt

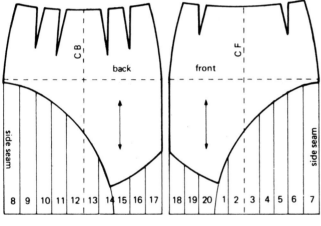

C B
back

C F
front

side seam

side seam

8 9 10 11 12 13 14 15 16 17   18 19 20 1 2 3 4 5 6 7

small
side flounce

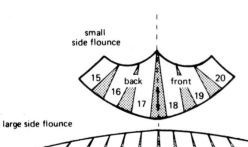

15 back front 20
16   19
17   18

large side flounce

1
2
3
4
5   6   7   8   9   10 11
back   side seam   side seam   front
12
13
14

24 Skirt with a flounce

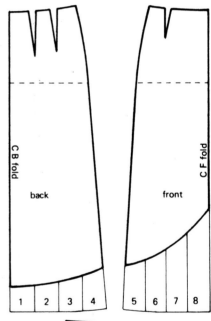

C B fold
back

C F fold
front

1 2 3 4   5 6 7 8

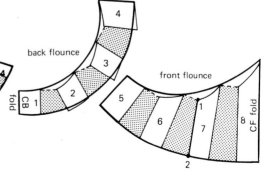

back flounce

4
3
2
1
CB fold

front flounce

5
6
7
8
1
2
CF fold

Straight waistbands

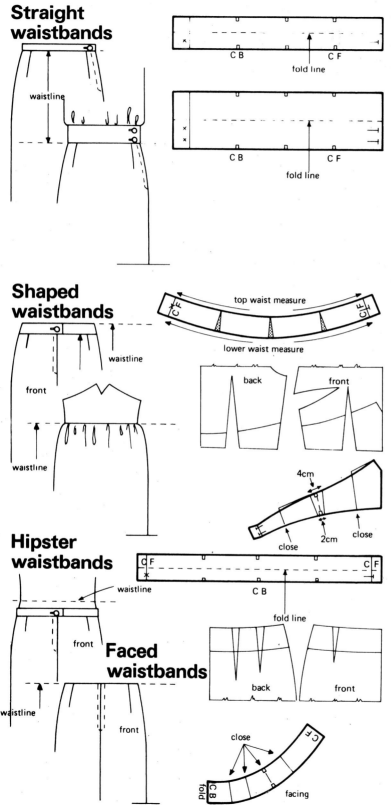

Shaped waistbands

Hipster waistbands

Faced waistbands

25 WAISTBANDS

Straight Waistbands These waistbands are satisfactory if they are set on the waistline and are made in widths from 2.5–8 cm.

Draw waistband exact length and double the width. Mark centre back, centre front and side seam; mark fold line. Add an underwrap of 4 cm. Mark any buttonholes required.

The waistline and waistband of a skirt can be drafted to include a substantial amount of ease (e.g. 10 cm) to enable the waistband to be elasticated.

Shaped Waistbands Waistbands set below the waistline or waistbands that reach high above the waist require shaping to fit the body.

Below Waist Remove the waistband depth from top of skirt pattern. Measure the new low waistline. Make a straight waistband the normal waist measurement; and single width. Cut waistband at centre back and side seams, open the lower edge till it becomes the low waistline measurement. Add underwrap and topwrap, mark buttonholes.

Above Waist Trace shaped bodice block. Draw in waistband on block. Cut out waistband; close darts and overlap side seams 4 cm at top, 2 cm at bottom. Trace round pattern. Add topwrap and underwrap, mark buttonholes.

Note All shaped waistbands have to be cut singly and faced.

Hipster Waistbands Mark lowered waistline on skirt pattern 5–6 cm below waistline and take new waist measurement for waistband.

Only very narrow straight waistbands can be used (maximum 2.5 cm). For deeper bands use the shaped waistband described above.

Faced Waistbands Trace round skirt pattern to hipline. Mark in the lower edge of facing.

Cut out facings; close darts and place side seams together. Trace round pattern (facing can be cut in two separate pieces).

Part One: Classic Form Cutting
7   FITTED TROUSER BLOCKS AND ADAPTATIONS

The Classic Tailored Trouser Block

MEASUREMENTS REQUIRED TO DRAFT THE
BASIC TROUSER BLOCK (example size 12)
Refer to the size chart (page 11) for standard
measurements.

Note   There is 1 cm ease in the waistline of the
trousers. The waistline of the trousers should always
be eased onto the waistband.

waist	70 cm	body rise	28 cm
hips	94 cm	waist to floor	104 cm
waist to hip	20.6 cm	trouser bottom width	22 cm

Front
Square both ways from 0.
0–1   body rise; square across.
0–2   waist to hip; square across.
0–3   waist to floor measurement; square across.
1–4   half the measurement 1–3 minus 5 cm; square
across.
1–5   one twelfth hip measurement plus 1.5 cm; square
up to 6 and 7.
6–8   quarter hip measurement plus 0.5 cm.
5–9   one sixteenth hip measurement plus 0.5 cm.
7–10   1 cm; join 10–6, join 6–9 with a curve touching
a point:
sizes   8–14   3 cm   from 5
sizes   16–20   3.25 cm   from 5
sizes   22–24   3.5 cm   from 5
10–11   quarter waist plus 2.25 cm.
Construct a dart on the line from 0; length 10 cm,
width 2 cm.
3–12   half trouser bottom width minus 0.5 cm.
4–13   the measurement 3–12 plus 1.3 cm (sizes 16–20
1.5 cm; 22–24 1.7 cm).
Draw in side seam through points 11, 8, 13, 12; curve
hipline outwards 0.5 cm.
3–14   half trouser bottom width minus 0.5 cm.
4–15   the measurement 4–13.
Draw inside leg seam 9, 15, 14; curve 9–15 inwards
0.75 cm.

Back
5–16   quarter the measurement 1–5; square up to 17
on the hipline, 18 on the waistline.
16–19   half the measurement 16–18.
18–20   2 cm.

20–21   2 cm.
21–22   quarter waist plus 4.25 cm; join 21–22 to
touch the horizontal line from 0.
9–23   half the measurement 5–9.
23–24   0.5 cm.
Join 21–19 and 19–24 with a curve touching a point:
sizes   8–14   4.25 cm   from 16
sizes   16–20   4.5 cm   from 16
sizes   22–24   4.75 cm   from 16
17–25   quarter hip plus 1.5 cm.
12–26   1 cm.
13–27   1 cm.
Draw in side seam through points 22, 25, 27, 26;
curve hipline outwards 0.5 cm, curve 25–27 inwards
0.5 cm.
14–28   1 cm.
15–29   1 cm.
Draw inside leg seam 24, 29, 28; curve 24–29 inwards
1.25 cm.
Divide the line 21–22 into three parts. Mark points 30
and 31. Using the line 21–22, square down from 30
and 31.
Construct darts on these lines 2 cm wide; length from
point 30 12 cm, length from point 31 10 cm.
Curve hemline down 1 cm at point 3.

Note   For extra ease in the crutch line see the
adaptation on page 102, ref. 4.

Trace off back and front sections. It is usual for the
back block to face to the left and the right block to
face to the right, particularly if the design requires
complicated adaptations.

TAILORED SHORTS
Shorts can be constructed from any of the trouser
blocks depending on the style.
Trace round trouser block required.
Draw a line parallel to the body rise line at depth
required.
Curve the back hemline downwards 1 cm.
Continue adaptation.

ALTERNATIVE LEG SHAPING
The fashion outline of trouser legs constantly alters;
the diagram shows alternative leg shaping. If classic
shaping is required, equal amounts are added or
subtracted to each side of each leg as shown in the
diagram.

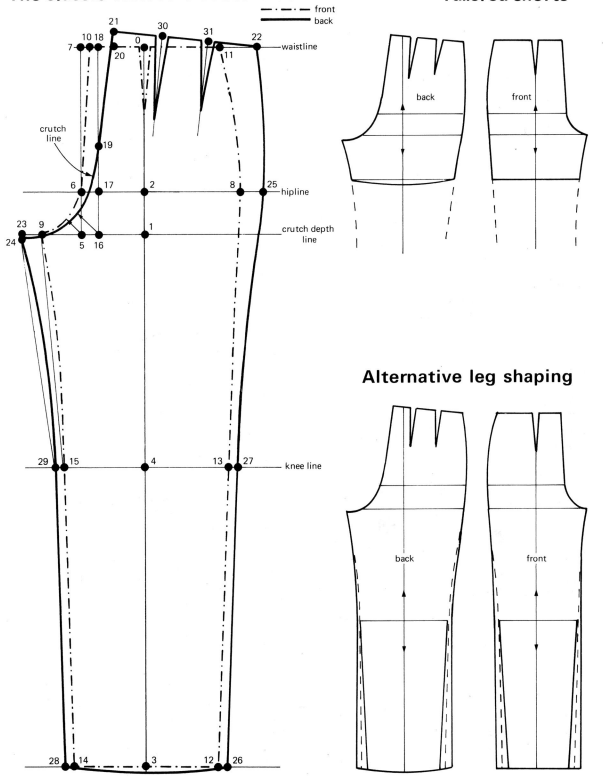

The classic tailored trouser block

— · — · front
——— back

crutch
line

crutch
line

waistline

hipline

crutch depth
line

knee line

Tailored shorts

back

front

Alternative leg shaping

back

front

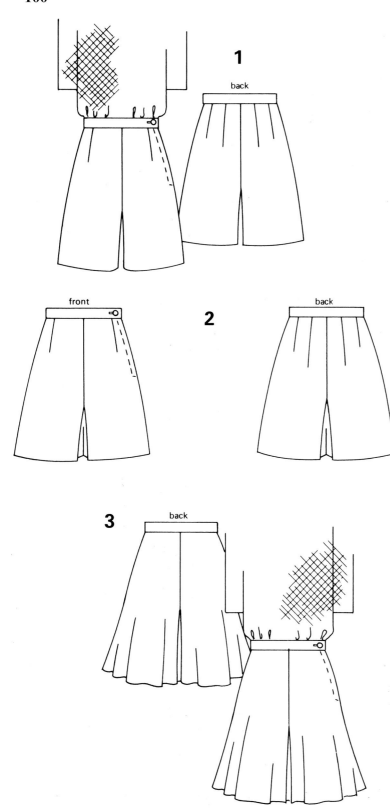

1 CULOTTES

Draw round straight skirt pattern, mark the hipline. Mark hemline depth. Cut off.

Back Mark 0 at centre back waist.

0–1 body rise plus 1.5cm.

0–2 finished length.

1–3 half 0–1 plus 1cm.

1–4 one eighth hip measurement plus 2cm; square down to hemline.

Join 3 to 4 with a curved line touching a point 3cm from 1.

Front Mark 5 at centre front waist.

5–6 body rise plus 1.5cm.

5–7 finished length; square across.

8 is midway between 5 and 6.

6–9 one eighth hip measurement less 2cm; square down to hemline.

Join 8 to 9 with a curved line touching a point 4cm from 6.

2 PLEATED CULOTTES

Trace round culotte pattern.
Separate inside leg sections from the skirt section.

On a new piece of paper trace round skirt sections. Add an 8cm vent pleat (total 16cm) to centre front and centre back.

Place inside leg sections to edge of pleat; trace round.

Fold pleats towards the side seams and cut out patterns.

3 FLARED CULOTTES

Trace round culotte pattern.

Back Drop vertical lines from the base of darts to hem. Cut out pattern and cut up the lines. Close darts to make flare at the hemline. Trace round pattern on a new piece of paper. Cut out.

Front Drop vertical lines from the front dart and a point midway between dart and the centre front. Close dart to make flare at the hemline, open the other vertical line to make the same amount of flare. Trace round pattern on a new piece of paper. Cut out.

1 Culottes

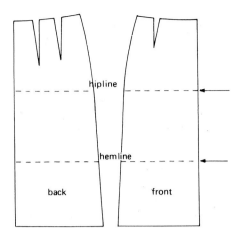

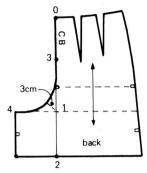

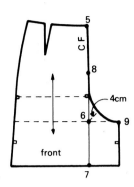

2 Pleated culottes

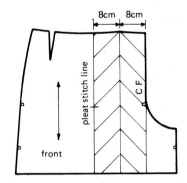

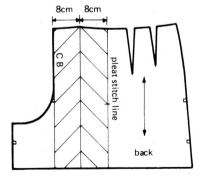

3 Flared culottes

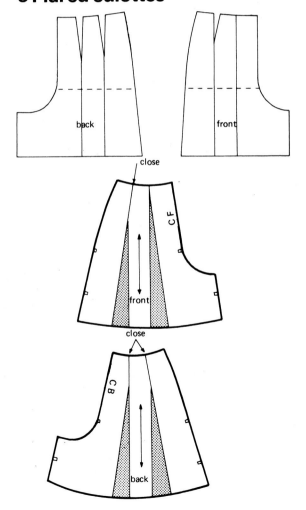

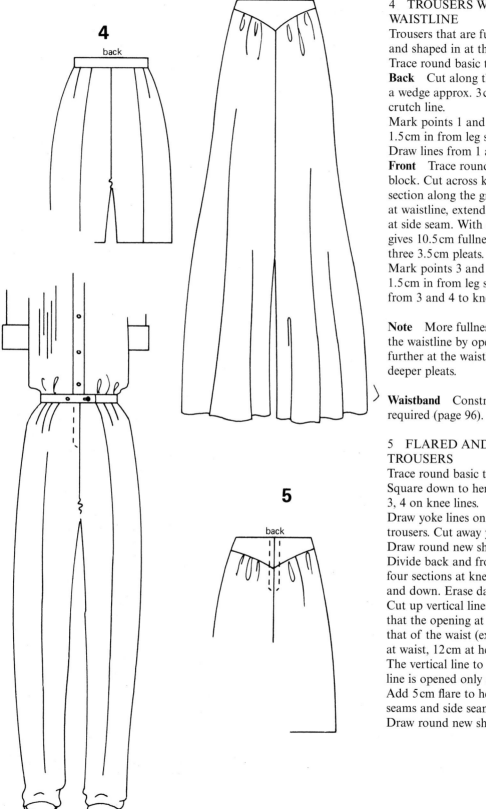

4

back

5

back

4   TROUSERS WITH PLEATED WAISTLINE

Trousers that are full at the waistline and shaped in at the hem.

Trace round basic trouser block.

Back   Cut along the hipline and open a wedge approx. 3 cm wide at back crutch line.

Mark points 1 and 2 on hemline 1.5 cm in from leg seam.

Draw lines from 1 and 2 to knee line.

Front   Trace round front trouser block. Cut across knee line, divide top section along the grain line. Open 5 cm at waistline, extend waistline by 3.5 cm at side seam. With dart allowance this gives 10.5 cm fullness. Divide this into three 3.5 cm pleats.

Mark points 3 and 4 on hemline 1.5 cm in from leg seam. Draw lines from 3 and 4 to knee line.

Note   More fullness can be added at the waistline by opening the grain line further at the waistline and making deeper pleats.

Waistband   Construct waistband required (page 96).

5   FLARED AND GATHERED TROUSERS

Trace round basic trouser block.

Square down to hem from points 1, 2, 3, 4 on knee lines.

Draw yoke lines on back and front trousers. Cut away yokes. Close darts. Draw round new shapes.

Divide back and front trousers into four sections at knee line. Square up and down. Erase darting.

Cut up vertical lines, open sections so that the opening at the hem is double that of the waist (example shows 6 cm at waist, 12 cm at hem).

The vertical line to the back crutch line is opened only at the hem.

Add 5 cm flare to hem of inside leg seams and side seams.

Draw round new shapes.

4 Trousers with pleated waistline 5 Flared and gathered trousers

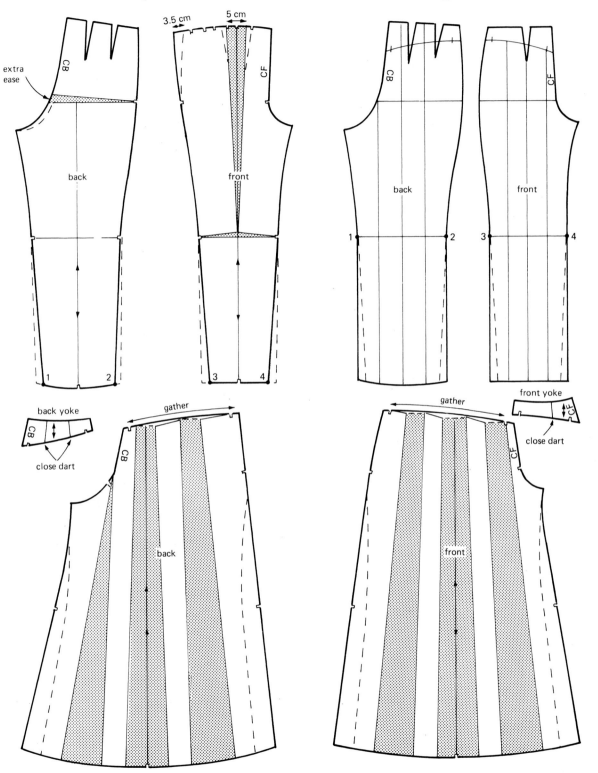

The Very Close Fitting Trouser/Jeans Block

MEASUREMENTS REQUIRED TO DRAFT THE BLOCK (example size 12)

Trousers or jeans made from close fitting blocks are often made from fabrics with slight stretch to provide a 'comfort fit'.

The close fitting trouser/jeans block is drafted so that the top of the waistband sits on the waistline. Jeans can be drafted to sit 2 cm below it (see instructions in brackets). The wedge in the back crutch line (see the jeans adaptation, points 17–34) should also be used for close fitting trousers.

Refer to the size chart (page 11) for standard measurements.

waist	70 cm	body rise	28 cm
hips	94 cm	waist to floor	104 cm
waist to hip	20.6 cm	jeans bottom	
waistband depth	4 cm	width	19 cm

Front
Square both ways from 0.
0–1 body rise minus 4 cm (6 cm); square across.
0–2 waist to hip minus 4 cm (6 cm); square across.
0–3 waist to floor measurement; square across.
1–4 half the measurement 1–3 minus 5 cm; square across.
1–5 one twelfth hip measurement; square up to 6 and 7.
6–8 quarter hip measurement minus 1.5 cm.
5–9 one sixteenth hip measurement minus 1 cm.
7–10 2 cm.
Join 10–6 and 6–9 with a curve touching a point:
sizes 8–14   3.25 cm from 5;
sizes 16–24   3.5 cm from 5.
10–11 quarter waist plus 1.5 cm (2 cm).
3–12 half jeans bottom width minus 1 cm.
4–13 the measurement 3–12 plus 2 cm.
Draw side seam 11, 8, 13, 12; curve 11– 8, out 0.25 cm; continue the side seam curve to 13.
3–14 half jeans bottom width minus 1 cm.
4–15 the measurement 3–14 plus 2 cm.
Draw inside leg seam 9, 15, 14. Curve in 9–15 0.75 cm.

Back
5–16 quarter measurement 1–5; square up to 17 on the hipline, 18 on the waistline.
16–19 half the measurement 16–18 plus 1 cm (2 cm).
18–20 2 cm.
20–21 2 cm.

21–22 quarter waist plus 4 cm (4.5 cm). Join 21–22 to touch the line squared out from 0.
9–23 the measurement 5–9 minus 0.5 cm.
23–24 0.5 cm. Join 21–19 and 19–24 with a curve touching a point:
sizes 8–14   4.5 cm from 16;
sizes 16–24   4.75 cm from 16.
17–25 quarter hip measurement plus 1.5 cm.
12–26 2 cm.
13–27 2 cm.
Draw side seam 22, 25, 27, 26; curve 22–25 out 0.5 cm, continue the side seam curve to 27 as shown.
14–28 2 cm.
15–29 2 cm.
Draw inside leg seam 24, 29, 28; curve 24–29 in 1 cm.
21–30 half the measurement 21–22; square down from line 21–22. Construct a dart on this line, width 1.25 cm (1 cm), length 8 cm.

6   BASIC JEANS ADAPTATION
Front   Trace off front section; mark point 6.
Draw in curved pocket line 31–32 and pocket bag.
Cut off side piece along the line 31–32; add 3.5 cm from 31–32.
Draw in fly piece shape to point 33, 1 cm below 6. Fly piece width 3.5–4 cm. Trace off fly piece. Trace off pocket bag along the line 31–32.

Back   Trace off back sections; mark points 17, 21, 22, 24, 25. Cut along hipline 17–25, open a wedge approx. 3.5 cm wide at 17.
17–34 1 cm; draw in new crutch line from 21–24. Draw in pocket design.
21–35 quarter the measurement 21–34.
22–36 quarter the measurement 22–25.
Cut off yoke along the line 35–36; close dart. Curve the lines 21–22 and 35–36.

Patch Pocket   Trace off back pocket.

Waistband   The straight waistband is cut 8 cm (11 cm) larger than the waist measurement to fit the lower waist positions.
Square both ways from 37.
37–38 twice waistband depth; square across.
38–39 waist measurement plus fly width; square up.
39–40 fly width; square up.
38–41 half the measurement 38–40; square up.
Mark fold line down the centre.

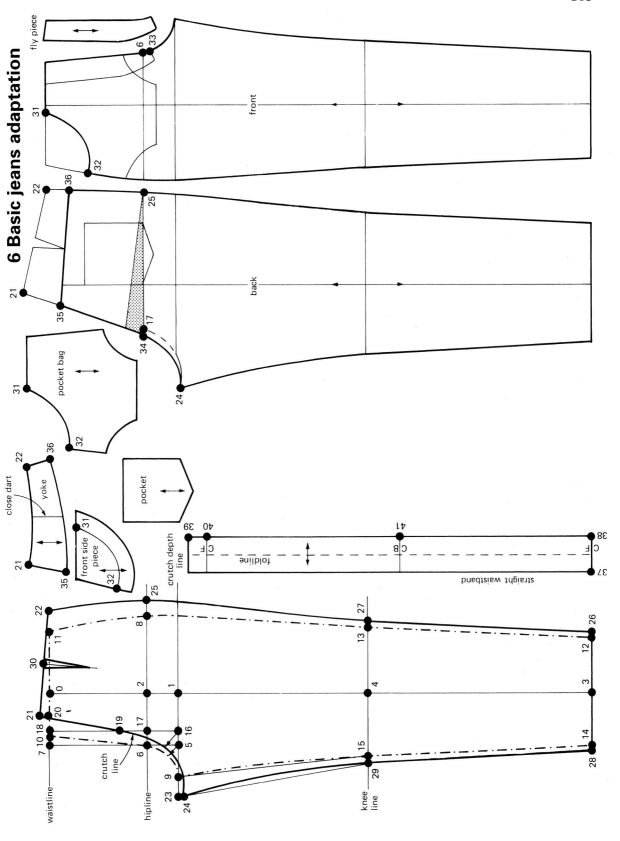

6 Basic jeans adaptation

fly piece

front

back

pocket bag

close dart

yoke

front side piece

pocket

crutch depth line

straight waistband

foldline

C F

C B

waistline

hipline

knee line

crutch line

7 Hipster jeans adaptation

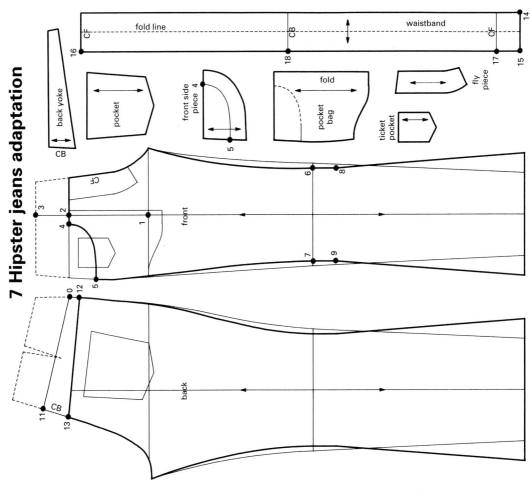

7 HIPSTER JEANS ADAPTATION

Trace off the basic jeans block with wedge at the crutch line.

Front Mark point 1 on crutch depth line of centre line.

1–2 body rise minus 11 cm; square across for new low waistline. Mark point 3 on old waistline.

Draw in curved pocket line 4–5 and pocket bag.

Draw in ticket pocket.

Cut off side piece along the line 4–5; add 3.5 cm from 4–5.

Trace off pocket bag. Trace off ticket pocket.

Draw in fly piece shape; fly piece width 4 cm.

Trace off fly piece.

Shape new side and inside leg seams.

Shape in approx. 0.5 cm at the knee line to 6 and 7.

Square down 5 cm from 6 and 7 to 8 and 9.

Add approx. 4 cm flare to each side of the hemline.

Join 8 and 9 to new hemline points.

Back Draw a line 10–11 parallel to the old waistline, the distance is the measurement 2–3 on front section. Draw in a new yoke line 12–13 from a point approx. 2.5 cm below 10.

Draw in back pocket.

Trace off back yoke. Trace off back pocket.

Shape new side and inside leg seams as for the front pattern.

Waistband Measure the waistline of the new draft. Square both ways from 14.

14–15 twice waistband depth; square up.

15–16 new waist measurement plus 4 cm fly width; square across.

15–17 4 cm fly width; square across.

17–18 half the measurement 16–17 square across. Mark fold line down centre of waistband.

Part One: Classic Form Cutting
8 COMPLEX ADAPTATIONS OF THE BODICE BLOCKS: DRESSES— JACKETS—COATS

These adaptations are all based on form cutting with the bust dart. However, the amount of darting that the designer uses should depend on the fabric selected.

Fabrics with stretch characteristics will expand to cover the form so many stretch garments are flat cut. However, it can be very rewarding to use them with all kinds of form cutting. This allows the designer to cut closer to the form yet still create some structure in the design.

Whilst many casual garments are 'flat cut', they can also be cut to the body shape (see page 124).

This book has been written for beginners. Although a tailored jacket block is included, together with a few tailored styles, the book *Pattern Cutting for Tailored Jackets: Classic and Contemporary* covers the subject of tailored garments in much greater depth.

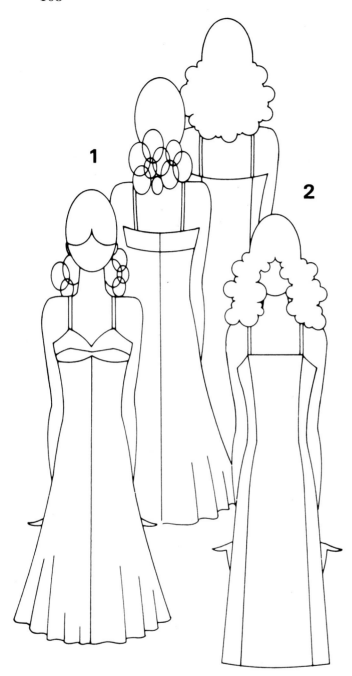

Lingerie and Form Fitting Dresses

For close fitting lingerie, decollete night and evening wear, widen the dart of the close fitting dress block and reduce some of the ease:
Trace round the close fitting dress block.
Reduce each side seam 1.5 cm at bust, 0.5 cm at the waist to 0.25 cm at the hips.
Double the width of the bust dart.

Some lingerie and most 'lingerie type' dresses made in fabrics with stretch, that are cut on the cross or are body-skimming rather than body-fitting do not always need the wider dart and some may even use a reduced dart.

1 'BRA' TOP

Trace round lingerie block to required length. Draw in shaped top of front and back bra. Draw horizontal line through bust point. Trace off bra sections. Cut out.
Bra Sections Close back dart, trace round. Widen bust dart by 1.5 cm. Cut across vertical line. Close top and bottom darts. Trace round upper and lower sections.
Skirt Rub out waist darts, take amount equivalent of dart shaping out at the seams, half at side seams and half at centre front and centre back seams. Add 5 cm flare to hem of front and back seams, 8 cm flare to side seams.

2 VERTICAL SEAMS

Trace round lingerie block to required length. Draw in shape of petticoat top. Widen bust dart by 1 cm. Drop vertical lines from the base of waist darts. Cut out panels, trace round. Shape seams of panels. Add 2 cm flare to hem of panel seams, 3 cm flare to hem of side seam.

Note The skirts or panels of the petticoats can be cut on the cross in woven fabric or on the straight in knitted fabrics. If non-stretch fabric is used a small opening may be required at the back or side seam.

3 STRAPLESS BODICE

Lower waistline 1 cm at centre front on lingerie block; join to centre back line.
Complete adaptation of the princess line petticoat to waistline or depth required. Trace off panels.
Shape in back panel at centre back waistline 1 cm.
Reduce both side seams by 1 cm at top edge only; redraw top edge shaping.
Shape waist of front panel seam on front and side front 1 cm.
Mark points 1, 2, 3 on front panel.
1–4 = one third measurement 1–2; 2–5 = one fifth measurement 2–3. Draw in new shaping at top edge.

Increasing the dart

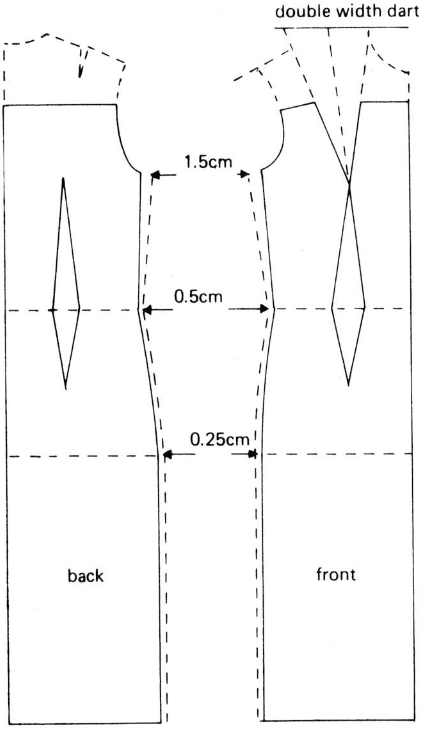

back

1.5cm

0.5cm

0.25cm

back   front

double width dart

1 'Bra' top

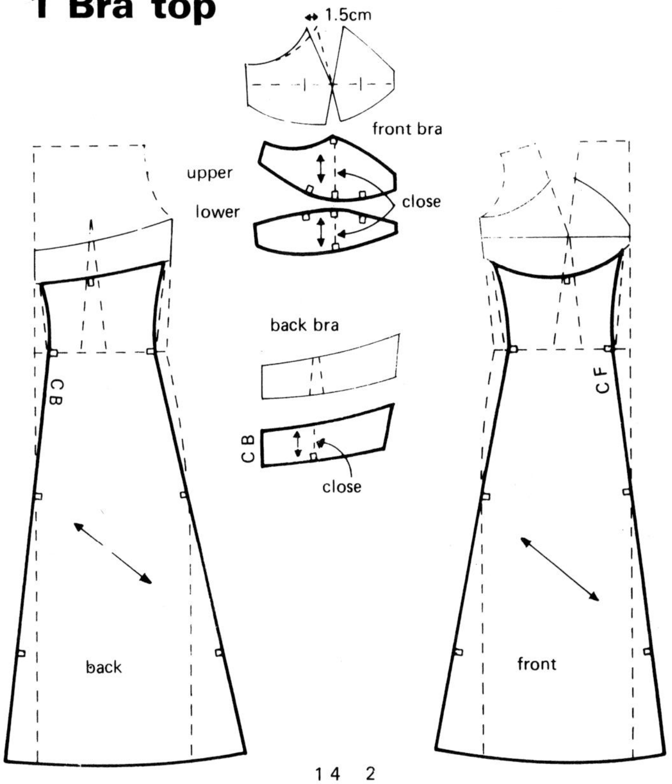

1.5cm

front bra

upper

lower

close

back bra

C B

close

C B

back

C F

front

2 Vertical seams

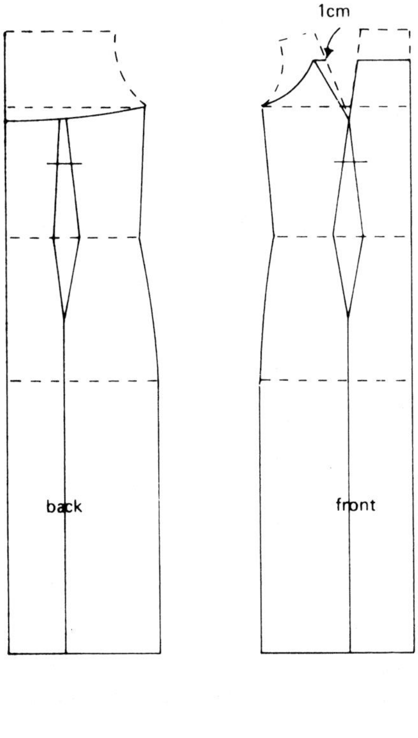

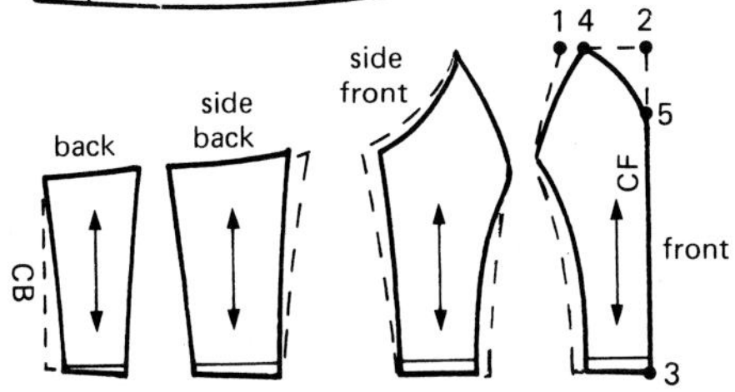

back   front

1cm

3 Strapless bodice

back   side back   side front   1 4 2   5   CF   front   3

C B fold   back   side back   side front   C F fold   front

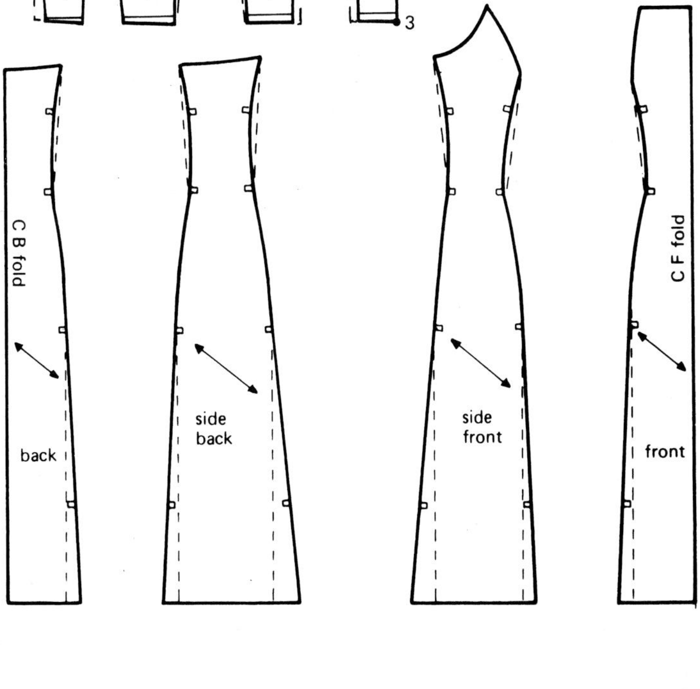

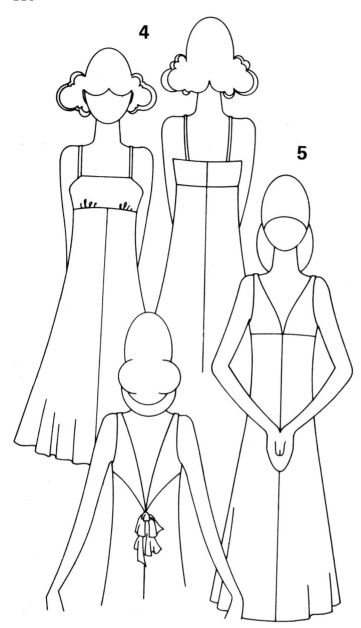

The skirts hang better if woven fabric is cut on the cross.

4 CAMISOLE TOP

Trace round lingerie block. Drop vertical lines from base of waist darts. Draw in camisole top. Shape the high waistline with slight curve. Cut away top sections. Shape side seams. Shape in front and back waist 2 cm.

Top Sections Close back dart, trace round section. Widen bust dart 1.5 cm. Close bust dart, trace round pattern.

Skirt Reshape waist darts from high waistline to base of darts. Cut out skirt. Cut up vertical lines. Close darts and insert 7 cm flare at hem. Grain line runs down centre of opening. Add 6 cm to hem of side seam and 4 cm flare to centre front and centre back seams.

5 'V' NECK

Trace round complete lingerie block. Draw in shaped waistline from back waist point.
Top sections

Back Draw in 'V' neck and armscye shape. Make 1 cm dart in neckline. Cut out section, close neck dart and waist dart. Trace round with smooth curved lines.

Front Draw in neckline (check distance from neck point equals that on back). Cut out section, close bust dart, trace round with smooth curved lines.

Skirts Rub out waist darts, shape in side and front seams as shown, the same amount that is removed by closing the darts in the upper sections. Cut out skirts. Trace round. Add 7 cm flare to hem of centre front and centre back seams, 10 cm flare to hem of side seam.

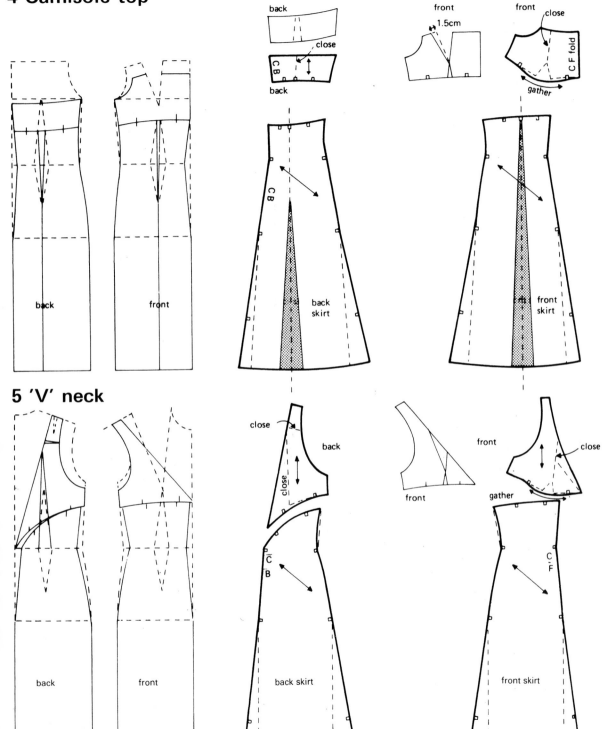

4 Camisole top

5 'V' neck

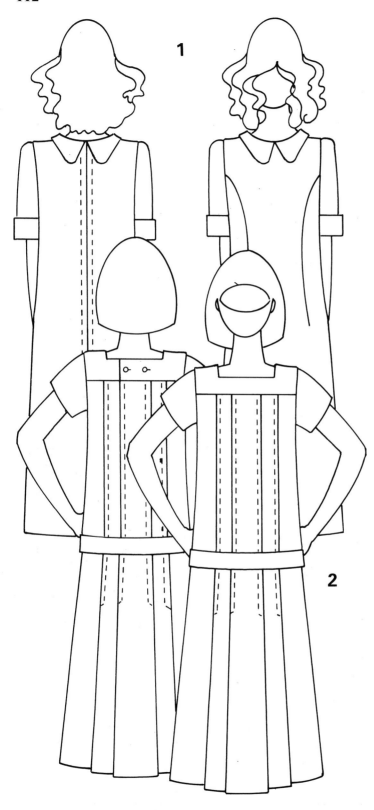

1

2

Dresses and 'Dressmaker' Jackets

Many styles are based on the shift dress, and the fit depends on whether a close fitting or easy fitting block is chosen for the adaptation. Shaping at the waistline can be varied.

1 BASIC SHIFT DRESS

Trace round one-piece dress block. Draw in curved line from armscye to front dart. Cut up side seam, cut out block.

Front Cut up curved line, close bust dart, trace round. Lower neckline. Shape side seam and top of dart. Add 3 cm flare to hem at side seam.

Back Rub out back waist dart. Lower neckline. Shape side seam. Add 3 cm flare to hem at side seam.

Collar Diagram shows two-piece flat collar (ref. 1 page 68).

Sleeve Design shows lengthened short sleeve (ref. 6 page 48) and straight cuff with facing (page 66).

2 STYLED SHIFT DRESS

Trace round easy fitting dress block without waist shaping. Cut up side seam, transfer bust dart to underarm.

Back and Front Sections Draw in square neckline, yoke lines and low waistband. Drop parallel pleat lines from back and front yokes.

Mark points 1 and 2 on back yoke line.

Back Bodice Trace off back bodice, cut up pleat lines, open approx. 5 cm; mark fold line down centre of pleats.

Back Yoke Trace off back yoke; mark point 3 at centre back, 3–4 is the measurement 1–2 on back yoke line. Mark buttonhole positions.

Front Bodice Trace off front bodice, cut up pleat lines, open approx. 5 cm; mark fold line down centre of pleats. Close bust dart (the dart then becomes a part of outer pleat).

Front Yoke Trace off front yoke.

Back and Front Skirts Trace off skirt sections; cut up pleat lines and open approx. 8 cm. Mark fold line down centre of each pleat.

Low Waistband Trace off back and front waistbands, join at side seam.

Sleeve Short sleeve (ref. 6 page 48).

Note The yokes are self faced.

1 Basic shift dress

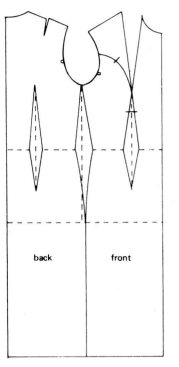

back   front

back

collar

collar

front

CB

CF fold

close

2 Styled shift dress

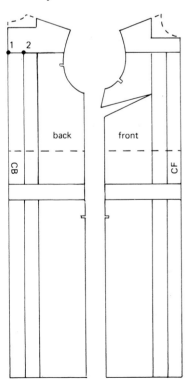

back   front

CB

CF

1 2

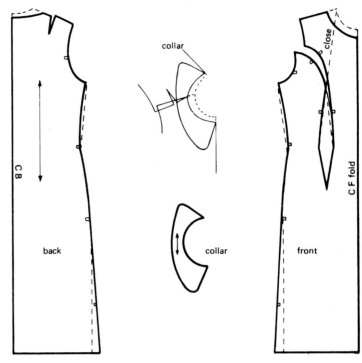

back yoke

CB

4 3

low waistband

CB   CF fold

front yoke

CF fold

CB fold

back
bodice

close
darts

front
bodice

CF fold

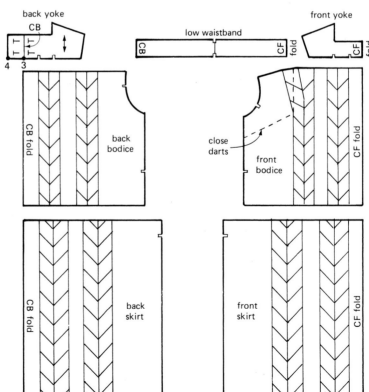

CB fold

back
skirt

front
skirt

CF fold

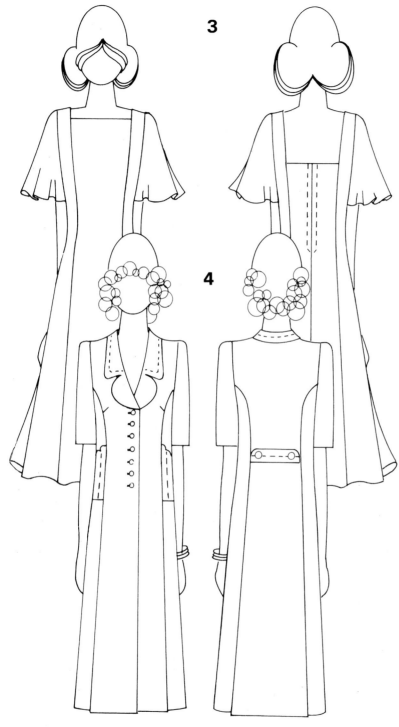

3 PRINCESS LINE

Trace round one-piece close fitting dress block. Take 2 cm off back shoulder (this includes dart allowance) and 1 cm off front shoulder. Transfer bust dart to centre shoulder, draw in front and back neckline. Lower back waist point 3 cm, shape in 1.5 cm. Reduce back dart 1.5 cm.

Drop panel lines from base of front and back waist darts. Cut out block, cut up side seams.

Front and Back Cut up panel lines, trace round panels, shape seams, add 3.5 cm flare to hem of panel seams, 5 cm flare to hem of side seams and 2 cm flare to hem of back seam. Add extended facings to top of front and back panel seams and to neck edge of side panel seams.

Sleeve Design shows very flared sleeve (ref. 10 page 50).

4 SEMI-FITTED PRINCESS LINE

Trace round one-piece dress block. Rub out side seam and waist darts. Mark balance points at underarm. Draw in side panels and shape waist 2.5 cm on each panel. Draw in neckline, take a 0.6 cm dart from front neckline. Draw a line from side panel to bust point. Cut out block and up panel seams.

Front Close bust and neck darts, trace round. Mark buttonholes, add buttonstand, small rever. Add 3 cm flare to side panel seam. Shape panel seam.

Side Panel Trace round, add 3 cm flare to panel seams, add a vent pleat (6 cm at top, 9 cm at bottom) to back panel seam.

Add extension 12 cm long, 4 cm wide for pocket. Shape seams.

Back Trace round, add 3 cm flare and pleat to panel seam as for side panel. Shape seam.

Draw belt shape at top of waistline.

Belt and Pocket Trace off belt shape. Draw pocket welt 12 cm long and 4 cm wide.

Collar Flat collar (ref. 3 page 68).

Sleeve Short sleeve (ref. 6 page 48).

Facing Trace a separate facing.

3 Princess line

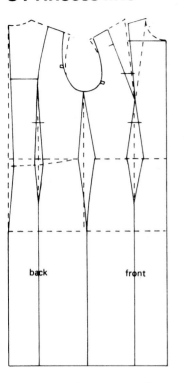

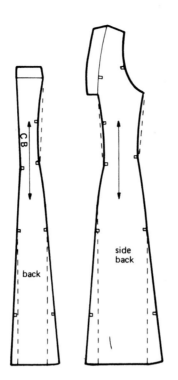

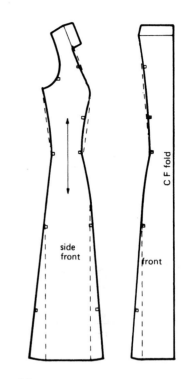

4 Semi-fitted princess line

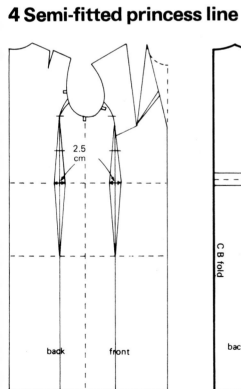

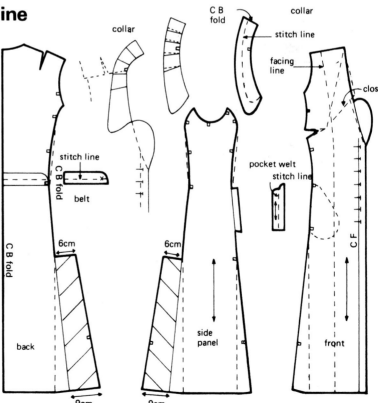

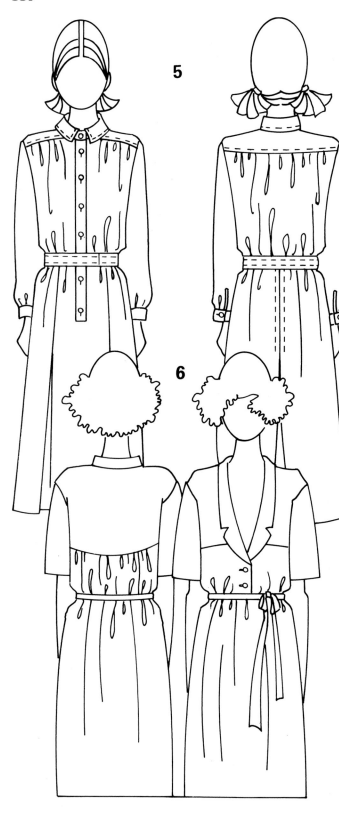

5   CLASSIC SHIRT DRESS
Trace easy fitting two-piece dress block (straight side seams on bodice).
Convert 0.5cm ease on back shoulder into a small dart.
Draw in strap line on front skirt and bodice 2cm each side of centre line.
Draft shirt armscye (widen bodice 2cm, lower armscye 1cm; ref. 24 page 54).
Mark panel line on front skirt.
Yokes   Draw back yoke line, slope down 0.5cm from shoulder dart to armscye edge.
Draw front yoke line. Cut off yokes. Close shoulder darts. Place front yoke to back yoke at shoulder line. Trace round pattern.
Back and Front Bodices   Trace bodices.
Cut off front strap. Square down from bust dart; cut up line, open approx. 4cm.
Add 4cm to centre back bodice.
Skirt   Trace round skirt block.
Construct pleats (ref. 4 page 82). Add 2.5cm flare to side seam.
Sleeve   Shirt sleeve (ref. 2 page 48).
Collar   Shirt collar (ref. 9 page 70).
Front Strap and Belt   Construct front strap, double strap width; join at waist. Construct belt, half length and twice width required.
Mark fold line at centre.

6   EASY FITTING DRESS
Trace easy fitting one-piece dress block and one-piece sleeve to required length.
Bodice Sections   Complete adaptation for dropped shoulder with lowered armscye (ref. 25 page 54).
Draw in yoke line on back and front.
Back and Back Yoke   Divide back yoke line into three sections, square down from each point.
Trace off back yoke. Trace off back section, cut up lines and open approx. 4cm; redraw curve.
Front Bodice   Trace off front bodice.
Cut along yoke line to base of bust dart; close bust dart.
Mark buttonholes; add buttonstand.
Construct classic roll collar (ref. 12 page 72).
Draw in facing line.
Trace off yoke and front bodice.
Collar Facing   Trace off facing.
Front Skirt   Trace off front skirt.
Sleeve   Complete adaptation for dropped shoulder with lowered armscye.
Belt   Construct belt, half length and twice width required. Mark fold line.

5 Classic shirt dress

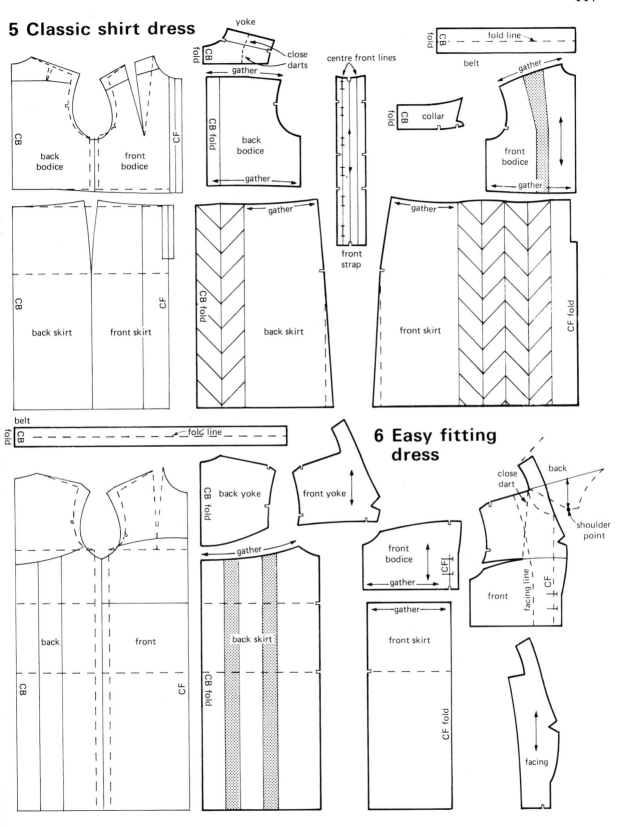

yoke

close darts

fold CB

gather

back bodice

CB fold

back bodice

gather

centre front lines

fold CB collar

fold line

fold CB

belt

gather

front bodice

gather

front strap

CB

back bodice

CF

front bodice

CB

back skirt

CF

front skirt

CB fold

back skirt

gather

gather

front skirt

CF fold

belt

fold CB

fold line

6 Easy fitting dress

CB fold

back yoke

front yoke

close dart

back

shoulder point

front bodice

CF

gather

facing line

CF

front

back

front

CB

CF

back skirt

CB fold

gather

gather

front skirt

CF fold

facing

7

8

9

For 'dressmaker' jackets use a dress block constructed from the close fitting or easy fitting bodice blocks.

7 JACKET – PLEATED PEPLUM

Trace dress block with waist shaping to length required. Hollow centre back waist 1 cm; drop front waistline 1 cm. Draw in panel seams and collar. Close bust dart. Draw in neckline. Cut along waist seam, panel, side seams. Trace round sections and collar. Shape seams; mark buttonholes and buttonstand. Cut facing as front.

Peplum Cut up centre of side panels; open 2 cm for flare. Add 4 cm vent pleats to panel lines and 8 cm at centre back for inverted pleat. Trace round, fold pleats, cut out. Add extended facing to centre front.

8 BASIC FITTED JACKET

Trace dress block without waist shaping to length required. Lower back waist 2.5 cm, shape in 1 cm. Draw in panel lines as shown, draw in required waist shaping on these lines and a small dart midway between side seam and front panel.

Draw in pocket and welt from small dart to back panel line. Trace off pocket welt and bag. Cut up panels.

Back Trace round, shape seams.

Side Panel Trace round, shape seams. Extend side seam at top of pocket the same measurements as width of dart. Cut along lines 1 and 2.

Front Close bust dart, trace round, shape panel seam, mark buttonholes, add buttonstand. Cut facing as front.

9 JACKET – FLARED PEPLUM

Trace dress block without waist shaping to length required. Draw shaped peplum line. Draw in two darts at back and front as shown. Cut up side seam, and along peplum line.

Back Trace round, shape seams, darts.

Front Close bust dart, trace round. Shape seams, shorten darts. Add scalloped buttonstand, mark buttonholes. Trace separate facing.

Peplums Close darts along waistline and open out hem to give required amount of flare. Trace round pattern.

7 Pleated peplum

8 Basic fitted jacket

9 Flared peplum

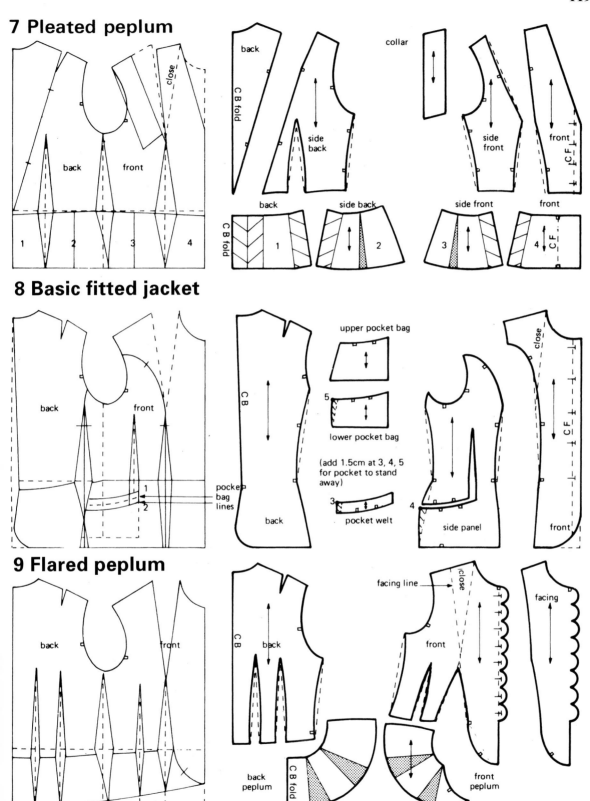

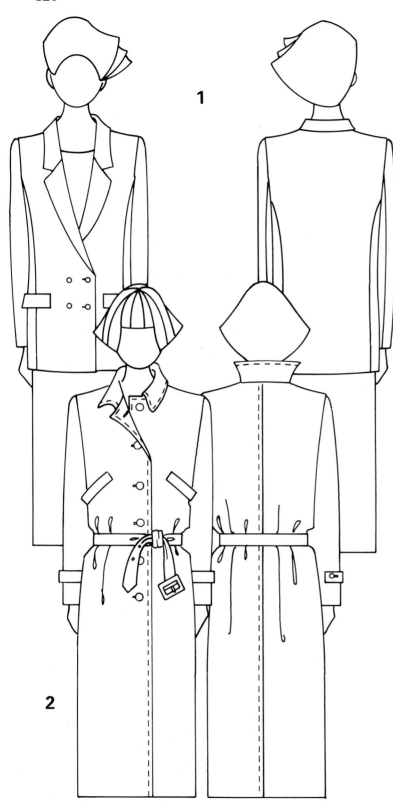

1

2

Jackets and Coats

1 SEMI-FITTED JACKET OR COAT

Trace jacket or overgarment block depending on fit of garment required. Draft block with reduced bust dart; transfer dart to centre shoulder.

Body Sections Drop vertical lines from back and front pitch points. Mark 1, 2, 3, 4 on back; 5, 6, 7 on front; 8 is midway 1–2; square across to 9. 3–10 and 6–11 1.5 cm; 4–12 and 7–13 2 cm. Draw back seam lines 9, 3, 12; 9, 10, 4. Draw front seam lines 5, 6, 13; 5, 11, 7. Draw in welt pocket.
Mark buttonholes, add buttonstand for double breasted front (ref. 3 page 38). Lower neckline and draw in required rever shape. Construct standard collar and rever (ref. 19 page 74) on new neckline. Draw in facing line.

Back Trace off back.

Side Panel Trace off side panel.

Front Trace front section; transfer 1 cm of bust dart to panel line (use as ease); the remainder to a dart in the neckline.

Collar and Facing Trace off collar and facing.

Sleeve Two-piece sleeve (page 24).

Pocket Trace off pocket welt, double the width, mark fold line down centre.

2 CLASSIC OVERCOAT

Trace overgarment block with reduced bust dart (example is half dart size). If extra ease is required in body, draft lowered armscye (ref. 23 page 54).

Back Trace off back section. Add 6 cm for vent at centre back. Add 2 cm flare and pocket facings to side seam.

Front Transfer bust dart to side seam. Draw in welt pocket if required. Lower front hemline 1 cm; join to side seam. Mark buttonholes, add buttonstand. Draw facing line, add extended facing. Add 2 cm flare and pocket facings to side seam. Draw pocket bag, trace off.

Sleeve Trace one-piece sleeve, complete lowered armscye if required.

Collar Construct convertible collar (ref. 8 page 70).

Belt Construct belt, length is half waist measurement plus 25 cm and twice width required. Mark fold at centre.

Straps and Pocket Welt Draft length required and twice width. Mark fold.

1 Semi-fitted jacket or coat

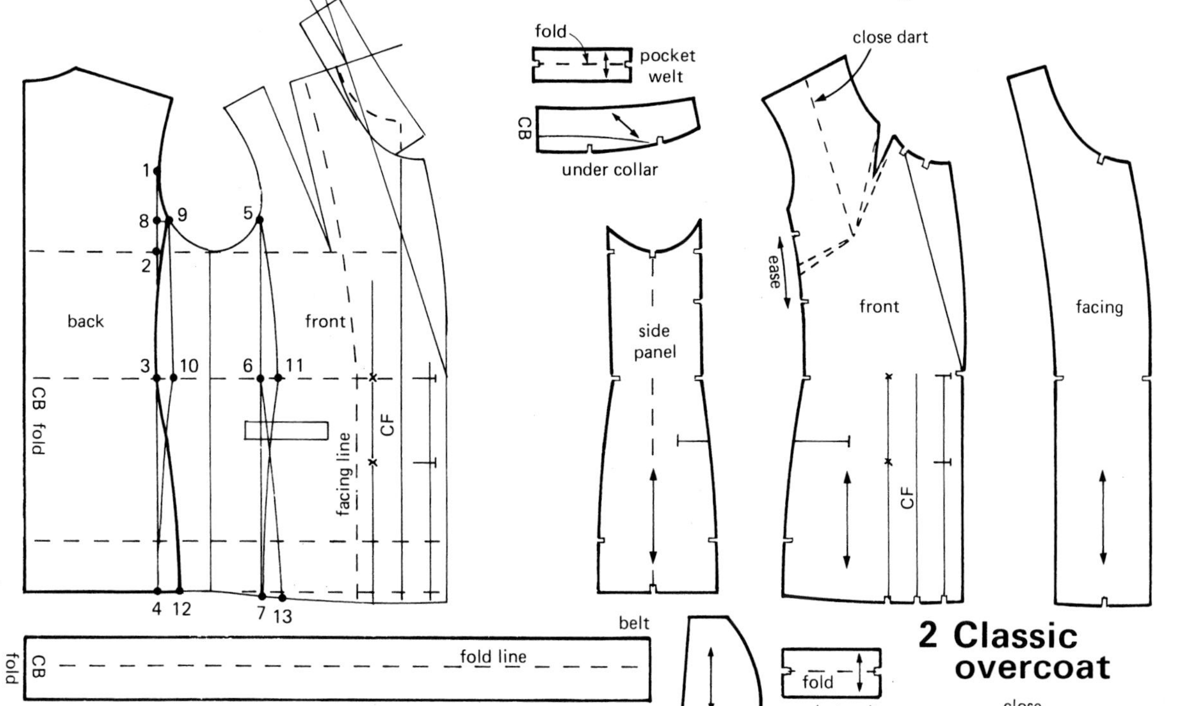

fold

pocket welt

close dart

CB

under collar

back

front

CF

CB fold

facing line

CF

side panel

front

ease

facing

close dart

1

8 9

2

5

3 10

6 11

4 12

7 13

belt

CB

fold

fold line

pocket bag

fold

pocket welt

2 Classic overcoat

CB

under collar

CB

back

front

CF

CB

back

CB

back

front

CF

facing line

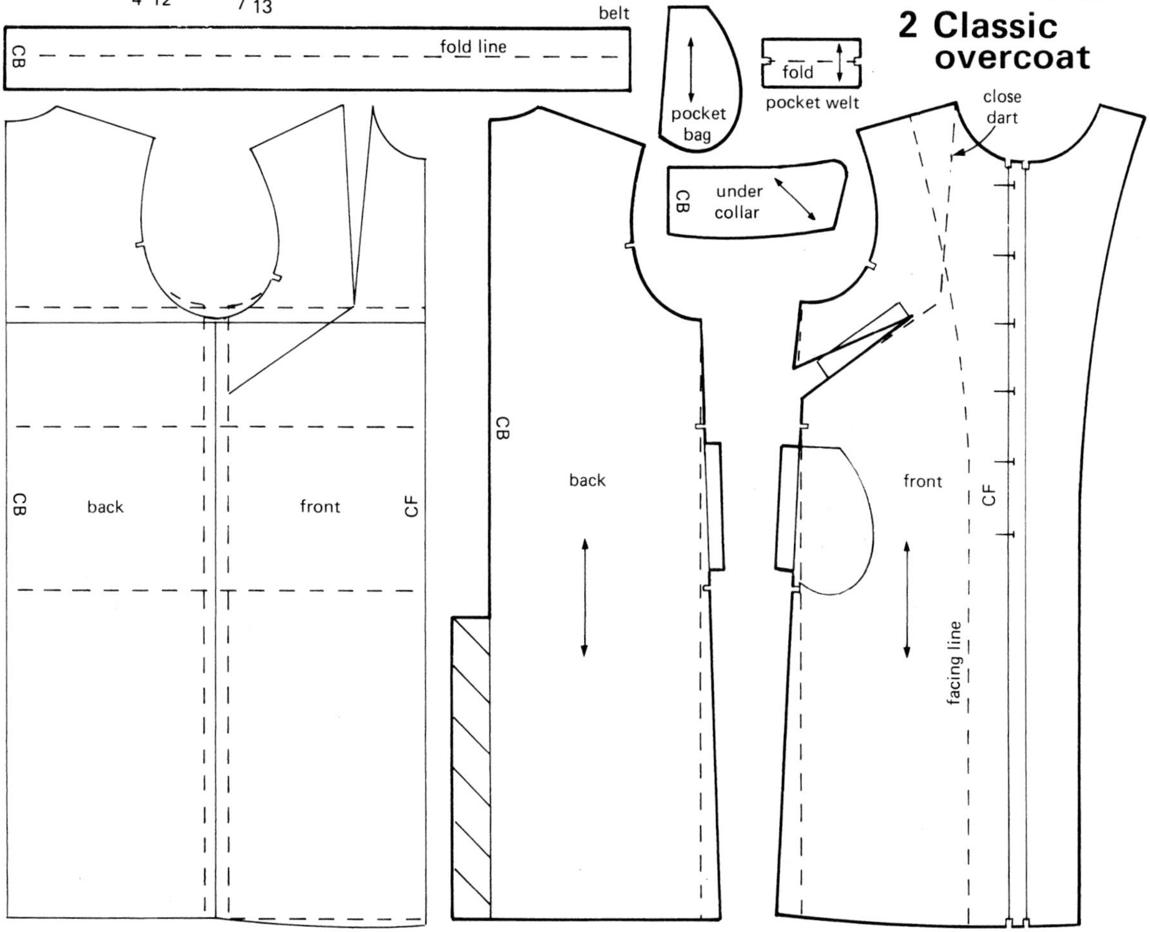

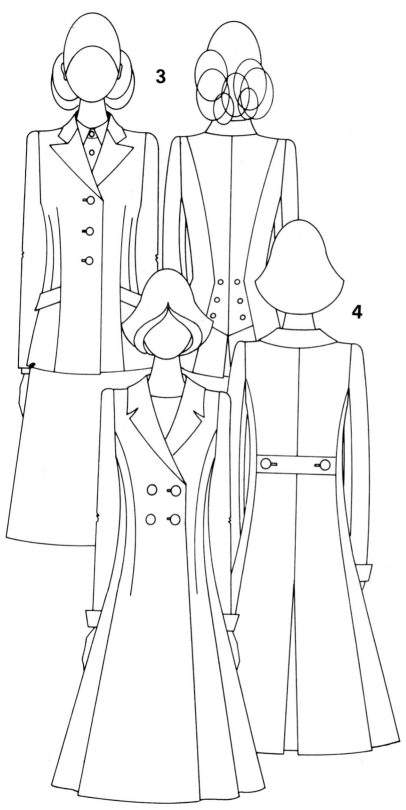

3   FITTED JACKET

Trace off tailored jacket block to length required. Draw in back panel lines, remark side seam 2.5 cm towards back. Shape waist and side seam as shown.

Divide front dart allowance into two darts. Add 1 cm flare to hem of back panel seam. Draw in pocket. Mark buttonholes, add buttonstand, construct a standard reefer collar and rever (ref. 18 page 74).

Trace off all sections. Close bust dart, shape darts and panel seams. Wheel off a front facing. Add 12 cm to centre back of lower back panel for an inverted pleat.

Sleeve   Draft two-piece sleeve.

4   FITTED COAT (SLIGHTLY HIGH WAIST)

Trace round overgarment block to the length required. (The tailored jacket block can be used for a close fit.) Mark in straight waistline. Extend to required length. Draw in panel seams. Shape in centre back seam 1 cm at waist and hem. Shape in approx. 3 cm at front waist dart and panel seams. Draw in belt shape.

For low rever draw in 0.6 cm dart at neckline. Close. Draw in button lines, mark buttonholes, add buttonstand. Construct a roll collar with a hollowed neck (ref. 16 page 72), swing back 5 cm. Draw in notch. Trace off all sections.

Back   Add 16 cm to centre back skirt for an inverted pleat. Shape panel seam, add 4 cm flare to hem.

Front and Side Panel   Shape panel seams, add 5 cm flare at hem. Add 2.5 cm flare at front edge. Add pocket facing to front seam. Close bust dart. Trace off front facing.

Sleeve   Draft two-piece sleeve (page 24). Construct shaped cuff (page 66).

Note   For padded shoulders raise shoulders and sleeve heads (ref. 8 page 48).

3 Fitted jacket

4 Fitted coat

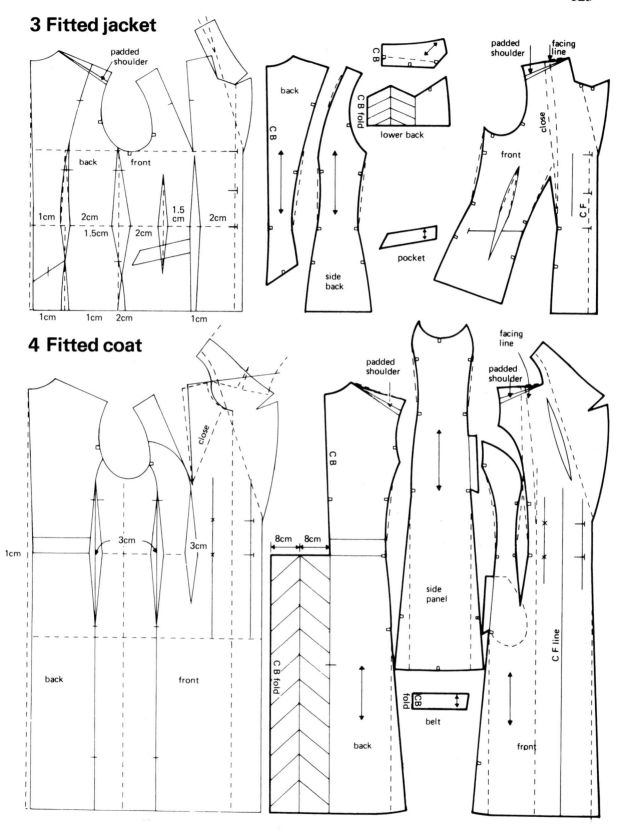

padded shoulder

padded shoulder

facing line

close

C B

back

front

1cm

2cm

1.5cm

2cm

1.5cm

2cm

1cm

1cm

2cm

1cm

back

C B

C B fold

lower back

side back

pocket

padded shoulder

facing line

close

front

C F

padded shoulder

facing line

padded shoulder

close

3cm

3cm

1cm

back

front

8cm

8cm

C B fold

back

belt

fold

C B

C B

side panel

C F line

front

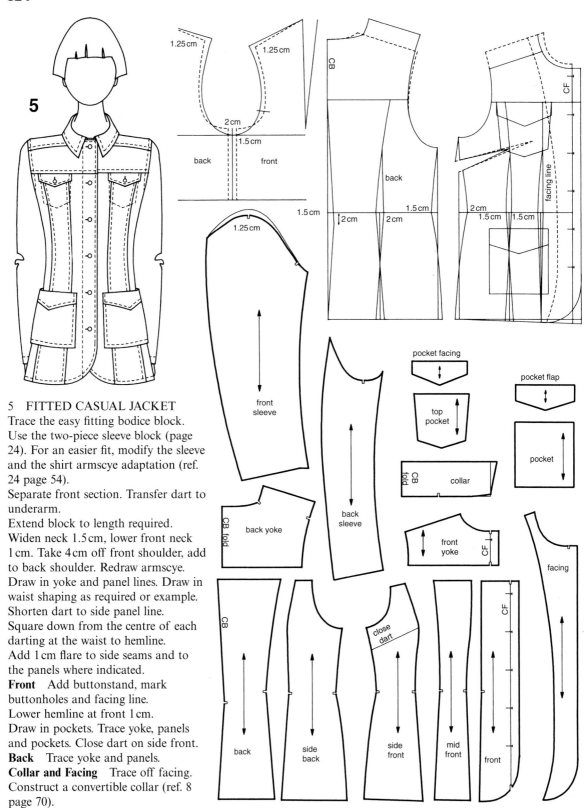

5   FITTED CASUAL JACKET

Trace the easy fitting bodice block.
Use the two-piece sleeve block (page 24). For an easier fit, modify the sleeve and the shirt armscye adaptation (ref. 24 page 54).

Separate front section. Transfer dart to underarm.

Extend block to length required.
Widen neck 1.5 cm, lower front neck 1 cm. Take 4 cm off front shoulder, add to back shoulder. Redraw armscye.
Draw in yoke and panel lines. Draw in waist shaping as required or example.
Shorten dart to side panel line.
Square down from the centre of each darting at the waist to hemline.
Add 1 cm flare to side seams and to the panels where indicated.

Front   Add buttonstand, mark buttonholes and facing line.
Lower hemline at front 1 cm.
Draw in pockets. Trace yoke, panels and pockets. Close dart on side front.

Back   Trace yoke and panels.

Collar and Facing   Trace off facing.
Construct a convertible collar (ref. 8 page 70).

Classic Coat and Jacket Hems and Seam Allowances

Seam allowances will vary with the style and the fabric; the example shows seam allowances on a basic jacket pattern.

Back and Front   Mark point A at facing line point on the front hemline.

A–B = 1 cm.

Add 1 cm seam to all seam edges.

Add 1 cm to the hem from point B to the front edge.

Add 4 cm hem allowance. Make a step at point B.

Facing   Mark point C at the collar point and point D at the break line.

Add 1 cm to all seam edges from C–D.

Add extra allowance to the outer edge of facing from C–D. (The amount will vary depending on the thickness of the fabric.)

Collars   The seam allowance for collars will vary with the type of manufacture or make-up (i.e. shaping of the under collar). Note that the top collar is cut with extra ease (ref. page 68).

For standard styles add extra ease (approx. 0.5 cm) to the collar style line from E–F and to the neck edge from G–H.

Sleeve   Add vents to back seam 10 cm long and 2 cm wide. Add 1 cm seam allowance to all seam lines. Add 4.5 cm hem allowance.

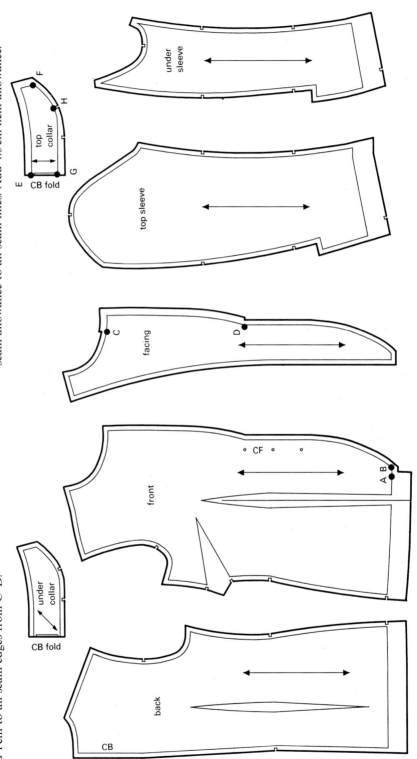

Classic Coat and Jacket Linings

Ease allowance is required in linings for two reasons:

(1) Cloth garments, particularly those made in woollen fabrics, 'spread' a little when they are cut out. Lining fabrics do not relax in the same manner. The amount of ease required is dependent on the fabric used; the example shown is a general guide.

(2) The linings should be loose enough to prevent the garment being distorted when the lining is inserted. The ease in the lining also allows for parts of the garment that come under stress from body movement. Particular stress points are the armscye and the centre back.

The lining patterns are made after seam allowance has been added to the garment piece patterns.

Body and sleeve linings are cut 2cm above cloth hemlines.

Back   Add 2cm at A for the centre back pleat. Add 1cm out and up at B; 1cm out and 0.5cm up at C; 0.5cm out at D and E.

Front   Add 1cm out and up at F; 1cm out and 0.5cm up at G; 0.5cm out at H and I. Add 1cm to the facing line for seam allowance.

Top Sleeve   Add 1cm up and 0.8cm out at J and K; 1cm up at L.

Under Sleeve   Add 1cm up and 0.8cm out at M and N; 1cm up at 0. Reshape underarm curve as shown. Add vent allowance to undersleeve.

Note   In the bespoke trade, linings are often cut by laying the cloth pieces directly onto the lining fabric; in manufacture, separate lining patterns have to be made.

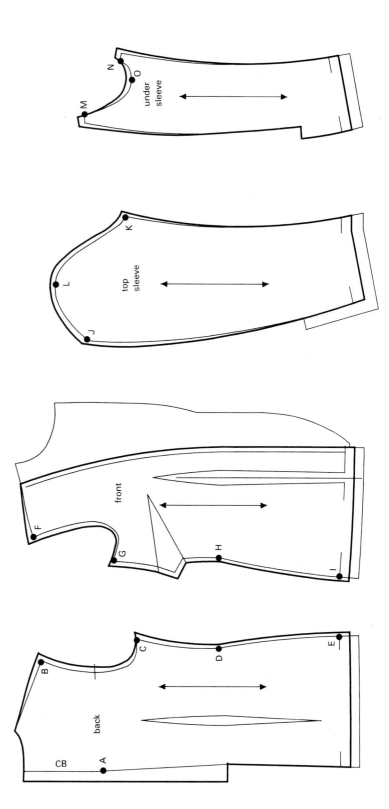

Part Two: Flat Cutting
9 EASY FITTING GARMENTS
(woven fabrics)

These adaptations are all based on flat cutting without using bust dart shaping or close fitting waist shaping. The technique is useful for garments that are flat-packed.

The basic blocks are used mainly for garments of easy fitting shape in woven fabrics as they have a substantial amount of ease included. They are particularly useful for sportswear and weatherwear overgarments.

Sleeve and collar adaptations from Part One can be used. Some style examples are shown to demonstrate their application. Most examples show the back and front sections facing the same way. This is used so that the grading points and instructions for both patterns will be the same. Flat cutting enables the use of these simple grading techniques.

SIZING
Sportswear and some casual wear manufacturers usually use sizing breaks of SMALL, MEDIUM, LARGE and XLARGE. The example sizings used in the following drafts are based on size Med., High Street *fashion* garments. See page 12.

Easy Fitting Trouser and Skirt Shapes
The Easy Fitting Trouser Block
For 'baggy' trousers and dungarees

MEASUREMENTS REQUIRED TO DRAFT THE BLOCK

The blocks can be drafted to size codes 8, 10, 12, 14, etc. or Sml, Med, Lge, XLge.

Example shown is for a size Med.; refer to the size charts (page 12) for standard measurements for High Street *fashion* garments.

waist	70 cm	body rise	28 cm
hips	94 cm	waist to floor	104 cm
waist to hip	20.6 cm	trouser bottom width (page 11)	22 cm

Front

Square both ways from 0.

0–1 body rise plus 1 cm; square across.

0–2 waist to hip; square across.

0–3 waist to floor measurement; square across.

1–4 half the measurement 1–3 minus 5 cm; square across.

1–5 one twelfth hip measurement plus 1.8 cm; square up to 6 and 7.

6–8 quarter hip measurement plus 1 cm.

5–9 one sixteenth hip measurement plus 1 cm.

7–10 1 cm.

Join 10–6 and 6–9 with a curve touching a point:

sizes   8–14 or Sml, Med.   3.5 cm   from 5
sizes   16–24 or Lge, XLge.   3.75 cm   from 5

10–11 quarter waist plus 5 cm.

3–12 half trouser bottom width minus 0.5 cm; join 8–12. Mark point 13 on knee line.

Draw in side seam; join 8–11 with a slight curve. Join 8–13 and 13–12.

3–14 half trouser bottom width minus 0.5 cm.

4–15 the measurement 4–13.

Draw inside leg seam, join 14–15; join 9–15 curving the line inwards 0.75 cm.

Back

5–16 quarter the measurement 1–5; square up to 17 on the hipline, 18 on the waistline.

16–19 half the measurement 16–18.

18–20 2 cm.

20–21 2 cm.

21–22 quarter waist plus 6 cm; join 21–22 to touch the horizontal line from 0.

9–23 half the measurement 5–9.

23–24 0.25 cm.

Join 21–19; join 19–24 with a curve touching a point:
sizes   8–14 or Sml, Med.   4.5 cm   from 16
sizes   16–24 or Lge, XLge.   4.75 cm   from 16

17–25 quarter hip measurement plus 2 cm.

12–26 1 cm.

13–27 1 cm.

Draw in side seam; 22–25 curve outwards slightly, 25–27 curve inwards slightly, join 27–26.

14–28 1 cm.

15–29 1 cm.

Draw inside leg seam; join 28–29; join 29–24 curving the line inwards 1 cm.

EASE IN THE BACK CRUTCH

Most easy fitting trousers, particularly dungarees, require extra ease in the back crutch line.

Trace off back trousers of required block.

Cut along the hipline and open a wedge approx. 3.5 cm wide at back crutch line.

Redraw back crutch line as shown.

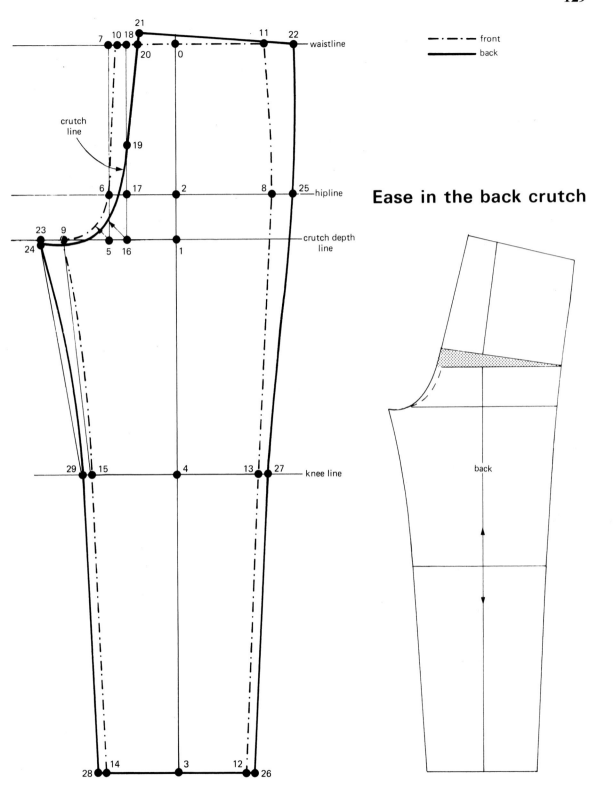

front
back

crutch
line

21
7 10 18
20 0
11 22 waistline

19

6 17 2 8 25 hipline

23 9
24 5 16 1 crutch depth
line

Ease in the back crutch

back

29 15 4 13 27 knee line

28 14 3 12 26

The Simple Trouser Block

MEASUREMENTS REQUIRED TO DRAFT THE BLOCK

The blocks can be drafted to size codes 8, 10, 12, 14, etc. or Sml, Med, Lge, XLge.

Example shown is for a size Med.; refer to the size charts (page 12) for standard measurements for High Street *fashion* garments.

hips	94 cm
body rise	28 cm
waist to floor	104 cm
high ankle	21 cm

Front

Square down and across from 0.

0–1 body rise plus 1 cm; square across.
0–2 waist to floor; square across.
1–3 half the measurement 1–2; square across.
1–4 quarter hip measurement plus 4 cm; square up to 5.
5–6 1 cm.
4–7 quarter the measurement 4–5.
4–8 one quarter the measurement 1–4 minus 0.5 cm.
Join 6–7 and 7–8 with a curve touching a point;

sizes   8–14 or Sml, Med.   2.75 cm   from 4
sizes   16–24 or Lge, XLge.   3 cm   from 4
2–9 half high ankle measurement plus 6 cm.
3–10 three quarters the measurement 1–4 plus 0.3 cm.
Draw inside leg seam; join 9–10 with a straight line, join 8–10 curving the line inwards 1 cm.

Back

5–11 3.5 cm.
11–12 3.5 cm join 12–0.
4–13 half the measurement 4–5.
8–14 the measurement 4–8 plus 0.5 cm.
14–15 1 cm.
Join 12–13 and 13–15 with a curve touching a point:
sizes   8–14 or Sml, Med.   5 cm   from 4
sizes   16–24 or Lge, XLge.   5.5 cm   from 4
9–16 2 cm.
10–17 3 cm.
Draw inside leg seam; join 16–17 with a straight line, join 15–17 curving the line inwards 1 cm.

Creating a One-Piece Pattern

Trace round back section (heavy line).
Trace round front section (dotted line).
Mirror the front and place the side seams together.

The Simple Skirt Block

The block has more ease than the basic skirt block. It can be used for skirts with elasticated waistbands. When used for hipster skirts, shape the side seam in further to fit a low waist measurement.

Front

Square down from 0.

0–1 skirt length required; square out.
0–2 waist to hip measurement; square out.
0–3 quarter hip measurement plus 0.5 cm; square down to 4.

0–5 waist measurement plus 4 cm; square up 1.25 cm to 6. Join 6–3.
Curve the hipline out 0.25 cm.
Join 0–6 with a curve.

Back

3–7 2 cm; square down to 8.
0–9 waist measurement plus 6.5 cm; square up 1.25 cm to 10. Join 7–10.
Curve the hipline out 0.25 cm.
Join 0–10 with a curve.

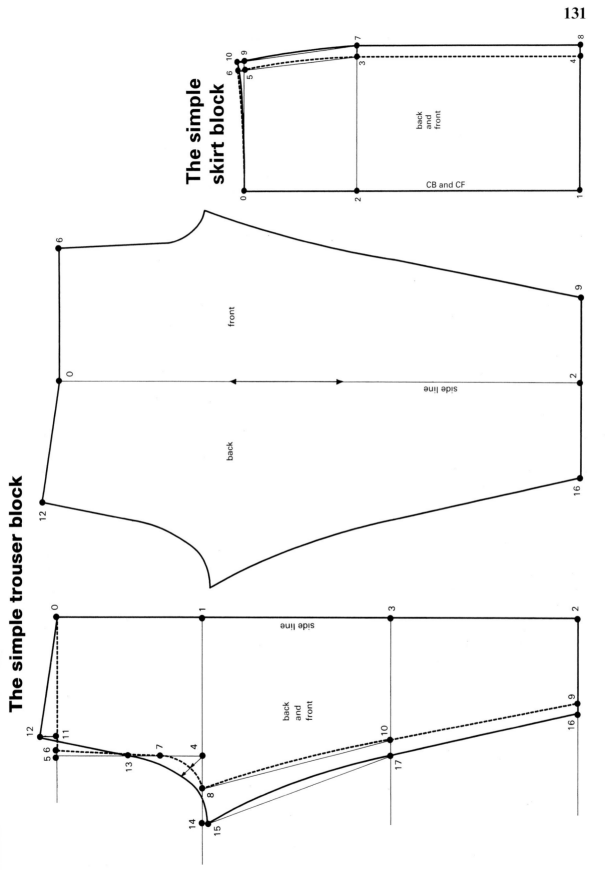

The simple skirt block

The simple trouser block

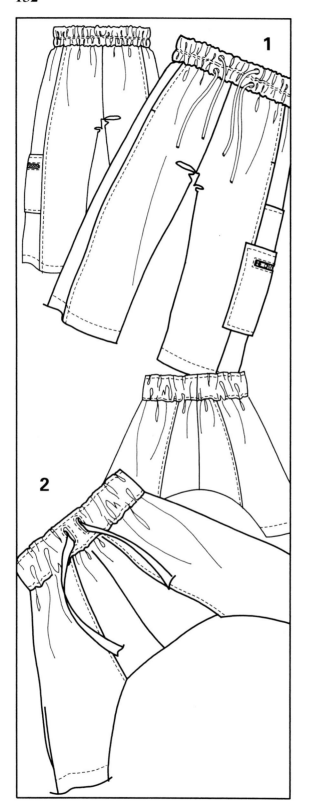

1 'BAGGY' TROUSERS

Trace off the back and front of the easy fitting trouser block.

Shorten to the required length.

If very baggy trousers are required, cut up the centre lines and open required amount.

Front Draw in side panel line.

Mark points 0–1 on the inside leg seam.

Extend the line from 1.

0–2 is one third distance 0–1; square down to 3.

4–5 = 1–3; square up to 6.

Draw in the pocket bag from the side panel line.

Draw in the front pocket.

Draw in the side pocket; mark points 7 and 8.

Trace off front and side front.

Back 9–10 and 11–12 are the measurement 1–3; square up to the inside leg seam and side seam.

Draw in the side panel line, width is the measurement 7–8 on the side pocket. Mark side pocket.

Trace off back and side back.

Pockets Trace off pocket bag, front pocket and side pocket.

Waistband construct a waistband: measurement of the waistline of the patterns created and twice the width required. Mark fold line down centre.

2 ONE-PIECE TROUSERS

Trace off the very easy fitting trouser block.

Back and Front Shorten to the required length.

Square down from 0 at the centre front to 1.

Square across to 2. Square up to 3, 3 cm above waistline.

Extend the back waistline to 3.

Gusset Draw a vertical line, length 110 cm.

Mark point 4 at the centre; square out.

4–5 approx. 24 cm.

Draw a line 8 cm long, parallel to the top of the vertical line.

Draw a line 12 cm long, parallel to the bottom of the vertical line.

5–6 is the measurement 0–1; square across.

5–7 is the measurement 2–3; square across.

Waistband Construct a waistband as above.

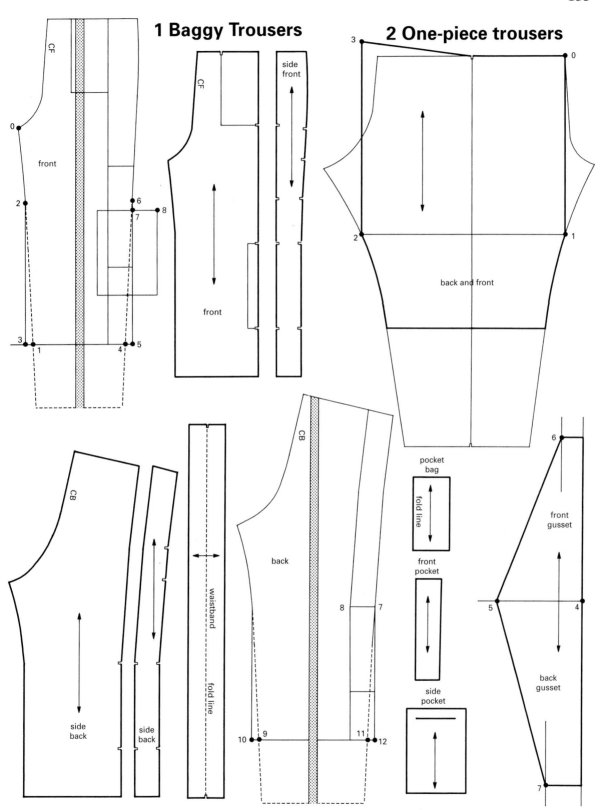

1 Baggy Trousers

2 One-piece trousers

CF

front

0

2

3 1 4 5

6
7 8

CF

side
front

front

back and front

3 0

2 1

CB

CB

back

side
back

side
back

waistband
fold line

CF
fold line

8 7

10 9 11 12

pocket
bag
fold line

front
pocket

side
pocket

6

front
gusset

5 4

back
gusset

7

Easy Fitting Body Shapes
The Basic Shirt Block

MEASUREMENTS REQUIRED TO DRAFT THE BLOCK

The blocks can be drafted to size codes 8, 10, 12, 14, etc., or Sml, Med, Lge, XLge.

Example shown is for a size Med.; refer to the size charts (page 12) for standard measurements for High Street *fashion* garments.

bust	88 cm	neck size	37 cm
nape to waist	41 cm	sleeve length	58 cm
armscye depth	21 cm	cuff size – shirts	21.5 cm
back width	34.4 cm	(page 11)	

Body Sections

Square up and down from 0; square across approx. 10 cm.

0–1 armscye depth plus 2.5 cm; square across.

0–2 neck to waist; square across.

0–3 shirt length required; square across.

1–4 half bust plus 9.5 cm; square up, square down to 5.

0–6 3.5 cm; square across to 7.

6–8 one fifth neck size plus 0.2 cm; square down to 9.

0–10 one third measurement 0–9; draw curve from 8–10.

6–11 one fifth armscye depth minus 0.5 cm; square out.

0–12 one fifth the measurement 0–1 plus 1 cm; square half way across the block.

1–13 half back width plus 2.5 cm; square up to 14 and 15.

15–16 1.25 cm; join 8–16.

14–17 half the measurement 12–14 minus 1.5 cm.

14–18 0.5 cm; join 17–18 with a curve

7–19 5 cm; square across.

19–20 one fifth neck size minus 0.6 cm.

19–21 one fifth neck size minus 1.6 cm.

Draw neck curve from 20–21.

19–22 one fifth armscye depth plus 0.5 cm; square out.

20–23 the measurement 8–16. Draw a line from 20 to touch the line from 22.

21–24 half the measurement 4–21 plus 1 cm; square across.

4–25 the measurement 1–13 minus 0.2 cm; square up to 26.

25–27 half the measurement 13–25; square down to 28 and 29. Draw armscye as shown in diagram, touching points 16, 18, 27, 26, 23; and to touch points 2.75 cm from 13 and 2.25 cm from 25.

21–30 1.5 cm buttonstand; square down.

30–31 3.5 cm facing; square down. Shape neckline.

12–32 2 cm (back pleat); square down.

Sleeve

Square down from 0.

0–1 one quarter armscye measurement (see measuring a curve on page 25): square across.

0–2 sleeve length minus cuff depth plus 2 cm ease; square across.

1–3 half the measurement 1–2; square across.

0–4 half armscye measurement; square down to 5.

0–6 half armscye measurement, square down to 7.

Divide 0–4 into four sections; mark points 8, 9, 10.

Divide 0–6 into four sections; mark points 11, 12, 13.

8–0 raise the curve: 1 cm at 9; 1.75 cm at 10.

Raise the curve at 11: 1 cm.

Hollow the curve at 13: 1 cm.

5–14 one quarter the measurement 2–5 minus 0.5 cm; join 4–14.

7–15 one quarter the measurement 2–7 minus 0.5 cm; join 6–15.

Mark points 16 and 17 on the line from 3.

14–18 1 cm; join 16–18 with a curve.

15–19 1 cm; join 17–19 with a curve.

20 midway 2–18; square up to 21.

21–22 one third the measurement 20–21.

20–23 0.75 cm; join 18–2 with a curve.

Cuff

Construct shaped cuff: length = cuff size plus 2 cm; cuff depth = approx. 7 cm. Mark buttonhole.

Draw curves at lower edge.

Collar

Construct a shirt collar (ref. 9 page 70).

Depth of shirt collar and stand approx. 8 cm.

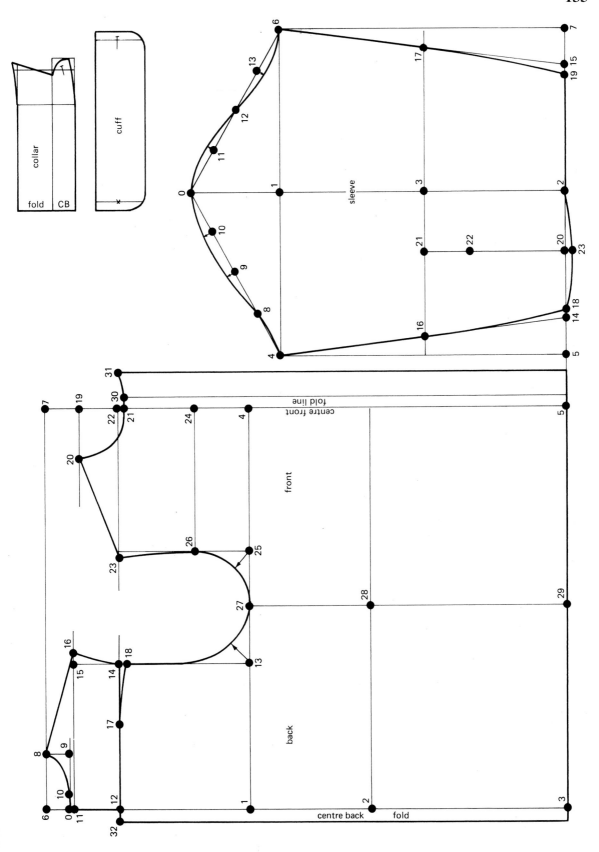

collar

fold   CB

cuff

sleeve

front

back

centre front   fold line

centre back   fold

The Basic 'Flat' Overgarment Blocks
For easy fitting jackets and overgarments

MEASUREMENTS REQUIRED TO DRAFT THE BLOCK

The blocks can be drafted to size codes 8, 10, 12, 14, etc. or Sml, Med, Lge, XLge.

Example shown is for a size Med.; refer to the size charts (page 12) for standard measurements for High Street *fashion* garments.

The main figures construct the jacket block, the figures in brackets the overgarment block.

bust	88 cm	shoulder	12.2 cm
nape to waist	41 cm	back width	34.4 cm
waist to hip	20.6 cm	armscye depth	21 cm
neck size	37 cm	sleeve length	58 cm

Back and Front Sections

Square down and across from 0.

0–1 back neck to waist plus 3 cm; square across.

1–2 waist to hip; square across.

0–3 quarter bust measurement plus 4.5 cm (7 cm); square down to 4 and 5.

0–6 2 cm.

6–7 armscye depth plus 4 cm (6 cm); square across to 8.

6–9 half the measurement 6–7; square out.

6–10 quarter the measurement 6–9 minus 0.25 cm; square out.

0–11 one fifth neck size plus 0.4 cm (0.7 cm); draw back neck curve.

7–12 half across back plus 3 cm (4.5 cm); square up to 13 and 14.

14–15 1.5 cm; join 11–15.

Draw in back armscye shape to touch points 15, 13, 8.

Front Section

0–16 one fifth neck size plus 0.4 cm (0.7 cm); draw in the front neck curve.

13–17 0.75 cm (1 cm).

Draw a line 0.75 cm below the line squared out from 10.

11–18 the measurement 11–15; draw front shoulder line to touch the new line at point 18.

Draw in the front armscye shape as shown in diagram to touch points 18, 17, 8.

Sleeve

0–1 half the measurement 6–7 on body block plus 1 cm; square across.

0–2 sleeve length plus 1 cm; square across.

0–3 the measurement of the armscye curve from 15–8.

2–4 two-thirds the measurement 1–3 plus 0.5 cm; join 3–4.

Divide 0–3 into six sections; mark points 5, 6, 7, 8, 9.

Draw in the back sleeve head:
hollow the curve 0.5 cm at 5;
raise the curve 1.5 cm at 8 and 9.

Draw in the front sleeve head:
hollow the curve 0.75 cm at 5;
raise the curve 1.75 cm at 8 and 9.

Sleeve Pitch Points

Some sleeve adaptations require pitch points on the sleeve and body sections.

Mark point 6 on the sleeve as a pitch point with a notch. Measure the sleeve curve from 3–6.

Measure along the armscye of the body sections the same distance. Mark the pitch points with a notch.

The 'Flat' Kimono Block

Body Sections

Trace round basic back body shape of jacket, or overgarment blocks with the front neckline and armscye depth line marked.

Mark points 0, 1, 2, 3, 4, 5.

3–6 1.5 cm. Join 2–6; extend the line.

6–7 the sleeve length.

Square out from the line 2–7 the measurement 2–4 on the block sleeve used plus 2 cm. Mark point 8.

4–9 quarter the measurement 0–1.

9–10 2 cm; square down to 11. Join 10–8.

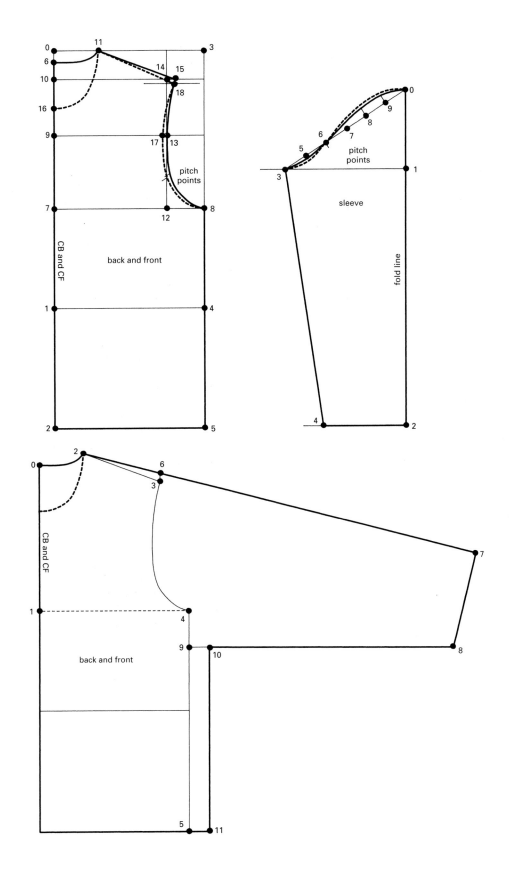

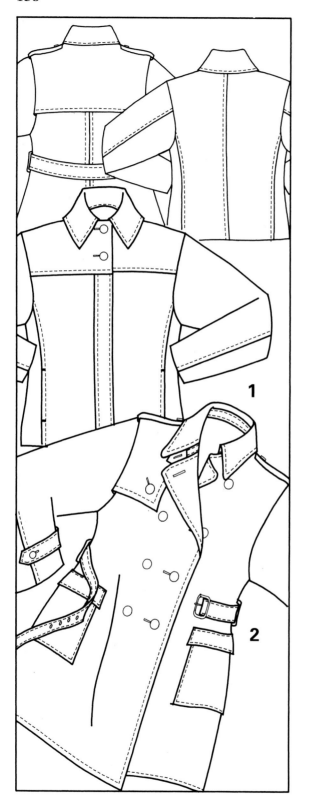

1 JACKET – INSET SLEEVE

Trace off the back, front and sleeve of the 'flat' easy fitting jacket block.

Back and Front Shorten to the required length.
Draw in vertical lines at the side panel positions.

Back Shape in the centre back seam 1 cm and lower the waist position 2 cm.
Shape in at the waist of the back panel line 2 cm.
Trace off the back.

Front and Front Yoke Shape in the waist of the front panel line 2 cm; square down to the hipline.
Draw in the front yoke line.
Draw in the buttonstand, mark buttonholes; mark the fly line.
Draw in the facing line. Draw in the pocket bag.
Trace off the front and front yoke.

Side Panel Trace off front side panel and reverse the section.
Trace off back side panel and join to the front panel at the side seam.

Sleeves Reverse front sleeve along the centre line.
Mark elbow line halfway down the underarm seam.
Draw a back seam line.
Separate the sleeves. Shape both sleeves 1 cm out at elbow and 1 cm in at the hem.

Facing and Fly Piece Trace off facing. Trace off fly piece along the fly line; reverse the piece along the fold line.

Collar Construct convertible collar (ref. 8 page 70).

Pocket Bag Trace off pocket bag.

2 TRENCH COAT – INSET SLEEVE

Trace off the back, front and sleeve of the 'flat' overgarment block.

Back and Front Lengthen to the required length.
Add 3 cm flare to side seam hem.
Draw in back and front flaps.

Back Add 5 cm pleat extension. Construct 10 cm pleat facing. Trace off back flap.

Front Lower front neck 1 cm.
Draw in buttonlines, add buttonstand and rever, mark buttonholes. Draw in facing line.
Trace off front flap.
Draw in pocket and pocket flap.

Sleeves Construct as above example. Draw in sleeve strap 3.5 cm. Trace off strap.

Facing and Collar Trace off facing.
Measure neck to centre front. Construct a shirt collar without button extension (ref. 9 page 70).
Construct a small collar tab the width of collarstand.

Pockets Trace off pocket and pocket flap.

Shoulder Strap Construct shoulder strap, length of shoulder and twice the width required.

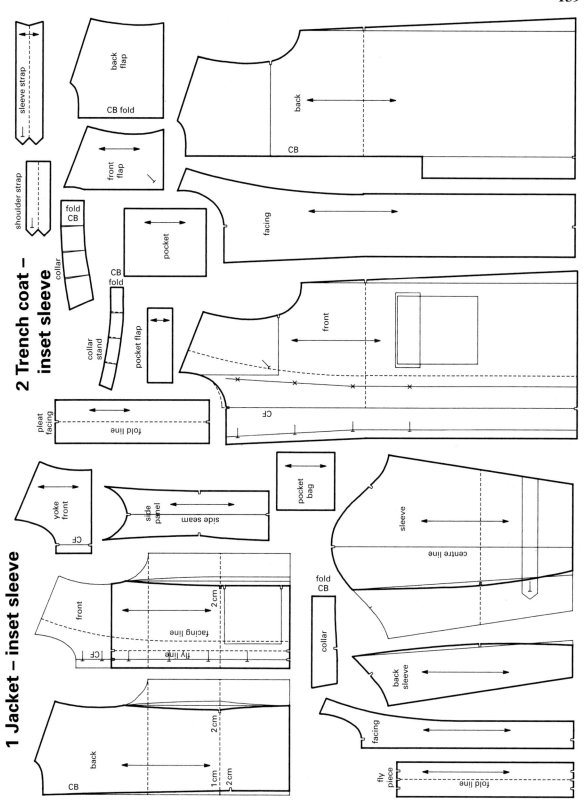

2 Trench coat – inset sleeve

sleeve strap

shoulder strap

collar

back flap

CB fold

front flap

fold CB

collar stand

CB fold

pocket

pocket flap

back

CB

facing

front

CF

pleat facing

fold line

1 Jacket – inset sleeve

yoke front

CF

side panel

side seam

pocket bag

sleeve

centre line

front

facing line

fly line

CF

fold CB

collar

back sleeve

facing

back

CB

2 cm

2 cm

1 cm

2 cm

fly piece

fold line

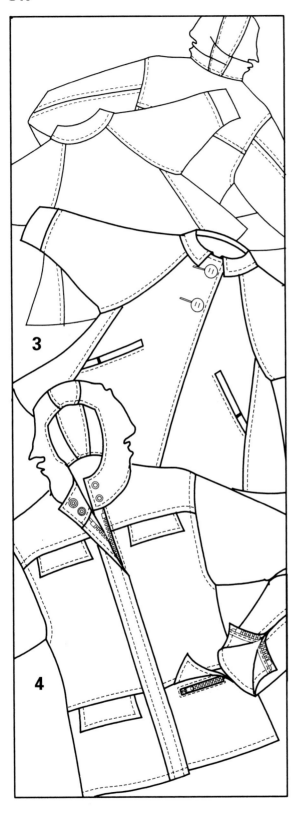

3   SWING JACKET/COAT – KIMONO SLEEVE

Trace off the back and front of the required 'flat' kimono block.

Back and Front   Extend to the required length.
Mark point 1 at the underarm. 1–2 5 cm; 1–3 5 cm; join 2–3 with a curve. Draw in raglan seams.
Mark 4 one third length of raglan seam. Join 3–4. Curve the sleeve seam.
Draw in side panel lines. Divide back into three sections, front and side panels into two sections.
Draw in the buttonstand, buttonholes and facing.
Back   Trace off back section. Cut up the dividing lines and open at the hem the required amount.
Front   Trace off front section. Cut up the dividing line and open at the hem the required amount.
Draw in pocket welt and pocket bag.
Back and Front Side Panels   Cut up the dividing line and open at the hem the required amount.
Sleeve   Trace off sleeves. Reverse front sleeve and join on the centre line. Cut along the lines 3–4 and open approx. 4 cm. Redraw the sleeve curves.
Draw lower sleeve line. Trace off lower sleeve.
Collar and Facing   Trace facing. Construct shaped convertible collar without stand (ref. 8 page 70).
Pockets   Trace off welt and pocket bag.

4   WEATHERWEAR – KIMONO SLEEVE

Many variations of this style can be applied.
Weatherwear is usually fully self lined.
Trace off the back, front and sleeve of the easy fitting 'flat' kimono block.
Attached hood only: lower back neck 0.5 cm; widen back and front neck 1 cm; lower front neck 1 cm.
Back and Front   Draw in armscye shape from approx. 5 cm past shoulder point 3 on the original block.
Take 1 cm darts from sleeve sections; two thirds length of back armscye, half the length of front armscye.
Mark point 1 at the underarm. 1–2 5 cm; 1–3 10 cm. Join 2–3.
Back   Draw in back yoke line. Trace off yoke.
Front Sections   Reverse front. Draw in front yoke and lower panel line. Draw in pocket flaps and pocket bags. Draw in pocket zip line. Draw in the fly piece approx. 2.5 cm each side of centre line.
Trace off the three front panels. Reduce the front edge of the panels by the width of the zip.
Sleeves   Trace off sleeves. Join on the centre line. Cut along the lines 2–3 and open approx. 3 cm. Redraw sleeve head and underarm with curves.
Draw in back seam line. Trace off back sleeve.
Fly Piece and Zip Extension   Trace off fly piece along the fly line. Trace off zip piece from the centre line. Reverse both pieces along the fold lines.
Pockets   Trace off pocket bags and pocket flaps.
Hood   Construct hood (ref. 5 page 149).

3 Swing jacket – kimono sleeve

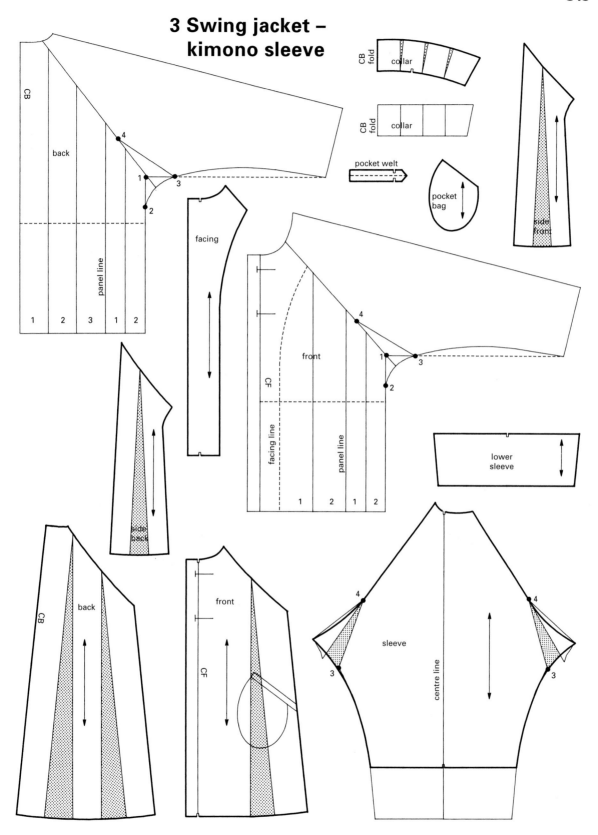

4 Weatherwear – kimono sleeve

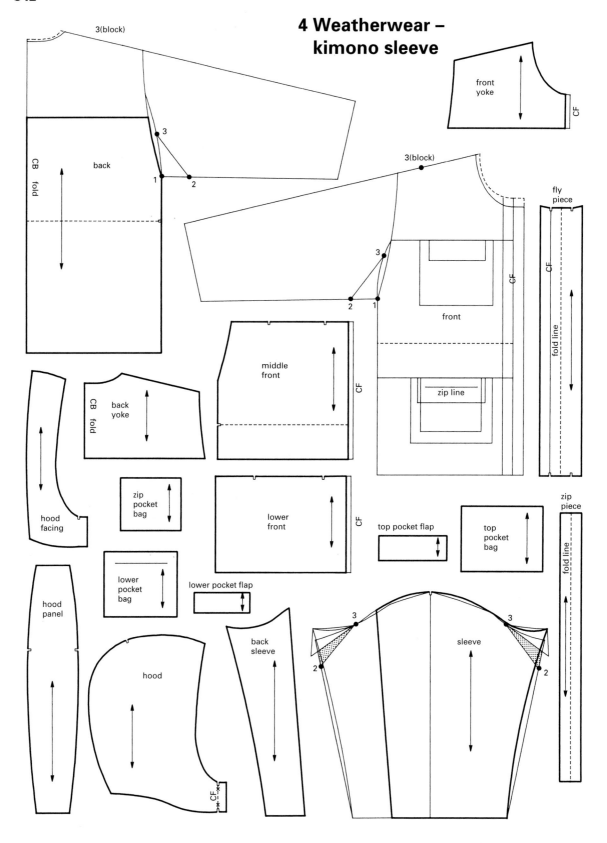

3(block)

CB fold

back

3

1

2

front yoke

CF

3(block)

CF

fly piece

CF

fold line

front

3

2

1

zip line

CB fold

back yoke

middle front

CF

hood facing

zip pocket bag

lower front

CF

top pocket flap

top pocket bag

zip piece

fold line

hood panel

lower pocket bag

lower pocket flap

back sleeve

hood

CF

3

2

3

sleeve

2

Part Two: Flat Cutting
10 EASY FITTING GARMENTS
(jersey and knitted fabrics)

SIZING
Sportswear and some casual wear manufacturers usually use sizing breaks of
SMALL, MEDIUM, LARGE and XLARGE. The example sizings used in
the following drafts are based on size Med., High Street *fashion* garments. See
page 12.

Easy Fitting Blocks for Jersey Wear

Blocks for Tee Shirts, Track Suits and Jersey Jackets

MEASUREMENTS REQUIRED TO DRAFT
THE BLOCK

The blocks can be drafted to size codes 8, 10, 12, 14, etc. or Sml, Med, Lge, XLge.

Example shown is for a size Med.; refer to the size charts (page 12) for standard measurements for High Street *fashion* garments.

The main figures construct the Tee Shirt Block, the figures in brackets the Track Suit or Fleece Jacket Block.

bust	88 cm	shoulder	12.2 cm
nape to waist	41 cm	back width	34.4 cm
waist to hip	20.6 cm	armscye depth	21 cm
neck size	37 cm		
sleeve length (jersey)	52 cm		

Body Sections

Square down and across from 0.

0–1 neck to waist; square across.

0–2 finished length; square across.

0–3 armscye depth plus 1 cm (4.5 cm); square across.

0–4 half the measurement 0–3; square across.

0–5 one quarter the measurement 0–4; square across.

0–6 one fifth neck size (plus 1 cm); square up.

6–7 1 cm; draw in neck curve.

3–8 half back width plus 0.5 cm (3.5 cm); square up to 9 and 10.

10–11 0.5 cm (1.5 cm); join 7–11.

3–12 one quarter bust plus 2 cm (4.5 cm); square down to 13.

Draw in armscye curve from 11 through 9 to 12.

0–14 one fifth neck size minus 1.5 cm (0.5 cm); draw in front neck.

Back and front are the same except for the neck curve.

Sleeve

Square down from 15.

15–16 half the measurement 0–3 plus 1 cm; square across.

15–17 sleeve length (jersey) plus 2 cm (5 cm); square across.

15–18 the measurement of the diagonal line from 11–12 on body section plus 2 cm; square down to 19.

18–20 one third the measurement 18–15.

Draw in sleeve head.

18–20 hollow the curve 0.6 cm.

20–15 raise the curve 1.75 cm.

19–21 one third the measurement 17–19; join 18–21.

Short Sleeve

15–22 sleeve length required; square across to 23.

23–24 2.5 cm; join 18–24.

RAGLAN ADAPTATION

Trace off block required.

Mark points 7, 9, 12, 18, 20.

Body Sections

Delete the curve from 9–12.

12–25 the measurement 18–20 on sleeve; curve the lines inwards 0.75 cm.

7–26 3 cm; join 25–26.

Cut away shaded sections.

Sleeve

Trace sleeve as full section.

Extend the centre line of sleeve.

Draw parallel lines each side of the centre line; the measurement of each line from the centre line is 3 cm.

20–27 the measurement 25–26 on the back.

20–28 the measurement 25–26 on the front.

Join 27–28 with a curve.

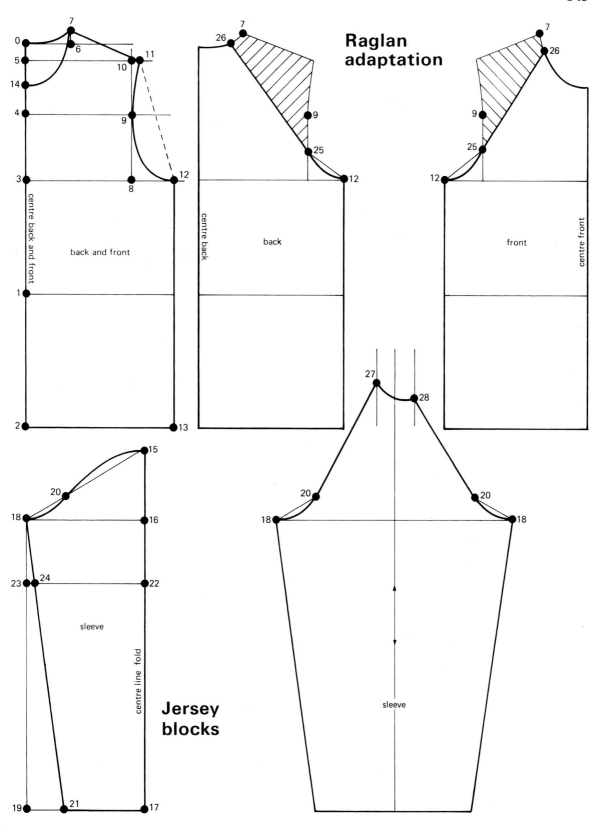

Raglan adaptation

Jersey blocks

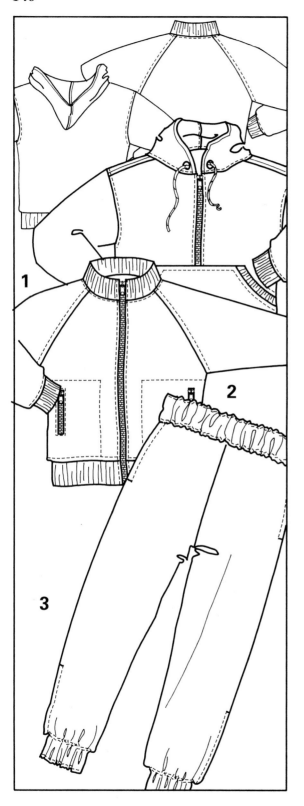

1 TRACK SUIT TOP – INSET SLEEVE

Trace off the track suit block.

Back and Front Shorten to the required length.
Shorten again by rib depth measurement.
Widen the neckline 1 cm at the shoulder; lower front neckline 1 cm.
Take a strip approx. 3 cm from the front shoulder and add to back shoulder.

Back Draw in back yoke line.
Trace off back yoke. Trace off the back section.

Front Draw in pocket shape.
Draw in facing line.
Trace off the front section.

Sleeves Reverse front sleeve along the centre line.
Hollow front curve of sleeve 0.7 cm.
Shorten sleeve by rib depth measurement.

Facing Trace off facing. Reduce centre front by half the zip width.

Hood Construct the Simple Hood to new neckline measurement (ref. 4 page 149).

Pocket trace off the front pocket.

2 FLEECE JACKET – RAGLAN SLEEVE

Trace off the track suit block.

Back and Front Shorten to the required length.
Shorten again by rib depth measurement.
Construct basic raglan adaptation (page 145).
Curve the raglan lines outwards 0.7 cm.

Back Trace off the back section.

Front Draw in pocket shape and zip pocket position.
Reduce centre front by half the zip width.
Draw in facing line. Trace off the front section.

Sleeves Reverse front sleeve along the centre line.
Hollow the raglan lines 0.5 cm.
Shorten sleeve by rib depth measurement.
Mark point 1 at point 25 on the block.
Mark point 2, 5 cm from the underarm point.
Cut along the line 1–2 and open approx 2.5 cm to 3.
Redraw the raglan and underarm line.

Facing Trace off facing. Reduce centre front by half the zip width.

Collar Construct straight rib collar two thirds the measurement of the neck measurement or a Standing Straight fabric collar (ref. 6 page 70).

Pocket Trace off pocket.

1 Track suit top – inset sleeve

2 Fleece jacket – raglan sleeve

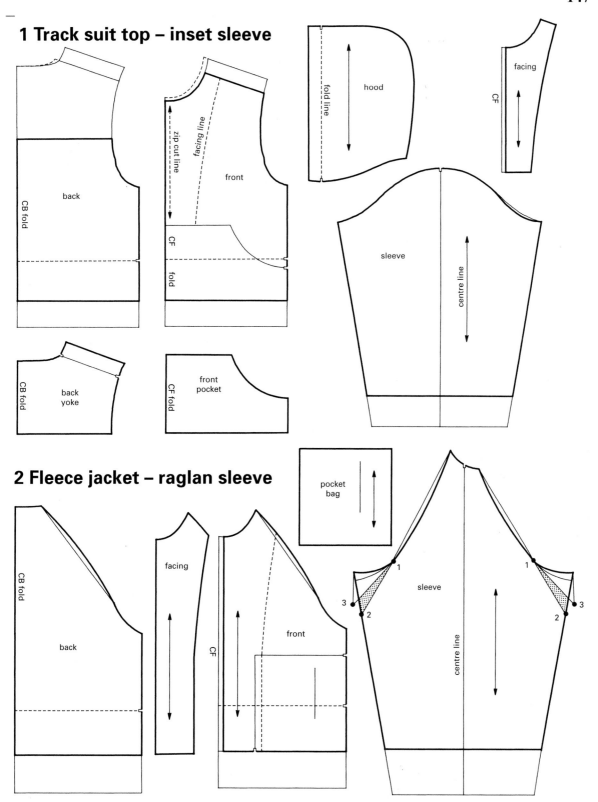

148

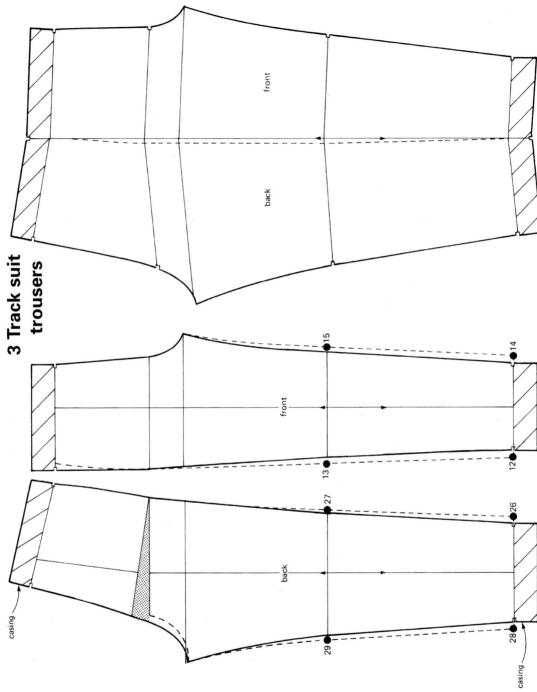

3 Track suit trousers

front

back

front

15

13

14

12

back

27

26

29

28

casing

casing

3 TRACK SUIT
TROUSERS
Trace off easy fitting
trousers.
Mark points 12, 13, 14,
15, 26, 27, 28, 29.
Insert ease at the back
crutch line (page 128);
measurement of the
seat wedge is 3.5cm.
Reduce the trousers at
the knee and hem if
required.
Square up from front
hipline to waistline.
Draw new side and
inside leg seams as
shown.
Add 5cm to hem and
waistline for casings.

Note The trouser leg
can be cut in one piece.
Draw a vertical line.
Place side seams of
front and back trousers
together at waist and
hem as shown.
Extra ease can be
inserted at the original
side seam position.

'SKI TROUSERS'
Trace close fitting
trouser block, insert ease
at crutch line. Narrow
legs to required width.
The trouser legs can be
cut in one piece as the
track suit trousers, but
a side dart will remain.

Hoods

MEASURE THE NECK
The neckline of hooded garments is usually lowered and widened. Measure the new neckline.

4 SIMPLE HOOD
Square down and across from 0.

0–1 three quarters the nape to waist measurement plus 4 cm; square out.

1–2 6 cm; square out.

Draw a line from 1, measurement of front and back neckline, to touch the line from 2.

Mark point 3; square up to 4.

1–5 back neckline measurement.

Draw in neck curve.

Raise the curve 0.5 cm from 1–5.

Lower the curve 1 cm from 3–5.

0–6 half the measurement 0–4.

0–7 quarter measurement 0–1 plus 2 cm.

7–8 2 cm. Draw in the head curve 1, 8, 6, 4.

Extend the front line approx. 4 cm for a facing.

5 GUSSETED HOOD
Square down and across from 0.

0–1 three quarters the nape to waist measurement plus 6 cm.

1–2 measurement of front and back neckline. Square up to 3.

2–4 3.5 cm; join 1–4.

1–5 Back neckline measurement.

Raise the curve 0.5 cm from 1–5.

Lower the curve 1 cm from 4–5.

3–6 one fifth the measurement 0–3; square down to 7.

0–8 half the measurement 0–6.

0–9 quarter 0–1 plus 2 cm.

9–10 3 cm.

6–11 2 cm.

11–12 2 cm. Draw in head curve 1, 10, 8, 12.

6–13 half the measurement 6–7.

4–14 7 cm. Draw in front curve 12, 13, 14.

Add buttonstand, mark stud positions.

Draw in facing line; trace off facing.

Gusset
Draw a rectangle; length = head curve measurement, width = 6 cm.

Mark points 0 and 1.

0–2 one third the measurement 0–1; square across to 3.

2–4 and **3–5** 1.5 cm. Draw in gusset curves.

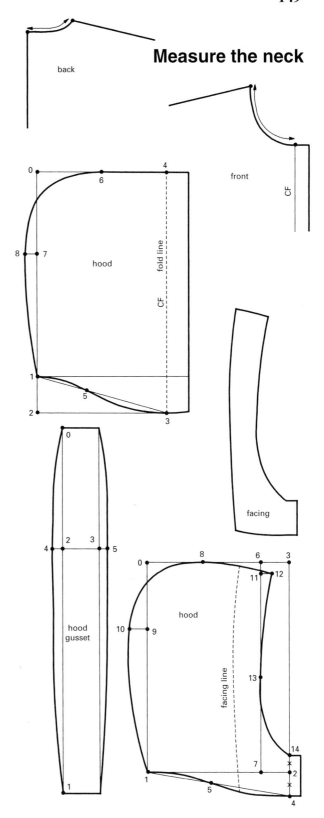

Measure the neck

Knitwear Blocks

Very easy fitting garments can be cut from simple basic shapes; this is particularly so if you are working with knitted garment shapes or with jersey fabric. The fabric will stretch over the complex areas of the body (i.e. the bust) or areas of the body that have extreme movement (i.e. elbows).

The basic grid for knitwear can be used for designing shapes for hand knitting or machine knitting. The examples show basic shapes, but far more complex shapes can be developed.

The Basic Grid

Note that this grid has no ease included; it is basic body measurements. Substantial extra ease must be added for movement and styling.

MEASUREMENTS REQUIRED TO DRAFT THE BLOCK

The blocks can be drafted to size codes 8, 10, 12, 14, etc. or Sml, Med, Lge, XLge.
Example shown is for a size Med.; refer to the size charts (page 12) for standard measurements for High Street *fashion* garments.

bust	88 cm	neck size	37 cm
nape to waist	41 cm	sleeve length	
armscye depth	21 cm	(jersey)	52 cm
shoulder	12.2 cm	waist to hip	20.6 cm
back width	34.4 cm		

Body Sections

Square down and across from 0.
0–1 1.5 cm.
0–2 one fifth neck size minus 0.2 cm.
1–3 armscye depth measurement; square across to mark armscye line.
3–4 2.5 cm; square across to mark bust line.
1–5 neck to waist measurement; square across to mark waistline.
5–6 waist to hip measurement; square across to mark the hipline.
0–7 one fifth neck size minus 0.2 cm; draw in back neck curve from 7–1; draw in front neck curve from 7–2.

6–8 quarter bust measurement; square up to the armscye.
Draw a line from 7 for the shoulder length measurement; construct the line at a 17° angle from the line from 0.
7–9 shoulder measurement.

1 KNITWEAR ADAPTATION SLEEVE – BASIC SHOULDER
Trace the basic grid; mark points 0, 1, 2, 6, 7, 9.
Mark point 10 on the centre back line at required length; square across.
10–11 is one quarter chest plus the amount of ease and styling requirements; square up.
Mark point 12 at armscye depth required.
Square across both ways at 9, using the shoulder line to square from.
Mark point 13 where the 'square across line' meets the line from 0.
Draw a line, to create the armscye shape, from 12 to touch the 'squared across line'. Mark this point 14.
Square out from 9 the jersey sleeve measurement, to point 15.
15–16 = cuff depth.
16–17 = width required at the top of the sleeve rib; square across to 18. Join 17–12.
Fold the section 7, 13, 9 along the shoulder line; mark point 19.
Trace back using the shoulder line 7–19.
Trace front using the shoulder line 7–13.
Trace sleeve; mirror the sleeve on the centre line.
Join point 14 to 14.

1 Basic shoulder

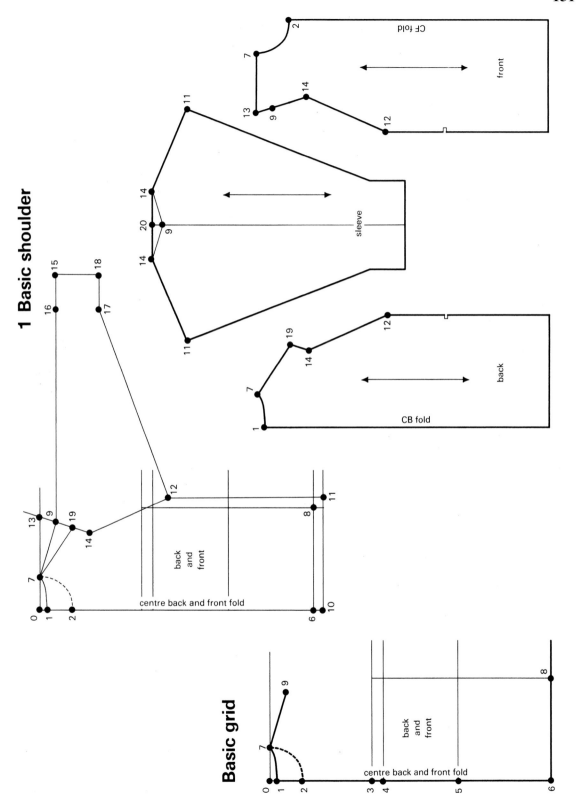

Basic grid

2 KNITWEAR ADAPTATION INSET
SLEEVE – EXTENDED SHOULDER

Trace the basic grid; mark points 0, 1, 2, 6, 7, 9.
Mark point 10 on the centre back line at required
length; square across.

10–11 is one quarter chest plus the amount of ease
and styling requirements; square up.
Mark point 12 at armscye depth required.
Extend the shoulder line to position required; mark
point 13. Draw in armscye shape from 12–13 as
required.
Square out from 13 the jersey sleeve measurement,
minus the shoulder extension to point 15. Square
down.

15–16 = cuff depth.

16–17 = width required at the top of the sleeve rib;
square across to 18. Join 17–12.
Trace front, back and sleeve sections.

Note Some knitted garments do not have any
armscye shaping. The body section side seam
continues from 12 until it meets the extended
shoulder seam. The sleeve is then drafted from this
new point.
Note that this method produces a very dropped
shoulder and surplus fabric in the area of the
underarm.

3 KNITWEAR ADAPTATION
RAGLAN SLEEVE

Trace the basic grid; mark points 0, 1, 2, 6, 7, 9.
Mark point 10 on the centre back line at required
length; square across.

10–11 is one quarter chest plus the amount of ease
and styling requirements; square up.
Mark point 12 at armscye depth required.
Extend the shoulder line from 9, the jersey sleeve
measurement, to point 13.

13–14 = cuff depth.

14–15 = width required at the top of the sleeve rib;
square across to 16. Join 15–12.
Draw a line from the underarm point 12 to point 17
on the front neck.
Draw a line from the underarm point 12 to point 18
on the back neck.
Trace off front, back and sleeve sections as shown.
Mirror the front sleeve and place the sleeve sections
together along the centre sleeve line.

Note Although this section concentrates on the basic
shaping, many variations of shape can take place by
the use of varying stitches to create different types of
fabric. This method can shape the garment internally.
For example, moss stitch creates a flat fabric. This can
be used with a form of ribbing that will shape the
garment into the body.

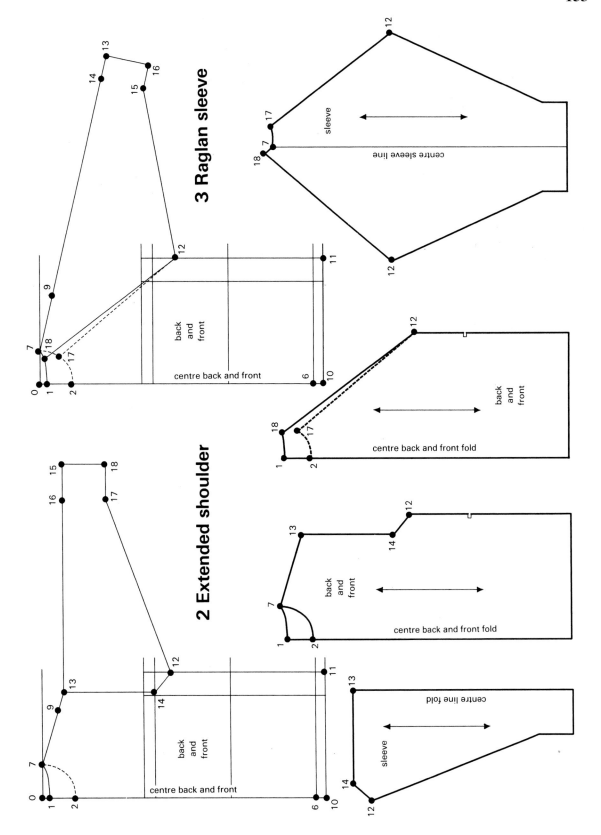

3 Raglan sleeve

2 Extended shoulder

Computers and Knitted Garment Shapes

The knitting industry is now highly computerized. Many machines can knit garments that employ fashioning to create internal shaping. Firm and stable knitted fabric is used to construct this type of garment. Garments constructed in loose or unstable knitted fabric, or highly patterned fabric, usually rely on the classic, simple, knitted shapes shown on the previous pages. Manufacturers of cheaper knitwear, which is cut from 'body blanks' and then overlocked, also use simple shapes in order to minimize fabric wastage.

The craft knitting industry, which uses domestic knitting machines, is now creating adventurous shapes and designs. Computer programs, which are surprisingly inexpensive, are available. These programs offer basic shapes which can then be modified, or the program will allow you to create your own shapes. Some programs have a grading system for sizing as well as individual sizing.

Part Two: Flat Cutting
11 CLOSE FITTING GARMENTS
(stretch and jersey fabrics)

SPECIAL NOTES

These blocks are constructed to be smaller than the body measurements and to stretch to the body shape. Some adjustments to the horizontal measurements may have to be made (this should be related to the stretch and relaxation of different fabrics). For more technical information and block construction see Chapters 2 and 7 in *Fabric, Form and Flat Pattern Cutting* also by the author.

Most designs in stretch fabrics are simple modifications of the basic blocks. The examples in this chapter demonstrate some particular techniques.

The sleeve measurement used is the jersey sleeve length, but this may still have to be adjusted to fabric stretch and relaxation properties.

SIZING

Sportswear and some casual wear manufacturers usually use sizing breaks of SMALL, MEDIUM, LARGE and XLARGE. The example sizings used in the following drafts are based on size Med., High Street *fashion* garments. See page 12.

Close Fitting Body Blocks

These blocks are drafted for maximum stretch, fine ribbed jersey or Lycra fabrics. Extra ease needed for less flexible jersey fabrics is shown in brackets.

MEASUREMENTS REQUIRED TO DRAFT THE BLOCK
The blocks can be drafted to size codes 8, 10, 12, 14, etc. or Sml, Med, Lge, XLge.
Example shown is for a size Med.; refer to the size charts (page 12) for standard measurements for High Street *fashion* garments.

bust	88 cm	neck size	37 cm
nape to waist	41 cm	armscye depth	21 cm
back width	34.4 cm	wrist	16 cm
sleeve length (jersey)	52 cm		

Body Sections
Square down and across from 0.
0–1   neck to waist plus 1 cm (0.5 cm); square across.
0–2   finished length; square across.
0–3   armscye depth minus 3 cm (1 cm); square across.
0–4   half the measurement 0–3; square across.
0–5   one eighth the measurement 0–4; square across.
0–6   one sixth neck size (plus 1 cm); square up.
6–7   1.3 cm; draw in neck curve.
3–8   half back width minus 2.5 cm (1 cm); square up to 9 and 10.
10–11   1 cm; join 7–11.
3–12   quarter bust minus 3 cm (1 cm); square down to 13 on the waistline, 14 on the hemline.
Draw in armscye curve, from 11 through 9 to 12.
13–15   3 cm (2 cm); draw in side seam 12, 15, 14.
0–16   one sixth neck size minus 1 cm (0.5 cm); draw in front neck curve.
Back and front are the same except for front neck curve.

Sleeve
Square down from 17.
17–18   half the measurement 0–3 plus 1 cm (0.5 cm).
17–19   jersey sleeve length plus 4 cm (2 cm); square across.
17–20   the measurement of the diagonal line from 11–12 on body section plus 0.5 cm.
20–21   one third measurement 17–20.
Draw in sleeve head. Hollow the curve 0.6 cm from 20–21; raise the curve 2 cm from 17–21.
19–22   half wrist plus 0.5 cm (1 cm); join 20–22.

Short Sleeve
17–23   sleeve length required; square across to 24.
24–25   1.5 cm; join 20–25 with a curve.

Leggings Block

hips	94 cm
body rise	28 cm
waist to floor	104 cm
high ankle	21 cm

Front
Square down and across from 0.
0–1   body rise minus 1 cm; square across.
0–2   waist to floor minus 8 cm; square across.
1–3   half the measurement 1–2; square across.
1–4   quarter hip measurement minus 2 cm; square up to 5.
5–6   1 cm.
4–7   quarter the measurement 4–5.
4–8   one sixth the measurement 1–4.
Join 6–7 and 7–8 with a curve touching a point:
sizes   8–14   2.25 cm   from 4.
sizes   16–22   2.5 cm   from 4.
2–9   half high ankle measurement minus 0.5 cm.
3–10   two thirds the measurement 1–4 minus 0.5 cm.
Draw inside leg seam; join 9–10 with a straight line, join 8–10 curving the line inwards 0.75 cm.

Back
5–11   4 cm.
11–12   3 cm; join 12–0.
4–13   one third measurement 4–5.
8–14   one fifth measurement 1–4.
Join 12–13 and 13–14 with a curve touching a point:
sizes   8–14   3.75 cm   from 4.
sizes   16–22   4 cm   from 4.
9–15   2 cm
10–16   3 cm.
Draw inside leg seam; join 15–16 with a straight line, join 14–16, curve the line inwards 0.75 cm.

Creating a One-Piece Pattern
Trace round back section (heavy line).
Trace round front section (dotted line).
Mirror the front and place the side seams together.
Add 2.5 cm facing at the top, 2 cm facing at the hem.

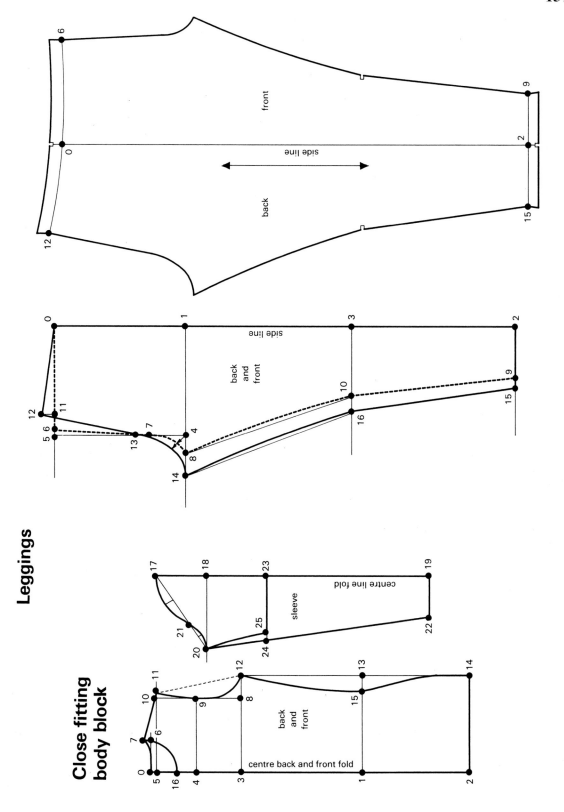

Leggings

Close fitting body block

1 CLOSE FITTING RIBBED TOP

Trace off the block for maximum stretch fabric to the required length.

Back and Front Sections Draw in the lowered neckline and cut-away armscye line. Draw in the width of ribbed edging around the neck and sleeves. Trace off the back and front sections.

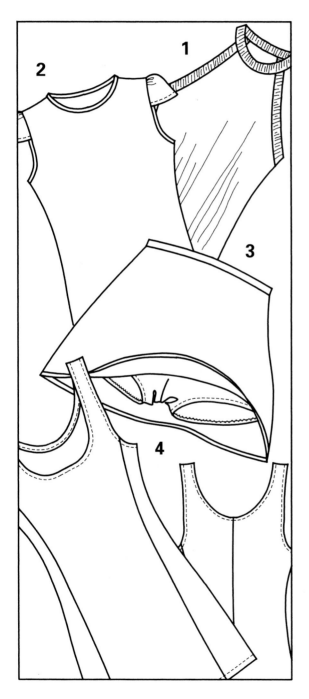

2 BASIC CAP SLEEVED TEE

Trace off the block for less flexible jersey fabric to the required length.

Back and Front Sections Draw in lowered neckline as required.

Sleeve Draw in the cap section on the sleeve.
Mark points 1 and 2. Measure the length.
Measure the same length on the bodice armscye point 3–4. Mark a notch at point 4.
Trace off the top cap section of the sleeve. Divide into four sections.
Draw a vertical and horizontal line.
Cut and open the sections as shown.
Trace round the new sleeve shape.

3 SPORTS SKIRT WITH PANTS

Back and Front Skirt Square out and down from 0.
0–1 waist to hip minus 6 cm.
0–2 skirt length.
1–3 quarter hip measurement minus 1 cm.
Square down to 4.
0–5 quarter waist measurement plus 1.5 cm.
5–6 1 cm; draw in waist curve.
4–7 2 cm; join 3–7. Join 3–6 with a curve.
Draw a vertical line from the centre of the waistline to the hem.
Cut and open at the hem approx. 3.5 cm.
Pants square down from 0.
0–1 waist to hip minus 6 cm; square out.
0–2 body rise minus 5.5 cm; square out.
1–3, 1–4 quarter hip measurement minus 3.5 cm.
Square up to 5 and 6, and down to 7 and 8.
5–9 2 cm. Join 3–9.
7–10 quarter 1–3 plus 1 cm; join 3–10 with a curve.
10–11 5 cm.
11–12 2.5 cm; join 10–12.
6–13 1 cm; join 0–13.
8–14 3.25 cm; square out.
14–15 quarter 2–8 plus 2.5 cm; join 4–15 with a curve.
15–16 5 cm.
16–17 2.5 cm; draw leg curve 17, 2, 12.

4 STRETCH DRESS

Trace off the block for less flexible jersey fabric to the required length.

Back and Front Sections Draw in lowered neckline as required. Draw in armscye line.
Draw in front panel line.
Trace off back and front sections.

Back Shape waist in 1 cm at a point 2 cm below the natural waistline. Add 1.5 cm flare to hem.
Front Shape waist 0.5 cm. Add 1.5 cm flare to hem.
Cut and overlap the neckline 0.5 cm.
Side Panel Shape waist in 1 cm. Add 1.5 cm flare to hem.

1 Close fitting ribbed top

2 Basic cap sleeved fee

3 Sports skirt with pants

4 Stretch dress

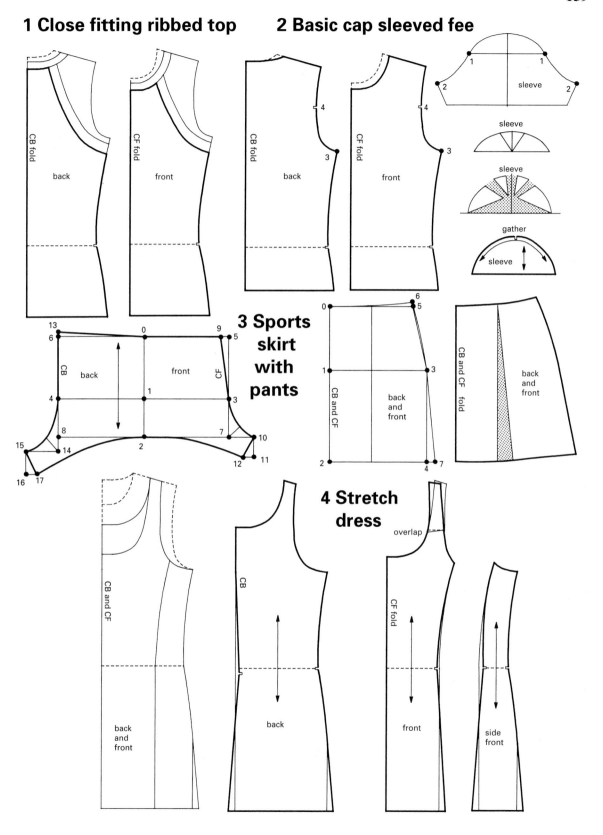

Bodyshapers

MEASUREMENTS REQUIRED TO DRAFT THE BLOCK

The blocks can be drafted to size codes 8, 10, 12, 14, etc. or Sml, Med, Lge, XLge.

Example shown is for a size Med.; refer to the size charts (page 12) for standard measurements for High Street *fashion* garments.

bust	88 cm	neck size	37 cm
nape to waist	41 cm	sleeve length	
armscye depth	21 cm	(jersey)	52 cm
back width	34.4 cm	wrist	16 cm

Back

Square down and across from 0.

0–1 neck to waist plus 1 cm; square across.
1–2 body rise; square across.
0–3 armscye depth plus 1.5 cm; square across.
0–4 half the measurement 0–3; square across.
0–5 one fifth the measurement 0–4; square across.
0–6 one sixth neck size; square up.
6–7 1.5 cm; draw in neck curve.
3–8 half back width minus 0.5 cm; square up to 9 and 10.
10–11 1 cm; join 7–11.
3–12 quarter bust minus 1.5 cm; square down to 13 on the waistline, 14 on the body rise line.
Draw in armscye curve, from 11 through 9 to 12.
1–15 quarter measurement 1–2; square across to 16.
16-17 3 cm.
13–18 4.25 cm. Draw in side seam.
2–19 one eighth bust measurement plus 1 cm; square across 3.5 cm to 20.
2–21 square out 6 cm for gusset line; join 21–17.
Draw in back leg; curve line 21–17 outwards 0.5 cm.
Draw in gusset curve; curve line 20–21 inwards 0.3 cm.
Trace off gusset. Draw a curved line from 21 to a point 0.5 cm above 2. Add 2 cm to the line 19–20.

Front

0–22 one sixth neck size minus 1 cm; draw in front neck curve.
2–23 half the measurement 2–19; square across 2 cm to 24; square up 2 cm to 25; join 25–17.
25–26 half the measurement 25–17.
Draw in front leg; curve line inwards 1.75 cm at 26.

Sleeve

Square down from 27.

27–28 half the measurement 0–3 plus 1 cm.
27–29 jersey sleeve length plus 3 cm; square across.
27–30 the measurement of the diagonal line from 11–12 on body section plus 0.5 cm.
30–31 hollow the curve 0.6 cm.

31–27 raise the curve 2 cm.
29–32 half wrist plus 0.5 cm; join 30–32 with a curve.

Short Sleeve

27–33 sleeve length required; square across to 34.
34–35 1.5 cm; join 30–35 with a curve.

Sleeveless Bodyshaper

12–36 2.5 cm.
11–37 4.5 cm; draw in new armscye curve 36–37.

Swimwear – Basic Shape

See diagram on page 161.

Back

Construct swimwear block as for bodyshaper block up to point 7.

3–8 half back width minus 4.5 cm; square up to 9 and 10 on the line from 0. Join 7–10.
3–11 quarter bust minus 4 cm; square down to 12 on the waistline, 13 on the body rise line.
Draw in armscye curve, from 10 through 9 to 11.
1–14 quarter measurement 1–2; square across to 15.
15–16 0.5 cm.
12–17 2 cm. Draw in side seam.
2–18 6 cm; join 16–18.
Draw in back leg; curve line 16–18 outwards 0.5 cm.
Lower bottom curve from 18 to 0.5 cm below point 2.

Front

3–19 half measurement 3–4. Draw front neck curve.
2–20 one sixteenth bust measurement plus 0.5 cm; square across 3.5 cm to 21. Square up 2 cm to 22. Join 16–22.
22–23 half the measurement 16–22.
Draw in front leg; curve line inwards 1.75 cm at 23.
2–24 measurement 2–20; square out 6 cm to 25.
Curve line 21–25 inwards 0.3 cm.
Lower bottom curve from 25 to 0.5 cm below point 24.

Swimwear – Bra Top

Trace off the front block, mirror front as shown.

3–26 half measurement 3–11 minus 2 cm; join 7–26.
Swing a line, the length of 7–25, to create a 10 cm dart at 26. Mark point 27.
Draw a line 4 cm long to touch the line from 5 at 28.
Draw in armscye line 11–28.
Draw in bra shape, draw neckline and seam line in bra cup.
Trace off top and bottom sections of the bra.
Close the dart in the top section.
Redraw bottom line and neckline if distorted.

Bodyshaper

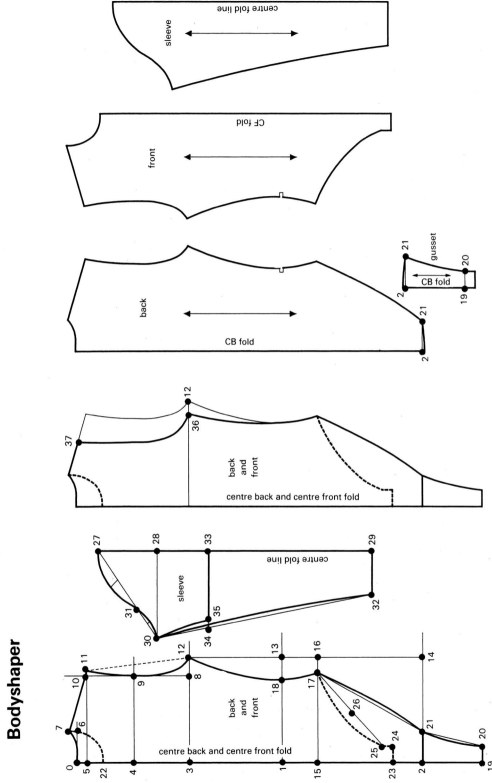

LARGER CUP SIZE

Lower Section
Draw a vertical line through the lower cup from bust point on top edge the required amount (example shows 1.5cm). Raise curve of top edge 0.5cm.

Top Section
Open dart line at the lower edge the same amount as the lower cup plus 1cm. Reshape lower edge as shown; ensure that the length A–B = C–D on the lower cup.

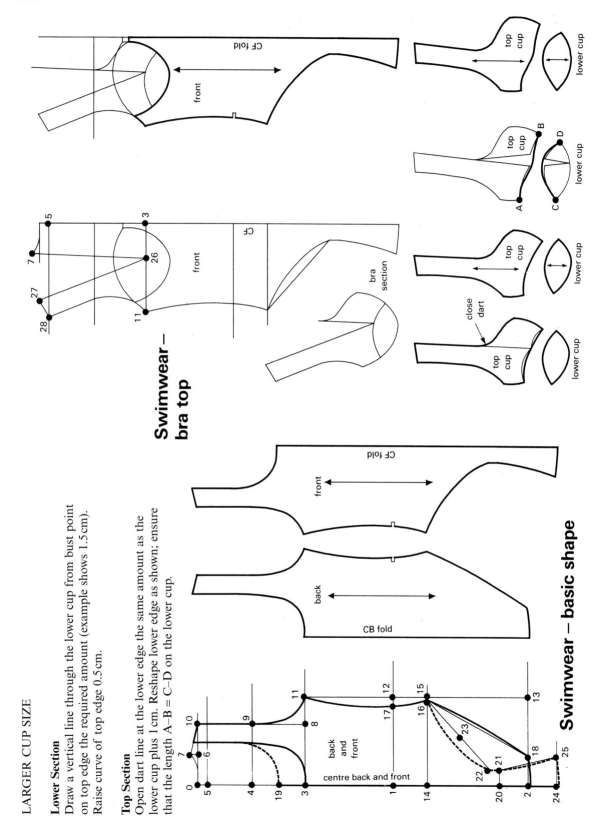

Swimwear – bra top

Swimwear – basic shape

Part Three: Size and Fit
12   BASIC GRADING TECHNIQUES

Many students find grading a difficult subject. Therefore, as this is an introductory book, examples of simple grading are demonstrated using the simplified size charts on page 12.

Grading for *form cutting* in this chapter is based on the size chart for codes 10, 12, 14, etc. This chart uses 5 cm intervals and an even grade between most sizes.

Grading for *flat cutting* is based on the size chart for High Street fashion sizes: Sml. Med. Lge. XLge. This chart uses 6 cm intervals and an even grade between all sizes.

Grading four sizes

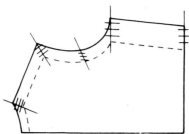

Measuring

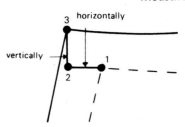

Pattern grading is a technique used to reproduce a pattern in other sizes. It must be done accurately; small errors unnoticed when one size is graded become difficulties when many sizes are required. An accurate method is to draft the smallest size, grade the largest size, then stop off the sizes between on lines drawn through the basic points (see diagram).

Grading machines and computers are available, but it is necessary for students to understand the principle of grading patterns. Although manufacturers have their own grading systems, once the principle is learnt

one can understand new methods quickly. The method used for finding a point by measuring horizontally then vertically is shown above. From base point 1 measure horizontally required measurement. Mark point 2, square across. Measure vertically required measurement point 3. Draw a line through the points 1 and 3 for a grading line. Points for further grading can be made along this line.

The methods shown demonstrate grading a basic pattern one size up. The lines through the basic points can be used to continue grading into further sizes.

Grading One Size Up – Form Cutting (5 cm intervals; size chart page 12)

Skirt for dress block

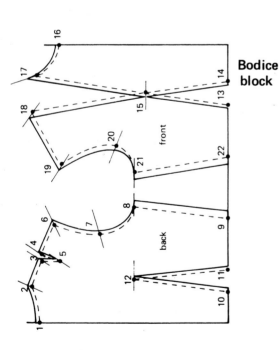

Bodice block

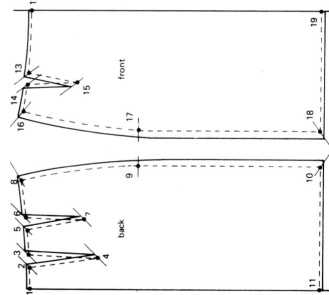

GRADING ONE SIZE UP FOR SIZES 10–18 AND 20–24 (size chart page 12).
Apply the figures to all sizes, except for the front bodice between size 10 and 12, refer to the intructions in brackets.

Back
1   measure 5 mm hor.
2   measure 5 mm hor. 2.5 mm vert.
3 4 5   measure 4.5 mm hor. 3 mm vert.
6   measure 4 mm hor. 4.5 mm vert.
7   measure 2 mm hor. 6 mm vert.
8 9   measure 10 mm vert.
10 11 12   measure 3 mm vert.

Front
13 14 15 measure 5.5 mm hor.
16 measure 6 mm (3 mm) hor.
17 measure 8 mm (5 mm) hor. 2.5 mm vert.
18 measure 8 mm (5 mm) hor. 8.5 mm vert.
19 measure 5.5 mm (4 mm) hor. 10 mm vert.
20 measure 1 mm hor. 10 mm vert.
21 22 measure 15 mm vert.

Skirt Block to fit Bodice Block for Two-Piece Dress Block
Back
1 measure 3 mm hor.
2 3 4 5 6 7 measure 3 mm hor. 3 mm vert.
8 measure 3 mm hor. 10 mm vert.
9 measure 12.5 mm vert.
10 measure 7 mm hor. 12.5 mm vert.
11 measure 7 mm hor.

Front
12 measure 3 mm hor.
13 14 15 measure 3 mm hor. 10 mm vert.
16 measure 3 mm hor. 15 mm vert.
17 measure 12.5 mm vert.
18 measure 7 mm hor. 12.5 mm vert.
19 measure 7 mm hor.

Sleeve
1 measure 6.5 mm vert.
2 measure 8.5 mm vert.
3 measure 2 mm hor. 2.5 mm vert.
4 measure 1 mm hor. 3.5 mm vert.
5 measure 4.5 mm hor.
6 measure 1 mm hor. 7 mm vert.
7 measure 1 mm hor. 8.5 mm vert.

Sleeve Block

Tailored Skirt Block

Tailored Skirt Block
Back
1 measure 3 mm hor.
2 3 4 measure 3 mm hor. 4 mm vert.
5 6 7 measure 3 mm hor. 8 mm vert.
8 measure 3 mm hor. 12.5 mm vert.
9 measure 12.5 mm vert.
10 measure 7 mm hor. 12.5 mm vert.
11 measure 7 mm hor.
Front
12 measure 3 mm hor.
13 14 15 measure 3 mm hor. 8 mm vert.
16 measure 3 mm hor. 12.5 mm vert.
17 measure 12.5 mm vert.
18 measure 7 mm hor. 12.5 mm vert.
19 measure 7 mm hor.

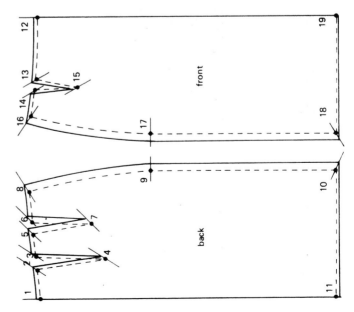

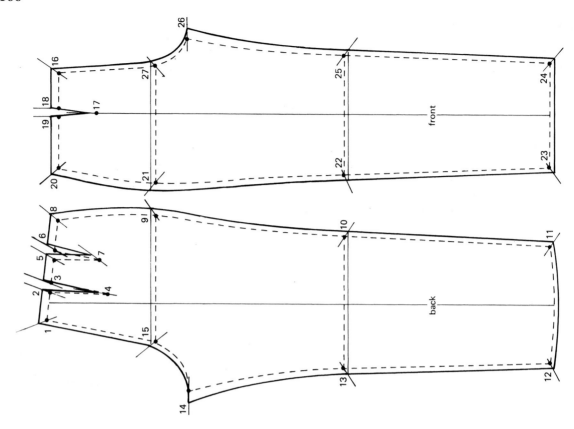

The Classic Tailored Trouser Block
Back
1 measure 7 mm hor. 3.5 mm vert.
2 3 4 measure 7 mm hor. 1 mm vert.
5 6 7 measure 7 mm hor. 4.5 mm vert.
8 measure 7 mm hor. 9 mm vert.
9 measure 4 mm hor. 9 mm vert.
10 measure 1.5 mm hor. 3 mm vert.
11 12 measure 3 mm hor. 2.5 mm vert.
13 measure 1.5 mm hor. 3 mm vert.
14 measure 9 mm vert.
15 measure 4 mm hor. 3.5 mm vert.

Front
16 measure 7 mm hor. 4 mm vert.
17 18 19 measure 7 mm hor.
20 measure 7 mm hor. 8.5 mm vert.
21 measure 4 mm hor. 8.5 mm vert.
22 measure 1.5 mm hor. 3 mm vert.
23 24 measure 3 mm hor. 2.5 mm vert.
25 measure 1.5 mm hor. 3 mm vert.
26 measure 7 mm hor.
27 measure 7 mm hor. 4 mm vert.

Grading One Size Up – Flat Cutting

GRADING FOR SMALL, MEDIUM, LARGE AND EXTRA LARGE SIZING
Refer to both of the size charts on page 12.

Grading Sizes – Mainstream Garments
Small = 8–10, Medium = 12–14, Large = 16–18, XLarge = 20–22.
The measurements for grading calculations should be used from the alternative sizes in the 5 cm size chart, i.e. 10, 14, 18, 22 for each of the above codes.

Grading Sizes – High Street Fashion
Small = approx. 8–10, Medium = 12, Large = approx. 14–16, XLarge = approx. 18.
Many garments in this group are sized in this way. This gives a 6 cm grade between the bust sizes. Examples of this type of grading are shown on the next two pages.

Back and Front
1   measure 6 mm hor.
2   measure 6 mm hor. 2.5 mm vert.
3   measure 5.5 mm hor. 8 mm vert.
4   measure 2 mm hor. 9.5 mm vert.
5 6   measure 15 mm vert.
7   measure 4 mm hor. 15 mm vert.
8   measure 4 mm hor.
9   measure 3 mm hor.

Sleeve
1   measure 3 mm hor.
2   measure 1 mm hor. 6 mm vert.
3   measure 9 mm vert.
4 5   measure 7 mm hor. 6 mm vert.
6   measure 9 mm vert.
7   measure 1 mm hor. 6 mm vert.

Flat Kimono Block
1   measure 6 mm hor.
2   measure 6 mm hor. 2.5 mm vert.
3   measure 5.5 mm hor. 18 mm vert.
4   measure 1 mm hor. 17.5 mm vert.
5   measure 1.5 mm hor. 15 mm vert.
6   measure 15 mm vert.
7   measure 4 mm hor. 15 mm vert.
8   measure 4 mm hor.
9   measure 3 mm hor.

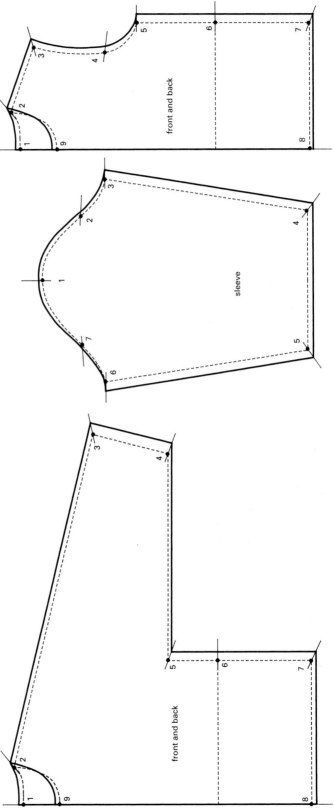

back

front

front and back

Grading One Size Up – Flat Cutting

GRADING FOR SMALL, MEDIUM, LARGE AND EXTRA LARGE SIZING

(High Street fashion 6cm grade between sizes). Refer to the size charts on page 12.

Flat Trouser Block

Back

1 measure 10mm hor. 4mm vert.
2 measure 10mm hor. 11mm vert.
3 measure 6mm hor. 11mm vert.
4 measure 2.5mm hor. 3mm vert.
5 6 measure 5mm hor. 3mm vert.
7 measure 2.5mm hor. 3mm vert.
8 measure 10mm vert.
9 measure 6mm hor. 4mm vert.

Front

1 measure 10mm hor. 5mm vert.
2 measure 10mm hor. 10mm vert.
3 measure 6mm hor. 10mm vert.
4 measure 2.5mm hor. 3mm vert.
5 6 measure 5mm hor. 3mm vert.
7 measure 2.5mm hor. 3mm vert.
8 measure 8mm vert.
9 measure 6mm hor. 5mm vert.

Flat Skirt Block

1 measure 4mm hor.
2 measure 4mm hor. 15mm vert.
3 measure 15mm vert.
4 measure 10mm hor. 15mm vert.
5 measure 10mm hor.

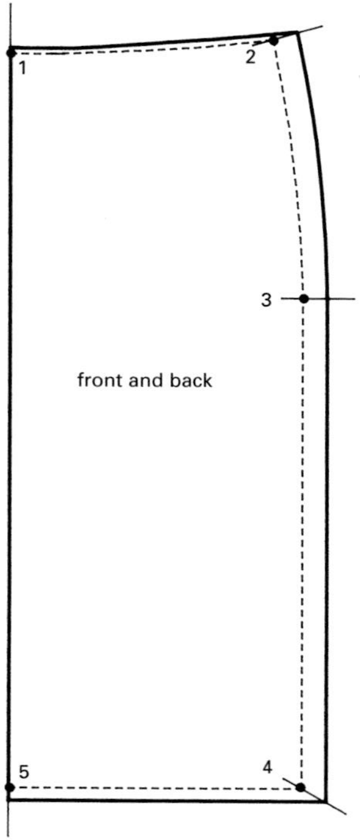

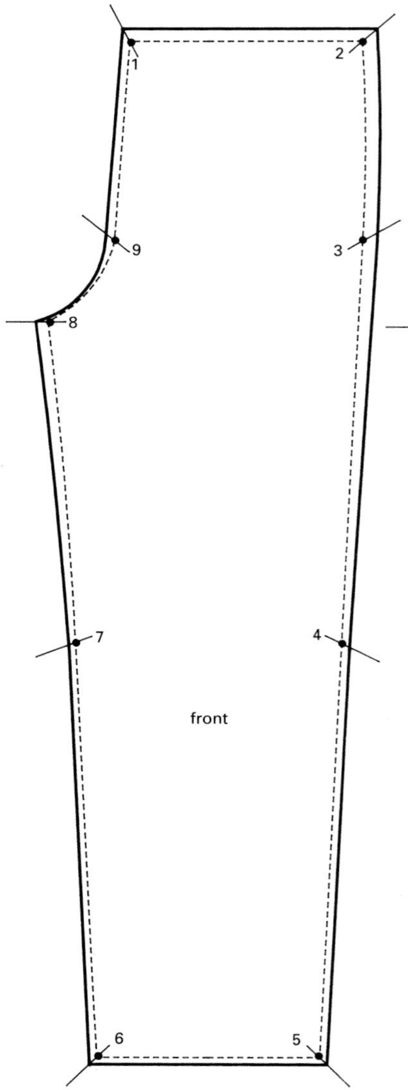

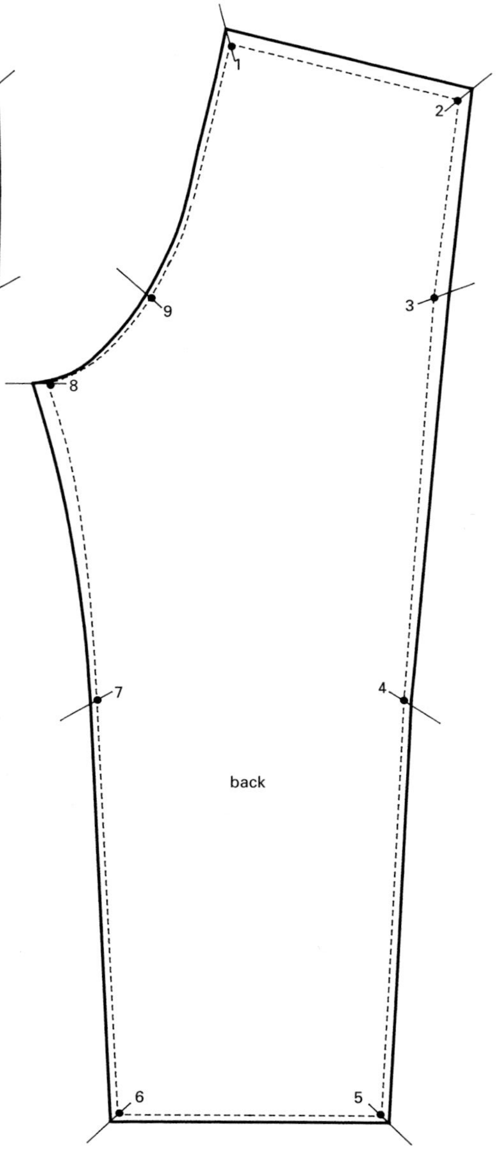

Part Three: Size and Fit
13 DRAFTING BLOCKS AND FITTING FOR INDIVIDUAL FIGURES

Drafting Blocks for Individual Figures

Drafting blocks for an individual figure is a simple operation. Use the instructions for the basic blocks (Chapter 1), but use personal measurements instead of the basic size chart.

Take the bust measurement. Unless this measurement is very large in proportion to the rest of the figure, the bust measurement determines the drafting size. Example bust 104 cm = size 20.

Note For a very large bust or for a 'dowager hump' back see page 178 before beginning the draft.

Copy the size chart shown below. Fill in the measurements shown in normal type from the size chart on page 11. For a bust size of 103.5 cm use those required for a size 20. All measurements shown in heavy type are those taken from the individual figure and then written on the chart.

It is a good idea to list the standard measurements at the side to compare them. If there are wide differences, the figure should be remeasured at these points and checked to see if it is in fact much wider or narrower than a normal figure.

	Personal measurements	Standard measurements	Comments on figure
1. BUST	**103.5**	104	nearest size
2. WAIST	**88**	86	larger waist
3. HIPS	**112**	110	larger hips
4. BACK WIDTH	**38.4**	38.4	
5. CHEST	**37.2**	37.2	
6. SHOULDER	**13.6**	13.25	wider shoulders
7. NECK SIZE	**41**	41	
8. DART	9.4	9.4	
9. TOP ARM	**32.2**	33.8	slimmer arm
10. WRIST	**17.5**	18	slimmer wrist
11. ANKLE	**25.9**	26	slimmer ankle
12. HIGH ANKLE	**22.9**	23	
13. NAPE TO WAIST	**43.5**	43	longer back waist meas.
14. FRONT SHOULDER TO WAIST	**46**	43.9	longer front waist meas.
15. ARMSCYE DEPTH	23.5	23	
16. SKIRT LENGTH	**71**		finished skirt length
17. WAIST TO HIP	21.8	21.8	
18. WAIST TO FLOOR	**110**	108	extra length
19. BODY RISE	**32.5**	30.8	longer body rise
20. SLEEVE LENGTH	**61.5**	60.5	longer arm

EXTRA MEASUREMENTS (GARMENTS) These are standard measurements (see page 11).

Taking Measurements

For extra guidance use the following instructions and the diagram opposite.

1 Bust . . . measure the figure at the fullest point of the bust, do not allow the tape to fall at the back.

2 Waist . . . take this measurement round the waist, make sure it is comfortable.
After taking the waist measurement tie a string firmly round the waist: this allows the vertical measurements to be taken accurately.

3 Hips . . . measure the widest part of the hips approx. 21 cm from the waistline. For hips that differ from standard measurement (hips 5 cm larger than bust) see page 180 for dress blocks.

4 Back Width . . . measure the back width 15 cm down from the neck bone at the centre back. Measure from armscye to armscye.

5 Chest . . . measure the chest 7 cm down from the neck point at the centre front (armscye to armscye).

6 Shoulder . . . measure from the neck to the shoulder bone.

7 Neck Size . . . measure the base of neck touching front collar bone.

8 Dart . . . standard measurement.

9 Top Arm . . . the arm must be bent, measure the biceps.

10 Wrist . . . take the wrist measurement with slight ease.

11 Ankle . . . measure around the ankle over ankle bone.

12 High Ankle . . . measure around leg just above the ankle.

13 Nape to Waist . . . measure from the neck bone at the centre back to the string tied around the waist.

14 Front Shoulder to Waist . . . measure from the centre of the front shoulder over the bust point to waist.

15 Armscye Depth . . . standard measurement.

16 Skirt Length . . . measure the skirt length from the string at the waist down to the required hem length.

Note Measure from the waist to floor at the back and front to check that the balance of the figure is even.

17 Waist to Hip . . . standard measurement.

18 Waist to Floor . . . measure from waist to floor at the centre back.

19 Body Rise . . . the subject should sit on a hard chair. Take the measurement at the side from the waist to the chair.

20 Sleeve Length . . . place the hand on hip so that the arm is bent. Measure from the shoulder bone over the elbow to the wristbone above the little finger.

The list of individual measurements should be carefully checked against the list of standard measurements and any great deviation accounted for. The blocks can then be drafted using the person's INDIVIDUAL measurements. If a figure fault is very pronounced consult the following section and adapt the block before making the toile.

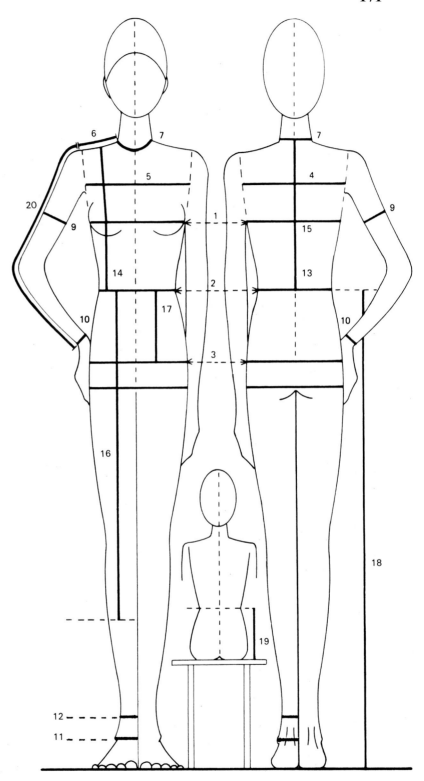

The two-piece dress block

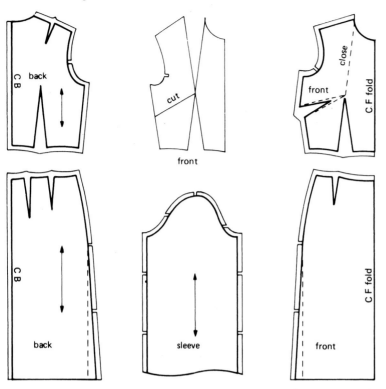

The tailored skirt block

Classic tailored trouser block

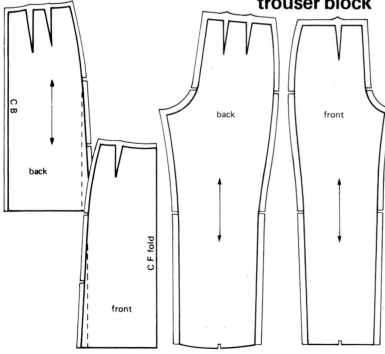

Making Toiles

The basic blocks must fit perfectly; therefore it is necessary to make them up into calico toiles to check the fit. Examples are given for making up the toiles of:

1. The two-piece dress block with the straight sleeve.
2. The tailored skirt block (page 78).
3. The classic tailored trouser block (page 98).

THE TWO-PIECE DRESS BLOCK
Draft the close fitting bodice and sleeve block. Follow the instructions on pages 14, 22 and 28 to produce the two-piece dress block.

Adjust waist darting if your waist differs from the standard measurements. If hips differ, see page 180. Transfer the bust dart to the underarm to make the fitting of the shoulders easier . . . draw a line from the underarm seam to the bust point. Cut along this line. Close the shoulder dart; this will open the new underarm dart. Shorten the dart by 2.5cm at the bust point.

Cut up the side seam of the skirt. Add 2.5cm flare to side seam at the hem, join to hip point.

THE TAILORED SKIRT BLOCK
For separate skirts not attached to bodices the tailored skirt provides a better fit, as it gives more shaping to the buttocks. It is useful to have a basic skirt block.

Draft the block (page 78). Separate at the side seam. Add 2.5cm flare to the side seam at the hem of the skirt; join to hip point.

CLASSIC TAILORED TROUSER BLOCK
Draft the classic tailored trouser block (page 98).

Cut out the blocks as shown in diagrams, add seam allowance of 1.5cm (no seam allowance at neck or hem of skirt, trousers and sleeves). Tack tape to waist of trousers and skirt.

Pattern Alterations for Fit

If the block has been drafted to personal measurements, it will provide a good fit unless there are special figure faults. Sometimes they are apparent and the block can be adapted before the toile is made up. Often they do not show until the toile is seen on the figure. The faults are then marked at fitting stage and the block is corrected.

FITTING THE TOILE
The person being fitted should be wearing the correct undergarments and shoes. She should stand in her normal relaxed position. Pin any openings.

1 Balance

The person being fitted should stand a distance away from the fitter to allow a general view. She should turn slowly. Note any obvious faults. Study the side seam; although the person may have an average figure her stance may cause the toile to swing and distort the side seam. See diagram opposite.

Note Make sure that it is the posture of the figure that is causing the distortion and not the figure protuberances, e.g. large bust, as this requires a different remedy.

Upright Figure

Cut across front block at bust and chest; open amount needed to bring front waistline down to its correct position. The alteration may be needed at chest or bust only. Trace round the new shape. Side bust dart will widen so that the side seams are of equal length.

Stooping Figure

Cut across the front block as explained above; overlap the amount to be removed. Trace round the new shape. The side bust dart will become smaller so that the side seams are of equal length.

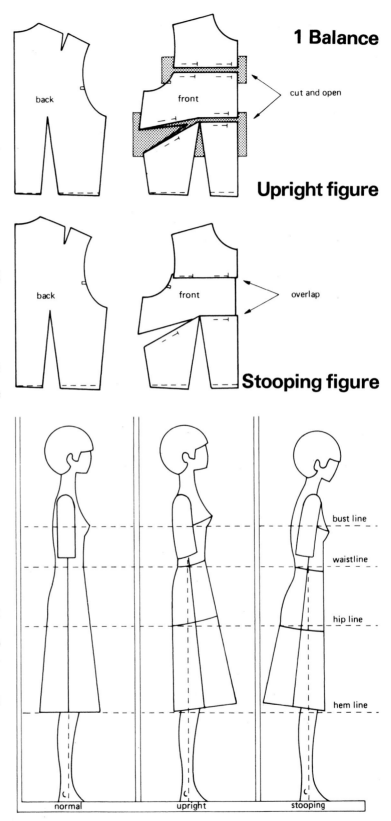

1 Balance

back   front   cut and open

Upright figure

back   front   overlap

Stooping figure

bust line

waistline

hip line

hem line

normal   upright   stooping

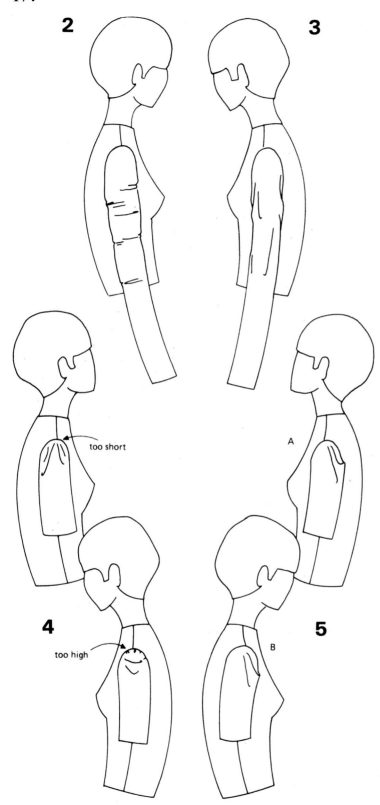

2

3

too short

A

4

too high

B

5

SLEEVES – MEASUREMENT PROBLEMS

2 Large Arm . . . the sleeve pulls tightly across arm and wrinkles. Cut block up centre line and across the sleeve head above back balance point. Open required amount as in diagram. Redraw the sleeve head. This increases the sleeve head measurement so the armscye is lowered approx. 1 cm. Remark the balance points to match sleeve.

Note   If top arm only is too tight, narrow the side seams to wrist after alteration.

3 Slim Arm . . . the sleeve sags and is shapeless.
Cut block up centre line and overlap required amount as in diagram. Redraw the sleeve head. This reduces the sleeve head measurement so the armscye is raised approx. 1 cm. Remark balance points to match sleeve.

SLEEVES – FIGURE PROBLEMS
4 Sleeve Head too Short . . . diagonal lines pull from shoulder point and there is too little ease in sleeve head. Slash across sleeve head and insert the required amount. This will give the ease required to sleeve head.
Sleeve Head too High . . . too much ease in the sleeve head which sags. Slash across sleeve head and overlap to reduce sleeve head.

5 Sleeve Pitch . . . the sleeve can drag to the left or to the right. Remove sleeve from garment and pin at the shoulder point so that the sleeve hangs correctly.
Remark the balance points on the sleeve.
This often means the underarm seams move out of line. If so, mark a balance point on sleeve to match to underarm.

Sleeves — measurement problems

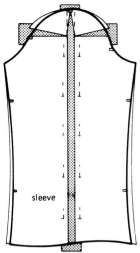

sleeve

2 Large arm

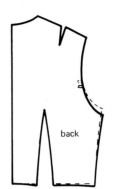

back

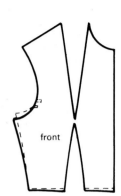

front

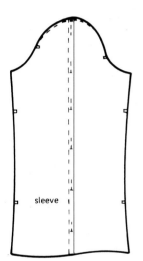

sleeve

3 Slim arm

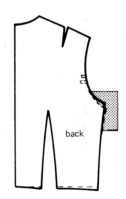

back

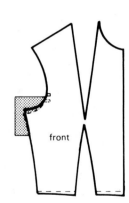

front

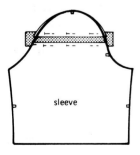

sleeve

Sleeves — figure problems

4 Sleeve head too short

5 Sleeve pitch

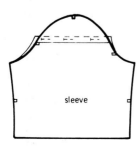

sleeve

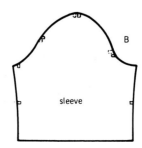

sleeve

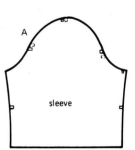

A

B

sleeve

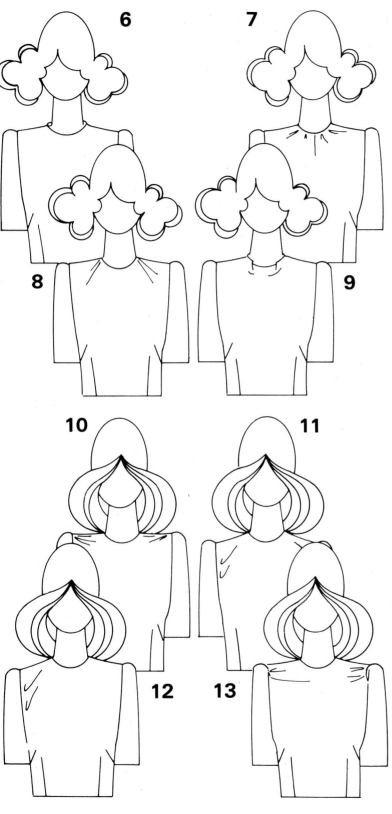

6

7

8

9

10

11

12

13

NECKLINES – FIGURE PROBLEMS

6 Wide Neckline . . . neckline sits too far away from the natural neckline. Raise the back and front neckline of block as required.

7 Tight Neckline . . . neckline grips the neck tightly and wrinkles. Lower the front and back neckline of the block the amount required.

8 Back Neck too Tight . . . neckline drags to the back causing diagonal wrinkles pulling from the neck. Widen back neck; add same amount to outer edge of shoulder so that shoulder measurement remains the same.

9 Front Neck too Loose . . . neckline is too full at the front.
Lower the shoulder line slightly at the neck point and fill in the front neck slightly as in diagram. Take the same amount from the outer edge of shoulder so that shoulder measurement stays the same.

SHOULDERS – FIGURE PROBLEMS

10 Square Shoulders . . . wrinkles pull from outer shoulder.
Slash armscye to neck point as in diagram and open required amount. Raise underarm so that the armscye measurement stays the same, raise balance marks.
If shoulders are well developed keep original armscye and raise sleeve head (ref 4 page 174).

11 Sloping Shoulders . . . sag lines appear at the sides of armscyes.
Slash armscye to neck point as in diagram; overlap required amount. Lower underarm so that the armscye measurement remains the same, lower balance marks.

12 Uneven Shoulders . . . alter one side of garment only.

13 Prominent Front Shoulders . . . garment pulls across the prominent front shoulder bones.
Slash armscye to neck point as in diagram; open required amount. Raise head of front sleeve slightly.

Necklines — figure problems

6 Wide neckline

7 Tight neckline

8 Back neck too tight

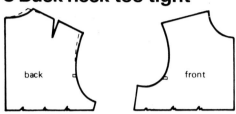

9 Front neck too loose

Shoulders — figure problems

10 Square shoulders

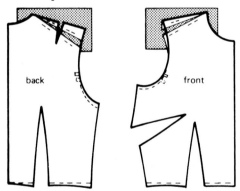

11 Sloping shoulders

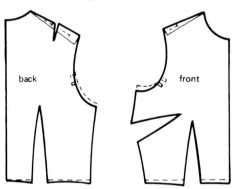

12 Uneven shoulders

13 Prominent front shoulders

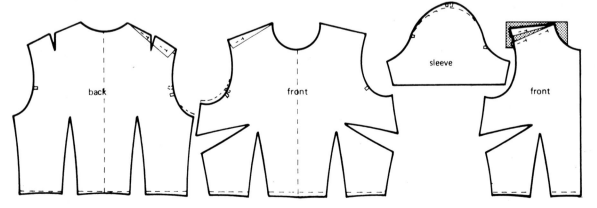

178

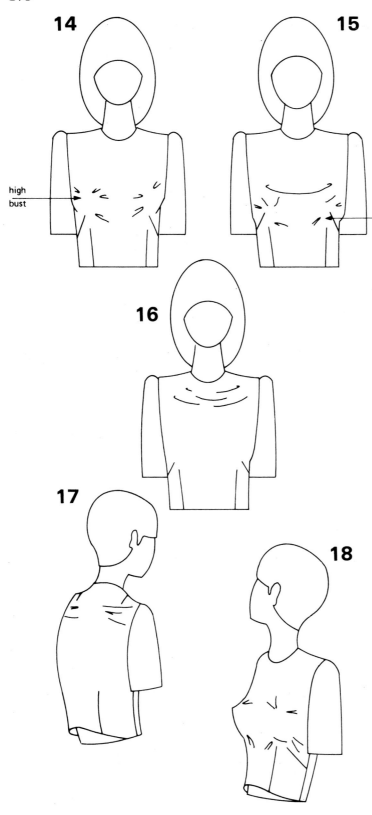

BODICE – FIGURE PROBLEMS

Most measurements should be correct as the block was drafted to individual measurements. The darting will have to be adjusted on the dress block if waist size differs from the standard.

14   High Bust . . . strain and wrinkles show across high bust line.
Mark dart point at the higher level required, redraw dart to this point.

15   Low Bust . . . fabric sags on normal bust line and pulls at dart point. Mark dart point at lower level required and redraw dart to this point.

16   Hollow Chest . . . the fabric sags across the chest area. Determine the amount to be removed. Lower front neck and shoulder point this amount. Redraw neck line. Join new shoulder point to outer shoulder with line.

17   Dowager Hump . . . a definite hump on the back pulls the fabric across the high back line; bodice rises up at the back. If the rest of the figure is normal, draft block to a standard back length and make the special alteration later. Slash across the high back line, open up the amount required. Straighten back seam to a vertical position, this will make a wider shoulder dart. Trace round pattern.

BODICE – MEASUREMENT PROBLEMS

18   Large Bust . . . fabric pulls across bust line and rises up at centre front. If figure is a basic smaller size except for large bust, draft a size smaller, then make alteration. Slash bodice vertically and horizontally; open the amount required. This will enlarge bust and waist darts.

Bodice — figure problems

14 High bust

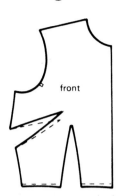

15 Low bust

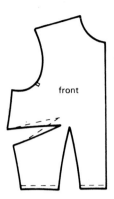

16 Hollow chest

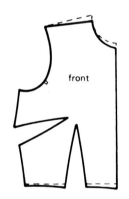

17 Dowager hump

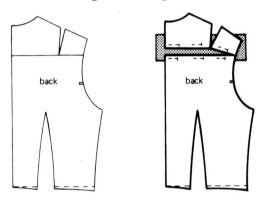

Bodice — measurement problems

18 Large bust

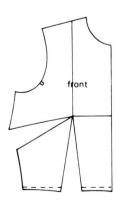
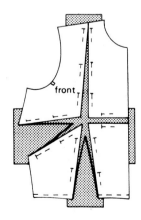
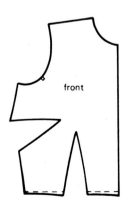

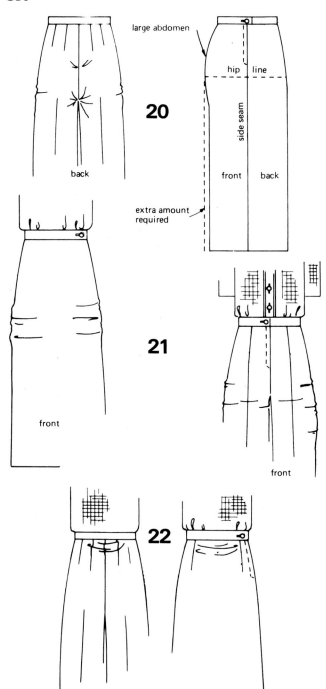

SKIRTS – TROUSERS – DRESS BLOCKS – MEASUREMENT PROBLEMS

Hips and waist sizes should be correct as they are drafted to individual measurements *except* the standard hip measurements and waist shaping on the dress block used for dresses and jackets.

19 Dress Blocks

Waist Darts adjust darts to measurements required keeping the shaping even.

Hips larger or smaller than standard cut up the side seam of the dress block, work out the difference between your hips and the standard hips for your bust size. Add or subtract one quarter the difference to back block and one quarter the difference to front block from hipline to hemline. Shape in to meet waist point.

Note On designs where the pattern has no side seam, complete the design then distribute the differences evenly on the panel lines.

20 Large Buttocks or Abdomen

. . . garments pull across the figure, drag at the crutch in trousers, or a skirt hem will rise at centre back or centre front. Although hip size is correct the garment may distort because the shape of the figure is uneven.

Add required length to the centre back or centre front waistline and at crutch on trousers. (Measure centre back to centre front between legs.) If the garment still distorts extra width can be inserted by slashing the pattern vertically and opening as shown. This will give a larger hip measurement, but an easier fitting garment is better for an obvious figure fault.

Note Also see 'Ease in the back crutch', page 128.

SKIRTS AND TROUSERS – FIGURE PROBLEMS

21 Thigh Bulge

. . . trousers or skirt pull across the thigh line.

Skirt add required amount to side seam from thigh to hem, shape the line to touch waistline at normal point.

Trousers add required amount to thighs at point 1. Draw a line from waist through point 1 to touch knee point.

22 Sway Back or Front

. . . trousers or skirt sag just below waist.

Reduce the 'waist to hip' length the required amount at centre back or centre front.

Measurement problems

19 The dress blocks

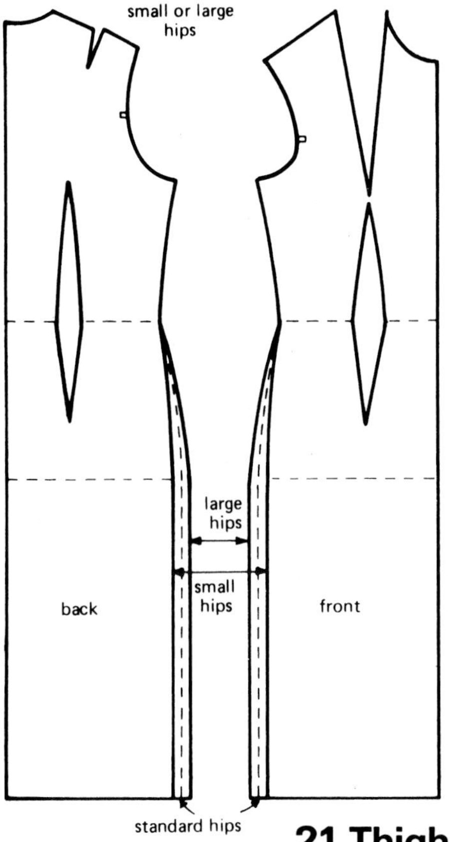

small or large hips

large hips

small hips

back

front

standard hips

20 Large buttocks or abdomen

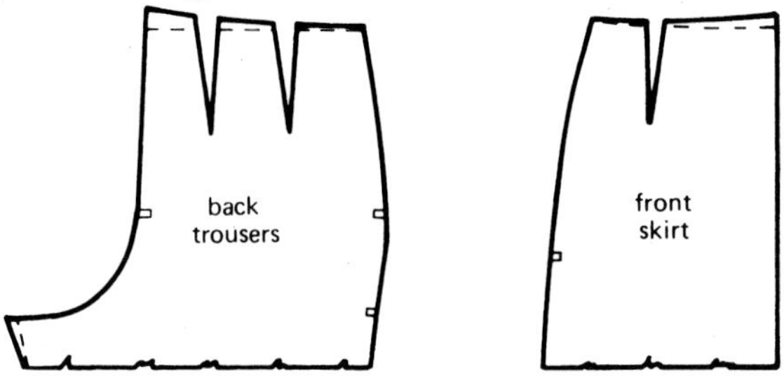

back trousers

front skirt

Extra amounts

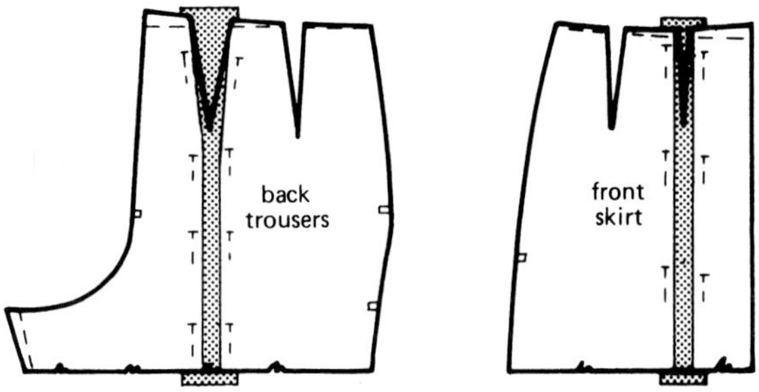

back trousers

front skirt

Skirts and trousers — figure problems

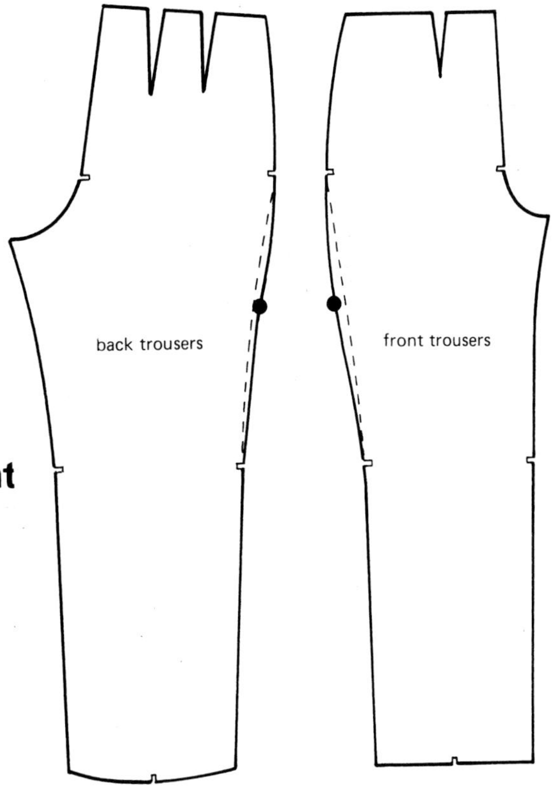

back trousers

front trousers

21 Thigh bulge

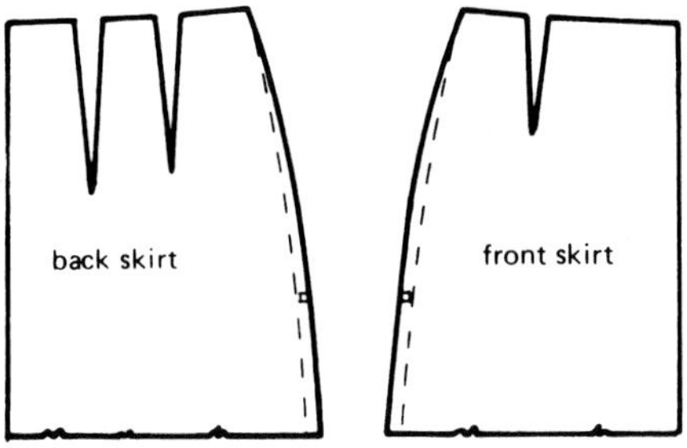

back skirt

front skirt

22 Sway back

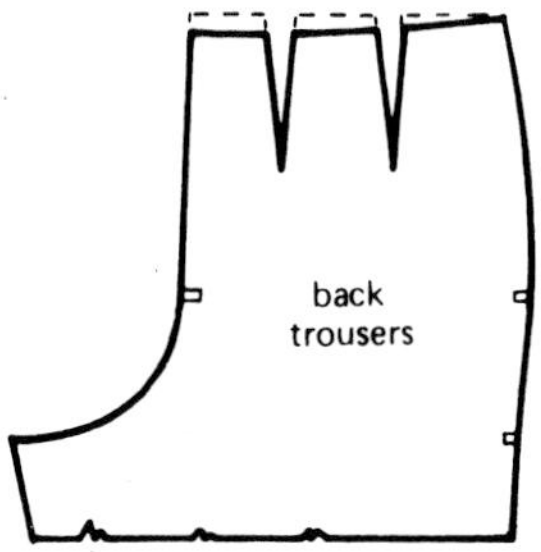

back trousers

Sway front

front skirt

182

Sway back   Long back

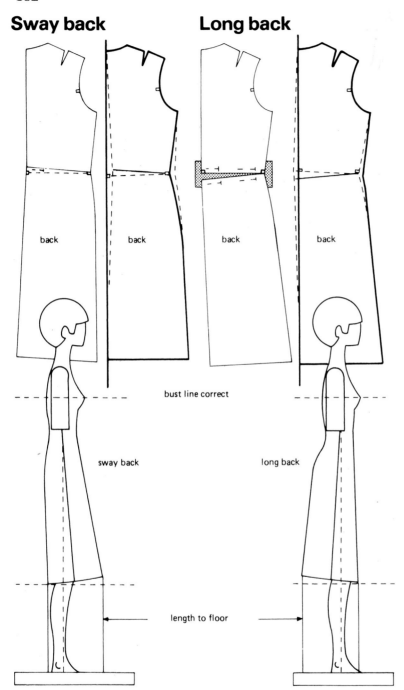

back

back

back

back

bust line correct

sway back

long back

length to floor

FITTING ONE-PIECE DRESSES AND JACKETS

Dresses and jackets without a seam at the waistline sometimes require a special alteration. This is when the figure has a sway back, or conversely a long back length in the centre area of the body between bust and hips.

Sway Back The dress or jacket will swing into the back of the figure.

Correction Measure front and back lengths to the floor to find out how much the back must be raised. Cut the pattern across the waistline and overlap the amount to be removed. Draw a vertical line on a new piece of paper; place neck and hem of altered pattern to this line. Trace round pattern. Reshape the side seam the same amount that is added by the distortion at the centre back seam.

Long Back The dress or jacket will swing away from the back of the figure.

Correction Measure front and back lengths to the floor to find out how much must be inserted into back length. Cut pattern at the waistline and open the required amount. (Place a piece of paper underneath the pattern and pin to this to hold the opening in place.) Draw a vertical line on a new piece of paper; place neck and hem of altered pattern to this line. Trace round pattern. Add to side seam the same amount that overlaps the centre back seam.

THE BLOCK PATTERN

When fitting the toile, pin the alterations that are required. Mark on the toile any instructions you need; mark with a pencil. Notes on bits of paper are often mislaid.

After fitting the toile all the alterations must be made to the block pattern. For very difficult adjustments, alter the block, alter the toile and re-fit to ensure that it fits perfectly.

A block pattern should be made in card or strong brown paper as it will be used many times. Some students prefer block patterns cut out in card so that they can trace round them; others prefer to have them drawn on a piece of paper to 'wheel' the outline onto a separate sheet underneath.

Part Four: Computer-Aided Design
14 COMPUTER-GENERATED DESIGN AND PATTERN MAKING

USING CAD IN CLOTHING MANUFACTURE

When computer-aided design (CAD) was first established in clothing manufacture, it was very expensive and could therefore only be bought by large companies. The full process from design to manufacture is usually an investment made by a manufacturer who makes a particular type of garment in large quantities. However, small companies can benefit from particular elements of CAD. The different processes of CAD can be of great advantage to a company; they can be described under the following headings:

- Design and Marketing
- Production Data Management
- Pattern Creation and Modification
- Sizing and Made-to-Measure
- Pattern Grading
- Lay Planning and Marker-Making.

Design and Marketing

Technological advances during the 1990s have produced revolutionary changes in communication. The Internet links the different sectors of the clothing industry and has become a vital part of many companies' operations. The Internet can link the designer with fabric and trimming suppliers, the garment manufacturers and the retailers, many of which can be overseas.

The word 'designer' is a broad description that covers many different functions. The area a designer may cover can range from the prediction or generation of the next season's range to pattern cutting and responsibility for the finished sample. This has to be checked in all sizes with cost lay plans, costings and manufacturing specifications. A designer in a large company may specialize in a particular area and be part of a team, whilst in a very small company a designer may have to perform all the above tasks.

The introduction of CAD into a company appears to have the effect of increasing the division between the generation of styles and pattern cutting. Pattern cutting is seen increasingly as a technical rather than a design process. When a company adopts new technology, a division often occurs because different types of software programs handle graphic data in different ways.

Imaging programs manipulate the data using screen pixels. The programs are used for idea generation, story boards, illustration and many forms of textile design. The software can offer much greater integration between fabric and garment design, offering new possibilities to the designer. A new generation of designers is emerging from the colleges, and many of them feel comfortable with the technology; they will undoubtedly increase the momentum of its application. Computers, their associated scanners and printers and some software programs are now relatively cheap and affordable even by very small companies and freelance designers.

Software programs that work in very high resolution are now available. They produce high-quality line output and photographic images. Today, fashion retailers demand a fast response; the advantages of modifying drawings and printing them with variations of colour and pattern are therefore obvious. Retailers make many decisions from virtual fabrics and virtual garments created by 2D and 3D textile and drape programs. Woven, knitted or printed fabrics can be realized on screen and printed by inkjet printers onto fabrics for instant sampling. Collections can be visualized by mapping fabrics onto sketches and photographs, thus creating virtual models and reducing the amount of samples needed each season. The large and medium size companies that supply the multiple retailers now see paint systems as an essential element of the early selection stages of the design process.

New developments in virtual reality are creating moving models and electronic fashion shows, or virtual store displays. It is now possible to access virtual models online through the Internet and see them from all angles as they rotate in real time. The garment image can be re-mapped with any of the different fabrics shown on the screen.

Pattern cutting programs are based on vectors that register and manipulate the data in the form of mathematical co-ordinates. It takes time to become skilled in working computer programs; therefore a choice of direction has to be made and there has become a direct distinction between the designer, now seen as a stylist (using *imaging programs*), and the pattern cutter.

A 2D storyboard incorporating many CAD images.
Photograph by permission of assyst bullmer

Draping a garment image with a fabric image.
Photographs by permission of NedGraphics

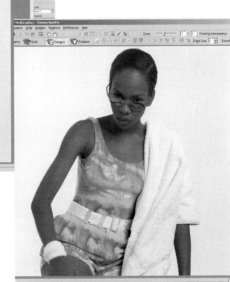

Production Data Management

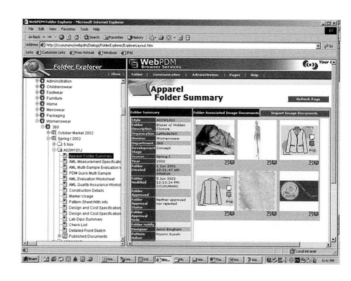

Students entering their first design position are often astonished at the amount of documentation that is required from the designer. Organization is central to the designer's work; rigorous notation of design styles, fabrics, trimmings and specifications are required.

Production data management (PDM) software controls the whole production process of the garment. The production cycle of a garment requires accurate information that can be accessed by all the departments in the company. A PDM system eliminates the repetition of identical information being processed. The information given by the designer on each style forms the foundation for the style to travel through the database as it enters the production cycle. The software allows authorized users to access and modify the sketches or photographs; the pattern, sizing and measurements; the fabric, linings, interfacings and trimmings information; the lay-plan and costing calculations; assembly instructions and making up procedures. External 'cut, make and trim' facilities in other factories and other sourcing information can also be accessed. The information can be constantly updated, with everybody being informed instantly about modifications.

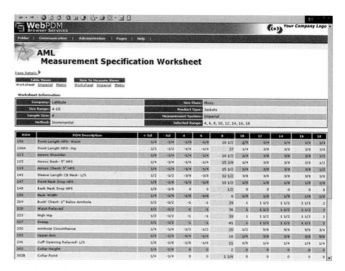

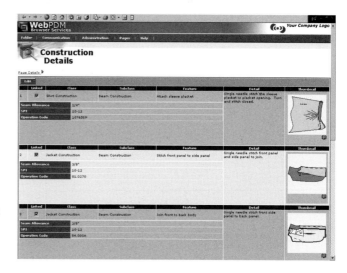

Pages from a PDM system showing: an overview, measurement data and a construction sheet.
Photographs by permission of Gerber Technology

Pattern Creation and Modification

SPECIFICATION DRAWINGS

Designers have to record styles by means of specification drawings. This is particularly important for the designer who delegates the pattern development of a style to a pattern cutter. The designer has to develop a concise means of communication within the design team as well as with the production staff. The technique of precise technical drawing, in correct proportion and measurements, can be aided by the use of a computer. The drawing can then be accurately interpreted into a first working pattern.

Accurate adaptations from specification drawings can be made of the type of design illustrated. Basic seam and pocket positions can be marked, pattern pieces can be traced off and modified.

MEANS OF PATTERN DEVELOPMENT

Designers use a range of techniques:
1. Modelling the garments on the dress stand.
2. Direct measurement.
3. Construction of patterns by instructions (usually basic styles in menswear).
4. Copy of an existing pattern.
5. Adaptation of a previous pattern.
6. Adaptation of blocks.

Some designers use a single technique, others combine them to achieve the final pattern, and it is possible to combine any of the above methods with the creation of computer-generated patterns. But, adaptations of blocks or previous patterns are the ways most companies use their pattern generation systems (PGS) because they are a means of quality control and sizing standards.

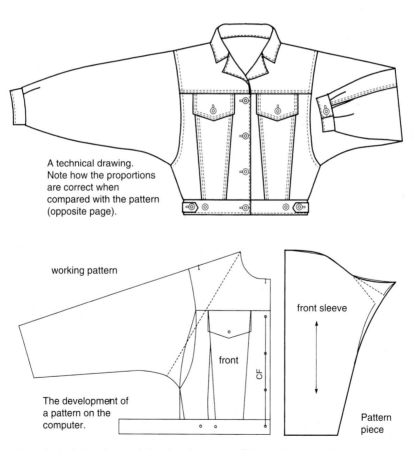

A technical drawing. Note how the proportions are correct when compared with the pattern (opposite page).

working pattern

front sleeve

front

CF

The development of a pattern on the computer.

Pattern piece

A technical drawing and the development of the pattern on the computer.
Note how the proportions of the pattern relate to the drawing.

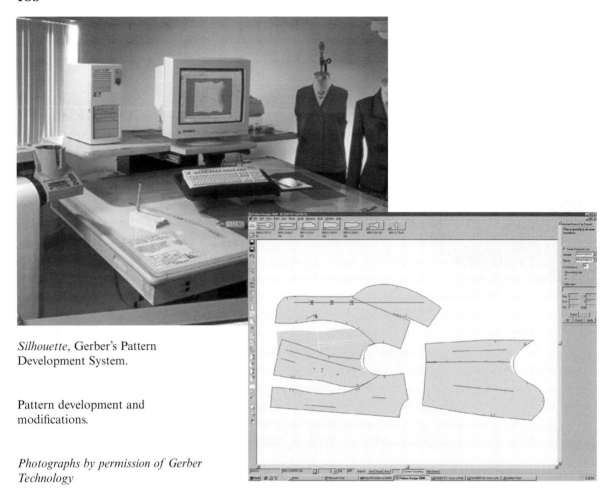

Silhouette, Gerber's Pattern Development System.

Pattern development and modifications.

Photographs by permission of Gerber Technology

PATTERN GENERATION SYSTEMS (PGS)

The systems are now very sophisticated. The 'natural environment' of the work table has been reproduced by working on a digitiser with personal tools and materials. The designer works in the same manner as manual pattern cutting, but the lines are recorded electronically. Sample calico toiles modelled on the stand or manually cut patterns can be traced into the system, refined to a production level and seam allowances added.

Although patterns can be drafted directly on the screen, the systems are particularly adept at adapting blocks or modifying patterns stored within the computer. They can perform many standard pattern adaptations such as swinging darts, adding pleats and fullness, etc. They also perform repetitive tasks such as adding seam allowances, instructions and labelling. The acknowledged value of PGS is that they systemize the procedure of creating an accurate pattern with many similar but slightly differing parts, such as lined jackets and coats. The ability to overlay and check the parts is crucial in this process. They can also associate parts so that any modification to the outer garment during the development process can be programmed to occur on associated pieces, such as the interlining or lining. Some systems (for example the assyst software) have 'macros' where the operator can teach the system to perform some drafting operations that are repetitive. The value of these systems for companies producing standard types of design, for example career wear, is recognized.

Some of the more advanced software can program the computer with instructions for drafting a particular style. This method can create patterns to individual sets of measurements, thus creating bespoke patterns for individual sizing.

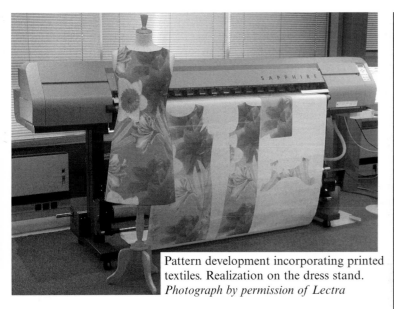

Pattern development incorporating printed textiles. Realization on the dress stand.
Photograph by permission of Lectra

Nautilus (2001)
Computer-aided
textile design created
in *Prostyle* Lectra.

Nautilus (2001)
modelled on the stand
using digitally printed
fabric produced with
Stork *Amber*
technology.

New Design Concepts: experimental and integrated garment and print design.
Design by Katherine Townsend. Photographs shown with her permission.

But, there is a temptation to modify previous styles. The sheer pace of the design cycle gives little space for innovative styling. It is not only the creation of the design, but the sourcing, costing, new production procedures and re-tooling of machinery which accompanies totally new concepts. Most of the systems excel at pattern modification or the development of basic styles from blocks or previous patterns. However, the generation of innovative fashion design of complex cut or fabric drape can be achieved far better by manual methods, where the 3D form of the shape can be modified during the pattern development process. But, the computer does not have to be dismissed from this or any other area of pattern cutting, it can be used as a part of any of the methods of pattern development.

The possibilities of integrating fabric design into pattern shape can be realized by using digital printing. Most of this form of printing has been used for the quick sampling of garments by creating short lengths of fabric or by pasting fabric images into garment pattern shapes. However, a few designers are creating new concepts of 2D to 3D design. Katherine Townsend uses the drape manipulation attributes of the technology to develop and change the print *during the process of garment design.*

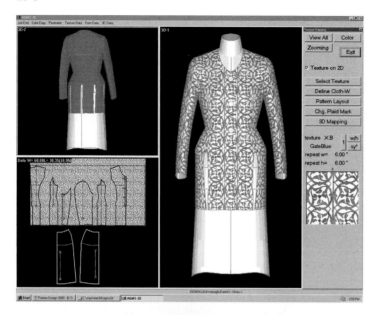

The Asahi virtual stand with 2D pattern pieces, created in Gerber Pattern Design, then mapped to the stand.

APDS-3D is a product of Asahi Ltd., licensed exclusively by Gerber Technology. Photograph by permission of Gerber Technology

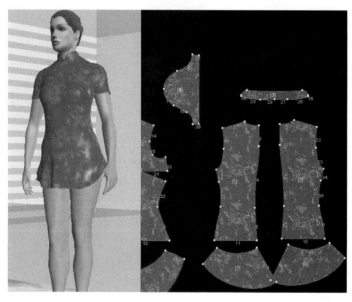

The program *V-Stitcher* by Browzwear in which the 2D garment pieces created in other CAD programs can be brought into *V-Stitcher* to be virtually stitched together to create a garment on a virtual model.
Photography by permission of Browzwear International Ltd.

3D SOFTWARE PROGRAMS

CAD suppliers have been working on research to create garment patterns directly on the 3D dress stand for decades. At least four CAD suppliers are offering or about to release differing versions of working within a 3D environment. The 3D program *V-Stitcher* by Browzwear is available in the UK through Gerber Technology who have also integrated it with their pattern cutting program. Most of the programs are based on 2D dress patterns that can be transferred onto a 3D stand or virtual body to give realizations of how the made-up garment will look. Although the characteristics of the fabric, particularly its draping qualities, can be entered to give a realistic image, the

most success has been with garments that fit closely to the body form. The stand or virtual body can be to modified to different shapes and sizes and some programs show the ease distribution.

The aim is to reduce the number of samples or toiles made up in the design room. However, only a few companies have installed the 3D programs. This is because experienced designers and pattern cutters, who have worked with pattern shapes and fabrics, can visualize 2D shapes as 3D images; therefore, many are using the current 2D computer programs with great skill. It is likely that designers will make more use of the 3D programs as they become increasingly sophisticated yet easier to operate.

Sizing and Made-to-Measure

An increasing number of companies are including made-to-measure in their product range. Different elements of the CAD process have made this direction feasible. Mass-customization offers not only a better fit, but also a wider choice of styles, fabrics, linings and trimmings.

THE PROCESS

The process begins with the customer's measurements being taken manually or by 3D scanning systems, which define not only the measurements of the customer, but also the shape in the form of a virtual figure which can be constantly updated.

Fabrics and styles can be selected within a store or via the Internet. Once the style is selected, the customer's measurements are compared to the nearest size of pattern stored in the system. A second layer of grade rules is then used to cover most basic alterations and variations in body stance. When new measurements are given, the system automatically modifies the pattern to the new measurements. Non-standard adjustments can be made in pattern design software. Any lining or interlining pieces are automatically adjusted; small pieces, such as pockets and collars, rarely need any adjustments. A lay plan is constructed for the modified pattern; this is sent directly to a single-ply cutter which cuts individual garments at high speed.

NEW SOFTWARE DEVELOPMENTS

The demand for made-to-measure software programs has led to new ways of developing the mathematics of pattern construction, parametrics. The patterns are constructed and defined by a set of dimensions, which can then be modified by typing in new measurements. If a point is dragged by the mouse, the system recalculates the entire model accordingly.

Measurements taken by body scanning, and style selection for made-to-measure.
Photograph by permission of Lectra

Pattern Grading

OVERVIEW

Grading is one of the main reasons why companies buy a CAD system. It will offer them more speed, accuracy and consistency in sizing their patterns than manually grading them. After the sample design has been accepted and the retailer has placed an order, the garment has to be produced in a range of sizes. Most larger companies are grading patterns by CAD.

Patterns created within PGS can pass directly into the grading sector. However, some companies using CAD systems are still cutting patterns manually. They have to input their patterns by digitizing the contour (see illustration page 188).

In order to get the information to construct graded patterns, the following sources are used:
- *Size charts of body measurements*
- *Garment specifications*
- *Manually nested patterns*
- *Grade rules provided by some CAD suppliers*
- *Copying grades from a previously graded similar pattern shape within the system.*

The grading of patterns by most CAD systems is based on identifying where specific points on the pattern have to be extended or reduced to create a new size. These points are moved by X and Y co-ordinates which tell the computer the direction of movement; measurements are given to identify the position of the new point. This co-ordinate movement is known as a grade rule.

CALCULATING A GRADE RULE

Grade rules are usually calculated to one-tenth of a millimetre. The amount of movement in the X direction is written first, followed by the Y direction. For example, the movement of the shoulder point between sizes is −4mm horizontally and 4mm vertically (see diagram).

The grade rule can be written in one-tenth of a millimetre (e.g. −40 40) or in centimetres (e.g. −0.4 0 0.4cm). It is the instruction across a range of sizes. Inconsistent grades between sizes can be registered. The same grade rule can be used at any point that requires the same grade. One grade rule is written as zero (00.0 00.0); it is used where no grade is required.

Companies often calculate many of the rules directly from size charts or garment specifications. However, manually graded 'nests' of blocks can be used. The nest is 'stacked' on one point, usually on the armscye depth line. The directions of the X and Y co-ordinates are registered from this point. Each graded point on the nest (these are beginnings and ends of lines and specific points, i.e. control points or notches) is measured. The measurements are checked with grading increments on size charts.

Grade rules can be copied from other patterns. Patterns with grade rules attached can be modified, and these grades will be retained on the new style.

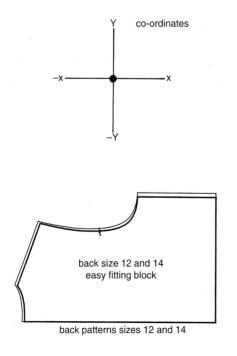

back size 12 and 14
easy fitting block

back patterns sizes 12 and 14

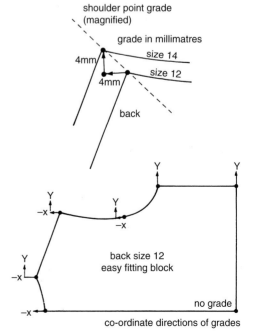

shoulder point grade
(magnified)

grade in millimatres

size 14

4mm

size 12

4mm

back

back size 12
easy fitting block

no grade

co-ordinate directions of grades

GRADE RULE LIBRARIES

A grade rule library is compiled of numbered grade rules used at the grade points. When the number is applied to a point, it will operate the grade. See diagram opposite.

The number of sizes, the size breaks and the names of the sizes have to be entered into the program. The grade rules for the pattern are then typed in to create a library for that size range.

Once the rules for a block or pattern are entered, any similar or adapted pattern can also be graded using the same grades. However, few patterns are exactly the same shape. This means that new grade rules have to be calculated by the grader and these rules added to the grade rule library.

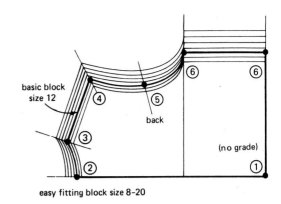

easy fitting block size 8-20

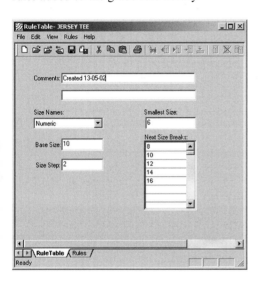

Examples of the screen displays of the input of sizes and grade rules.
By permission of Gerber Technology

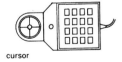

cursor

DIGITISING PATTERNS

If a pattern has been cut manually it has to be digitised into the system. The pattern is placed on the digitiser and the pattern profile is entered into the computer using a cursor. The centre of the cursor's cross hairs is placed on the points to be graded and the grade rules entered. These points and other points define the lines, curves and corners of the pattern. Folds and the grain line are also entered. Notches and drill holes for pocket positions or buttonholes can also be recorded.

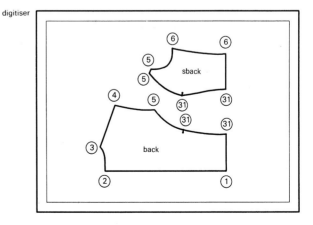

GRADING THE PATTERN

Pattern pieces constructed in the PGS pattern cutting software or digitised into the system can be realized on screen. Grade points can be identified with a screen cursor and the grade rule number can be entered. Some systems do not use grade rule libraries but attach the rules to the pattern piece and copy rules from one pattern piece to another. When the grade points have been added, an instruction to grade the piece is given. This order will generate a nest of grades over the range of sizes, using the grade rules attached to the piece or from rules stored in the grade rule library. The patterns can be drawn out on a plotter for checking, or sent directly through the system for lay planning and cutting.

FURTHER GRADING TECHNIQUES

Sophisticated grading techniques are now included in many programs. Perpendicular grading calculates the grades with reference to the angle of another line; tangent grading techniques control points along a line or the length of the line itself. If a pattern is split, the system will grade the new seam lines proportionally. If a line is altered on a pattern, it is possible for it to be modified automatically through all the grades. 'Walking' graded pieces allow seams to be checked for fit along the making up lines.

A number of companies are developing systems based on parametrics. Any sizes are based on the measurements made to construct the pattern. Any new sizes are generated not through point movements, but through measurement changes.

Some small clothing companies do not have pattern cutting or grading expertise, so some software companies offer a range of patterns of basic garments (with alternative sleeves and collars), already graded. Instead of copying individual grade points from other patterns, *EasyGrading* from Investronica allows a company to lay a pattern over a similar graded shape in the system to copy all the grades. These short-cut techniques are useful for companies with a narrow product base; however, they do restrict their styling capabilities.

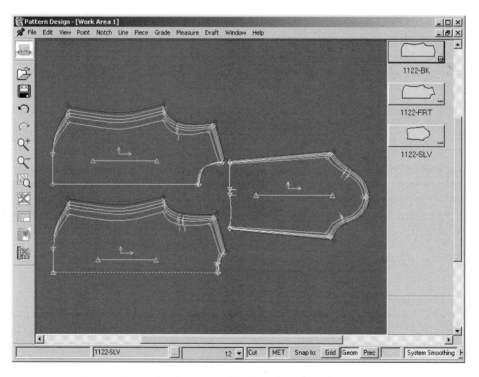

Example of a screen display of graded pieces.
By permission of Gerber Technology

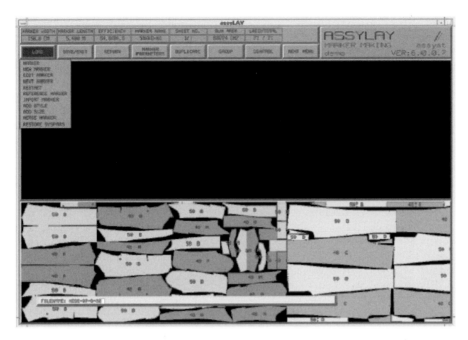

A marker-making software program screen display.
By permission of assyst bullmer

Lay Planning and Marker-Making

CREATING MODELS

Throughout the clothing industry most companies making substantial quantities of garments are using CAD systems. They bought them principally for marker-making, which offers accuracy, speed and fabric utilization.

To cut a garment by CAD the first procedure is to create 'models' for the style. A model is created by calling up the style's pattern pieces (stored in the system) that have to be cut in a particular fabric. If there are different fabrics used in the style, or if there are interlinings or linings, a number of 'models' will have to be made.

A MARKER ORDER

Order processing for production lay plans can be very complex. There can be as many as eight fabrics in a jacket, each requiring a model and separate lay plan (marker). In addition, a large order with many sizes will increase the number of markers. The length of the cutting tables restricts the marker length. Therefore, the distribution of the number of garments and sizes in a marker is crucial to the fabric utilization figures. Cut Order Planning software can

distribute the sizes into different markers to give the best fabric utilization for the order.

The marker for each fabric needs the following instructions:

1. Piece names
2. Sizes
3. Number of pieces
4. Fabric constraints (single or double-ply, face-to-face, nap)
5. Any blocking of areas
6. Any buffering around pieces
7. Matching of checks, patterns.

MARKER-MAKING

The pattern pieces for the marker appear on the screen and can then be placed manually by an operator 'dragging' the pieces into position. Many options allow the grouping of pieces and the dynamic alteration or matching of pieces. The standard of automatic marker-making has improved in speed and fabric utilization and is now used more often than manual functions. The system will try different ways of placing the pieces in the lay until the best fabric utilization is achieved.

E-COMMERCE MARKER-MAKING

Direct web-based marker-making is now available from assyst bulmer, and it offers the service to clothing manufacturers. Its advantage is the power of the main computer which offers quality markers twenty four hours per day every day. It works at a very fast speed regardless of whether or not a customer has broadband connections. The service is aimed at manufacturers who are short of staff, have peak workloads, are wanting to expand production, or those who have production spread around the world. It is important for manufacturers to realize that compatibility between systems is no longer a problem, that data can be transferred between different CAD systems.

PLOTTING AND CUTTING

The markers can be plotted out or cut automatically on high-speed, deep-ply cutters that can cut many layers of fabric, or on single-ply cutters for custom-made garments. Gerber's *InVision* uses an intelligent vision system to simplify and improve plaid and stripe matching. The operator uses the advanced camera and optics system to precision match the fabric cutting.

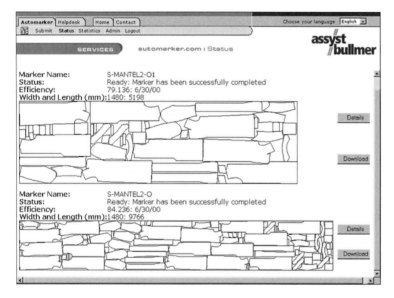

E-commerce automatic marker-making.
Photograph by permission of assyst bullmer

Deep-ply cutting on the 'Turbocut' knife plotter.
Photograph by permission of assyst bullmer

Appendix: Aliquot Parts

If a calculator is not available for working out fractional parts, the following table can be used. The table covers most of the popular sizes. (Figures in columns marked with an asterisk are calculated to one decimal place.)

NECK SIZE (cm)

	$*\frac{1}{8}$	$*\frac{1}{5}$
34	4.3	6.8
35	4.4	7
36	4.5	7.2
37	4.6	7.4
38	4.8	7.6
39.2	4.9	7.8
40.4	5.1	8.1
41.6	5.2	8.3
42.8	5.4	8.6
44	5.5	8.8
45.2	5.7	9

CONSTRUCTING A CIRCLE

Some patterns use circles as a base for their construction. The following calculations can be made to obtain the radius required to construct a circle.

The circumference of a circle is the measurement around a circle.
The radius is a line from the centre of the circle to the outer edge.
To construct a circle the radius must be known.
Radius = circumference divided by 6.28.

Working example Waistline measurement is 68 cm, a circle is required whose circumference is 68 cm.
Radius = 68 ÷ 6.28 = 10.8
Construct a circle, radius 10.8 cm, its circumference will be 68 cm.

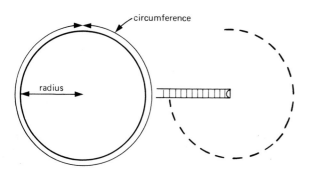

BUST, WAIST AND HIP (cm)

	$*\frac{1}{16}$	$*\frac{1}{12}$	$*\frac{1}{6}$	$*\frac{1}{4}$	$*\frac{1}{2}$
60	3.8	5	10	15	30
61	3.8	5.1	10.2	15.25	30.5
62	3.9	5.2	10.3	15.5	31
63	3.9	5.3	10.5	15.75	31.5
64	4	5.3	10.7	16	32
65	4.1	5.4	10.8	16.25	32.5
66	4.1	5.5	11	16.5	33
67	4.2	5.6	11.2	16.75	33.5
68	4.3	5.7	11.3	17	34
69	4.3	5.8	11.5	17.25	34.5
70	4.4	5.8	11.7	17.5	35
71	4.4	5.9	11.8	17.75	35.5
72	4.5	6	12	18	36
73	4.6	6.1	12.2	18.25	36.5
74	4.6	6.2	12.3	18.5	37
75	4.7	6.3	12.5	18.75	37.5
76	4.8	6.3	12.7	19	38
77	4.8	6.4	12.8	19.25	38.5
78	4.9	6.5	13	19.5	39
79	4.9	6.6	13.2	19.75	39.5
80	5	6.7	13.3	20	40
81	5.1	6.8	13.5	20.25	40.5
82	5.1	6.8	13.7	20.5	41
83	5.2	6.9	13.8	20.75	41.5
84	5.3	7	14	21	42
85	5.3	7.1	14.2	21.25	42.5
86	5.4	7.2	14.3	21.5	43
87	5.4	7.3	14.5	21.75	43.5
88	5.5	7.3	14.7	22	44
89	5.6	7.4	14.8	22.25	44.5
90	5.6	7.5	15	22.5	45
91	5.7	7.6	15.2	22.75	45.5
92	5.8	7.7	15.3	23	46
93	5.8	7.8	15.5	23.25	46.5
94	5.9	7.8	15.7	23.5	47
95	5.9	7.9	15.8	23.75	47.5
96	6	8	16	24	48
97	6.1	8.1	16.2	24.25	48.5
98	6.1	8.2	16.3	24.5	49
99	6.2	8.3	16.5	24.75	49.5
100	6.3	8.3	16.7	25	50
101	6.3	8.4	16.8	25.25	50.5
102	6.4	8.5	17	25.5	51
103	6.4	8.6	17.2	25.75	51.5
104	6.5	8.7	17.3	26	52
105	6.6	8.8	17.5	26.25	52.5
106	6.6	8.8	17.7	26.5	53
107	6.7	8.9	17.8	26.75	53.5
108	6.8	9	18	27	54
109	6.8	9.1	18.2	27.25	54.5
110	6.9	9.2	18.3	27.5	55
111	6.9	9.3	18.5	27.75	55.5
112	7	9.3	18.7	28	56

CHAPTER INDEX
Part One: Classic Form Cutting

Part One: Classic Form Cutting – Continued

Part Two: Flat Cutting

Part Three: Size and Fit

Part Four: Computer-Aided Design

Appendix: Aliquot Parts

Blackwell
Publishing

Blackwell Publishing
C/o Marston Book Services
P O Box 269
Abingdon
Oxford, OX14 4YN

Tel: +44 (0) 1235 465500
Fax: +44 (0) 1235 465555
Email: direct.order@marston.co.uk

Metric Pattern Cutting for Menswear

Including unisex clothes and computer aided design

Third Edition
Winifred Aldrich

Since the first edition was published in 1980, *Metric Pattern Cutting for Menswear* has become established as the standard work on the subject. The book has been designed especially for students so that they can transfer many of the skills that they have gained in their studies of pattern cutting for women's wear. It gives them the opportunity to be more creative in developing fashion styles for menswear and also to experiment with unisex designs. This companion volume to *Metric Pattern Cutting* follows the same style, with concise text accompanied by numerous clear illustrations and diagrams.

The third edition updates the size charts and discusses the problems of metric conversions and sizing. It also includes a new section on flat cutting, which is used for most casual wear and sportswear garments. New blocks have been added as well as grading for Small, Medium, Large and XLarge sizing. There is also a comprehensive chapter on computer aided design for menswear.

168 pages •ISBN-10: 0 632 04113 7
•ISBN-13: 978 0 632 04113 8

Blackwell Publishing

Blackwell Publishing
C/o Marston Book Services
P O Box 269
Abingdon
Oxford, OX14 4YN

Tel: +44 (0) 1235 465500
Fax: +44 (0) 1235 465555
Email: direct.order@marston.co.uk

Metric Pattern Cutting for Children's Wear and Babywear

Third Edition

Winifred Aldrich

This expanded and updated book on children's and babywear contains hundreds of stylish illustrations, clear, concise instructions and a new range of updated size charts. It is a companion volume to Metric Pattern Cutting and is essential for students who wish to specialise in the design, cutting and manufacture of clothes for children.

The children's wear market has changed remarkably over the last decade. It reflects the more casual but fashion-conscious lifestyle of children and reacts quickly to changes in fashion and new fabric developments. Children's wear has become a more exciting and innovative market and this is encouraging more students to become children's wear designers.

Two important new sections have been added in this new edition. Babywear has been included for the first time and it is offered from a fashionable as well as a practical perspective. Second, a whole new section is devoted to simple flat cutting. These additions are a response to the phenomenal growth in casual clothes for babies and children, particularly the garments made in jersey or stretch fabrics.

192 pages •ISBN-10: 0 632 05265 1
•ISBN-13: 978 0 632 05265 3

Blackwell
Publishing

Blackwell Publishing
C/o Marston Book Services
P O Box 269
Abingdon
Oxford, OX14 4YN

Tel: +44 (0) 1235 465500
Fax: +44 (0) 1235 465555
Email: direct.order@marston.co.uk

Fabric, Form and Flat Pattern Cutting

Winifred Aldrich

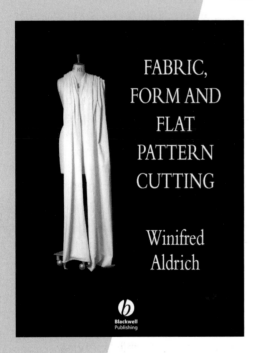

This book is unique but essential reading for students of garment design. Pattern cutting books rarely integrate the application of fabric into the process of garment cutting, but the fabric informs and often determines the methods to be used. Selecting the fabric, recognising its qualities and using the most appropriate cutting method is one of the most difficult aspects of a designer's training. The process is made even more difficult because an ever-increasing range of new fabrics is available to designers who often have to select fabric ranges in stressed situations. Whilst designers may know the technical requirements for a particular product range, such as absorbency or washability, it is equally important that they recognise the handle of the fabric and estimate its qualities with reference to cutting.

The book identifies the five principal fabric characteristics which will determine the form of the garment shape. It then demonstrates, through numerous examples, how these factors are crucial in the selection of pattern cutting procedures.

It is a good designer who knows how to work in harmony with a fabric or how to create interesting discords without losing control of the design. Students who have completed basic pattern cutting modules should now use the book to understand the complexities of integrating the fabric with the design.

206 pages •ISBN-10: 0 632 03917 5
•ISBN-13: 978 0 632 03917 3

Blackwell
Publishing

Blackwell Publishing
C/o Marston Book Services
P O Box 269
Abingdon
Oxford, OX14 4YN

Tel: +44 (0) 1235 465500
Fax: +44 (0) 1235 465555
Email: direct.order@marston.co.uk

Pattern Cutting for Women's Tailored Jackets

Classic and Contemporary

Winifred Aldrich

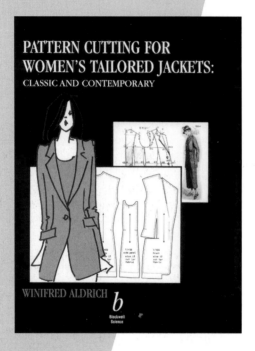

This book has been written for students who have mastered the basic principles of pattern cutting and have become interested in cutting tailored garments. A large number of garments can claim to be 'tailored', and the term is often confusing; therefore, the book starts by explaining the history of cutting tailored clothes. It describes the evolution of the tailored jacket through the eighteenth and nineteenth century and defines the legacy that has been left for designers and cutters.

The book then demonstrates, by examples, the different approaches to cutting tailored garments today. The major practical part of the book is divided into three sections:

- Classic bespoke cutting
- Engineered cutting and manufacture
- 'Style' cutting variations.

Any student, who wishes to become a designer or cutter in one of these areas, will find this book valuable. The type of make-up or manufacture of garments is vastly different in each sector of the trade and this affects the cutting techniques to be used. It is important that students understand the possibilities and the limits of each sector before they select a career.

The first chapter of the book is well illustrated with many unique historical images of tailored garments and cutting practices. The practical section includes many photographs of current manufacturing processes and contains the kind of clear illustrations, instructions and diagrams for cutting garments that are associated with the author's previous books.

120 pages •ISBN-10: 0 632 05467 0
•ISBN-13: 978 0 632 05467 1